The Horizontal Revolution

Morris A. Graham
Melvin J. LeBaron

Foreword by Stephen R. Covey

The Horizontal Revolution

Reengineering Your Organization Through Teams

Jossey-Bass Publishers • San Francisco

Substantial discounts on bulk quantities of Jossey-Bass books are available to corporations, professional associations, and other organizations. For details and discount information, contact the special sales department at Jossey-Bass Inc., Publishers. (415) 433–1740; Fax (415) 433–0499.

For sales outside the United States, please contact your local Paramount Publishing International Office.

Manufactured in the United States of America. Nearly all Jossey-Bass books and jackets are printed on recycled paper that contains at least 50 percent recycled waste, including 10 percent postconsumer waste. Many of our materials are printed with either soy- or vegetable-based ink; during the printing process these inks emit fewer volatile organic compounds (VOCs) than petroleum-based inks. VOCs contribute to the formation of smog.

Library of Congress Cataloging-in-Publication Data

Graham, Morris A.
    The horizontal revolution : reengineering your organization through teams / Morris A. Graham, Melvin J. LeBaron.—1st ed.
        p.   cm.—(The Jossey-Bass management series)
    Includes bibliographical references and index.
    ISBN 0-7879-0046-X
    1. Work groups. 2. Employee motivation. I. LeBaron, Mel.
II. Title. III. Series.
HD66.G7 1994
658.4'036—dc20   94-31341
                                                              CIP

FIRST EDITION
HB Printing   10 9 8 7 6 5 4 3 2 1   Code 94129

The Jossey-Bass Management Series

Contents

      In Balance   181

      Part Three: Keeping the Revolution Alive   213

7.   Reward Success: Tracking Performance and
      Sharing the Gains   215

8.   Revolutionary Prescriptions: Continuous Learning
      and Hard Work   247

      Epilogue: Guiding the Transformation to Teams   283

      References and Recommended Readings   287

      Index   293

Foreword

The Horizontal Revolution is a timely piece of instruction for teachers, trainers, managers, and organizational leaders. This book responds to a new horizontal leadership model of teaming and coaching, which develops and renews people at all levels. The concept of a horizontal organization includes ideas familiar to devotees of high-commitment/performance teaming, process reengineering/decentralizing, empowerment, customer focus, and principle-centered leadership. Within this revolution, people across the organization are called on to assume more account-ability and exercise decision-making authority and to be trained in the application of self-managing principles in order to become more than equal to the new challenges of our dramatically chang-ing times.

Guiding people and organizations into a new horizontal cul-ture is no easy feat. It isn't as simple as reengineering an outside-in approach—scrapping your organization chart, mashing middle managers, and dropping all departmental barriers. Externally imposed approaches may elicit short-term gains but are a breed-ing ground for mistrust, negative feelings, and lack of work force responsiveness. Instead, the authors of *The Horizontal Revolution* champion an inside-out approach—focusing first on develop-ing principle-centered teams that sustain a continual process of renewal—an upward spiral of growth that leads to progressively higher forms of responsible independence and effective inter-dependence. Ultimately, these teams will take on the knowledge, skill, desire, and opportunity to succeed in a way that leads to collective organizational success. The new culture becomes high-trust, win-win where helpful system structures are created to reinforce people working together effectively.

In this new culture of trust and open communication, people working interdependently in cross-functional teams are able to generate creativity, improvement, and innovation beyond the total of their individual capacities. Horizontal functioning becomes the practical process in which teams plan, execute, and control their own performance within an agreed-upon stewardship. This win-win condition facilitates effective autonomy in which teams have access to the primary elements of empowerment—knowledge, skill, desire, and opportunity. To keep a lean management staff from choking on a glut of decisions, authority is reinvested in high-leverage team leadership and self-directed activity.

In many ways, this book is a complement to and extension of my work and teachings. Morris Graham and Mel LeBaron have given us a powerful presentation of principles, values, and practices that align people as the most valuable organizational asset. The realization of a high-trust team culture comes through an organization's commitment to integrity, maturity, and abundance mentality. Teams with integrity make and keep commitments to themselves, to the customer, and to the organization. Individuals within these teams are able to express their ideas and feelings with courage balanced with consideration for the ideas and feelings of others. People with abundance mentality assume that there is plenty out there for everybody. They deeply value the contribution of others and recognize unlimited potential for teaming together. Teams with a high degree of integrity are free to interact with true synergy and creativity, unrestrained by the doubt and suspicion that permeate low-trust cultures. Clearly, it is my experience that without principles and values to guide these processes, people will lack a true sense of personal contribution to the work.

These are spirited times. I am particularly impressed with the sense of destiny, commitment to people and excellence, and passion for renewal shown by Morris and Mel in this book. I admire their willingness to lean toward the artistic and penetrating instincts required for success at work. I also believe that we must build better business—and be able to live with ourselves and each other—to get things done that need to be done. Applying principles and values to learning, leadership, teaming, and coaching is absolutely required for effective work and workplace behavior.

Finally, this book inspires me to action because it is not based on theory or hearsay. Morris and Mel have actually done the things they write about. They are supreme coaches and yet they are extremely coachable. They learn as they go and cause others to do the same. They have helped many, and I'm sure they will help the reader to realize that the imagination that goes into team structure is as important as the imagination that goes into producing products and services. *The Horizontal Revolution* reaffirms that our imagination should never run away with our judgment. Herein is a profound structure and process for giving power to people and impacting the people of power. It is the emotional, mental, and physical move many of us need to make. I am personally grateful that Morris and Mel have given us such an insightful and practical road map for our journey. This inside-out approach is so needed today, and the awareness of that need is literally flooding sophisticated organizations that have learned, and continue to learn, the flaws of outside-in.

September 1994   Stephen R. Covey
Chairman of Covey Leadership Center
and author of the best-selling
The 7 Habits of Highly Effective People
and *Principle-Centered Leadership*

Preface

A horizontal revolution is reinventing the U.S. workplace. Unlike the Industrial Revolution, which was machine-based, the horizontal revolution is people-based. The Industrial Revolution altered our way of living. The horizontal revolution is altering our way of working.

The revolution taking place today is the organizational movement from hierarchical, function-based structures to horizontal, integrated workplaces organized around empowered individuals and self-directed work teams as the means to achieve sustainable business process changes and extraordinary organizational redesign. Organizations can no longer rely exclusively on the wisdom of a few at the top. The thinking skills and responsiveness required to deal with the multitude of customer demands, cultures, technological advances, competitors, and possible futures means that every employee must be intelligently and fully involved. The horizontal revolution is built upon both efforts for efficiency and process redesign and requirements for flexibility and involvement. New skills for building trust, collegiality, adaptability, teaming, and coaching are its vehicle. Shared power, information, and rewards are its hallmarks. Individuals and teams that are empowered, that make their own decisions, and that serve clear business processes and purposes are its heart and soul.

Background of This Book

Ours is a voice from the frontline trenches. We have worked as coaches in those trenches—where people encounter people, where the sense of ownership, commitment, and mutual goals begins. Guiding various stages of the revolution for such corporations as General Electric, Disney, ITT, Otis, Marriott, and Litton, we have created learning experiences and learned the necessary continuity of day-after-day coaching in a workplace. We have also learned the consequences of that nurturing, witnessing amazing shifts in workplace roles, goals, and souls. New visions and missions for work effectiveness have become new agendas for focusing on the process of working together. Self-direction, shared ownership, and shared gains have become a vital part of action plans and business strategies for applying unique talents and insights to reengineering objectives.

The center of a business is people working with business processes in high-involvement teams that meet together weekly and meet occasionally with a coach providing the coaching skills necessary for all individuals to constantly reinvent themselves. Therefore, our approach integrates process reengineering and teaming/coaching. It is analogous to first going on a diet and then keeping the weight off. Sadly, over the long course, most organizational process-reengineering diets do not work because fundamental work styles have not been altered enough to sustain long-term changes. Corporate weight stays off only when teaming/coaching and other new and creative approaches to human interaction permanently replace old ways of doing things, when organizations help people adapt to change; understand the stages of change; diminish defensive, blaming, and rationalizing behaviors; and take on increased ownership and accountability throughout the organization.

The horizontal revolution requires everyone to feel and heed new life-enhancing principles: passion comes before politics; compassion comes before compulsion; and reality before rhetoric. People at work have for too long spun their wheels while only the political treads hit the road.

Audience

We wrote this book to be both a supercharger for those who have already joined the revolution but want to change more rapidly and effectively, and a navigational manual for those who need to get on course with their restructuring, realigning, and reengineering efforts. *The Horizontal Revolution* was written also for executives who want to better understand the workings of horizontal change in the workplace and who think about, and are in a position to initiate, job and organizational redesign. If you are a modern executive, you need to get things done in a more efficient and cost-effective way, to get employee buy-in, and to get employees to be more self-directed. This book will help you develop your coaching skills for the new workplace.

Overview of the Contents

The Horizontal Revolution presents a doable process executives and managers can use to redefine their organizations around teams. We present proven prescriptions, insights, techniques, and skills for redistributing ownership and responsibility and minimizing the us-them conditions that prevent teams from creating high-performance results. As we discuss further in the Introduction, we show you how to make your workplace a center of learning and leadership, a place in which work is integrated around the generation of both greater productivity and more humane relationships.

Part One (Chapters One through Four) discusses staging the horizontal revolution. Chapter One shows managers how to establish the up-front involvement and initiatives needed to roll out the revolution through teams. It introduces the first stage of a four-stage model for revolution and describes how to deal with barriers to change so that camps of resistance will not be left to smoulder, ultimately flaring up again to stall the revolutionary process. Street

fighting tactics are discouraged and practical ways to air disagreements and build coalitions are fully described, since a fully effective
team implementation requires integration of all restructuring
processes with behavioral conversion. Chapter Two develops the
settling-in stage of the revolution and ways of helping work teams
struggle with the inevitable gaps between expectation and reality.

In Chapter Three, we examine the new horizontal roles for
managers, team members/leaders, coaches, facilitators, recorders,
and the steering and design teams, using a new analogy to describe
the way individuals in an empowered group can think of themselves, their common mission, and their flexible functions. We also
show how horizontal functioning best fits strategies that integrate
profit centers around customers. In Chapter Four, we discuss the key
tools that transform teams into the building blocks of the horizontal revolution, focusing on workouts and process mapping.

Part Two (Chapters Five and Six) describes how to lead the
team-powered organization. Team-based organizations require
better, stronger, and situationally correct leadership, not less leadership. Chapter Five stresses commitment over control as the paradigm for horizontal leadership and describes how team leaders can
be more elastic. Chapter Six presents a unique coaching process
for horizontal functioning along with practical coaching tools for
remedying substandard performance on horizontal teams.

Part Three (Chapters Seven and Eight) shows you how to keep
the revolution alive. Chapter Seven features a refashioned approach
to sponsoring, monitoring, and recognizing people's progress,
endorsing a horizontal redistribution of wealth. Chapter Eight sup-
plies additional prescriptions for staying organizationally healthy
and fit. Because the maintenance of the horizontal revolution is
often difficult to plan and dangerous to coach, additional tools are
included here for both initiators and implementers.

When we first began to put our work together in the mid 1980s,
we saw an *evolution* taking place in the workplace. With the
pressure and panic over change, rapid-fire redesign efforts, and

downsizing, and the fear and anxiety these events have brought to managers, that evolution has become a *revolution*. We have seen it, felt it, lived it, and not least, reflected deeply upon it. It is as real as an earthquake and vivid as the sunrise. This book is our understanding of what that revolution means and how businesses can thrive by joining it.

Acknowledgments

Our learning experience has been enhanced through our interactions and involvements with some significant colleagues and teachers, and a host of wonderful team and organizational people along the way. Notable in this regard are John Ravens of Ravens & Associates (U.K.); Colin Ingleton of Edinburgh University; Chris Argyris of Harvard University; Ken Bishop, Larry Frame, Wally Smith, and Ron Birdsong of Litton: Guidance and Control Systems; Sandra Kowen and David Porteus of GE Capital; Jack Zenger of Zenger-Miller; Keith Fulton, Larry Langston, Bruce Schmidt, Dave Godair, Jon Storbeck, and the many able warriors at Disney; Maury Jacques and George Boyadjieff at Varco International; and our associates Bill Martin and Gary Entwhistle for their faith and encouragement over the years. We also give much thanks to organization development writer/consultant Richard Beckhard for his extensive review of our initial work and his recommendations. Major support and encouragement from Bill Hicks and Cedric Crocker of Jossey-Bass inspired and ignited us in this endeavor. And we offer our special appreciation to Winnie and Joan.

September 1994

Morris A. Graham
Laie, Hawaii

Melvin J. LeBaron
Brea, California

The Authors

Morris A. Graham is an established organizational psychologist, professor, consultant, and manager, and the president of Graham & Associates, an organization development and consulting firm. He has directed organization development projects and training both nationally and internationally, holding positions as a national director of the American Society of Training and Development's HRD-Consultancy Network, a manager in the London-based International Federation of Training and Development Organisations, and a consultant/trainer with the National Productivity Board of Singapore and the Zenger-Miller Training and Consulting Group. Graham has been a professor at the Scottish School of Business, Edinburgh University, and the Marriott School of Management, Brigham Young University, and was founder and director of the international organizational development program at Brigham Young University, Hawaii. Graham studied organizational development at Edinburgh University and received a Ph.D. degree (1974) in cross-cultural organizational psychology from the University of Arizona. His work has focused on developing and revitalizing team-based organizations into high-performance systems. He regularly delivers addresses to, conducts seminars for, and consults with major companies on how to design, implement, and coach horizontal work systems.

Melvin J. LeBaron is a prominent workplace coach and consultant. He is the founder of Mel LeBaron Learning Systems and president of Workable Workplace Systems and has worked with more than 200 business, industrial, and governmental organizations in five countries, using innovative techniques for building work teams; motivating high-performance, creativity, and leadership; and providing people with the principles and skills to maintain new directions in life. LeBaron received his Ed.D. degree (1971) in administrative leadership from the University of Southern California (USC). For nineteen years, he served as a faculty member and administrator with the USC School of Public Administration, and he has also served as visiting faculty at eight colleges and universities. He also has been chief-of-party for a U.S. State Department management training program and mayor and city councilmember for Brea, California (where he lives). Artistic and innovative in his work, LeBaron is credited with having a particular talent for creating change in the workplace and for providing much needed principles and prescriptions for the complex workplace problems of today. The author of thirty-two publications, he currently focuses on integrating skills and artistry into the processes identified in this book.

The Horizontal Revolution

Introduction: Revolutionary Change for Revolutionary Times

These are revolutionary times. Organizations are smashing and flattening their hierarchies, reengineering their key processes, and creating multifunctional teams that reach across departments to manage these processes. Horizontal revolutions are taking place everywhere in a new approach to survival in today's world of pervasive and relentless change, an approach that demands an intense focus on customer needs and superior process designs and executions, that assumes that knowledge and skills are domain specific and too complex to be nested within hierarchies, and that requires multifunctional teams to manage the new order of specialty coordination and work inventiveness.

A tacit acceptance of this horizontal revolution underlies all the corporate talk of pushing decision making down to the lowest possible level, driving out unnecessary work, paying people for results, and using horizontal teams to manage and improve core processes because these teams intensify focus and commitment, build core skills, spread knowledge to those who need it in order to perform, and deliver dramatic improvements in efficiency and speed.

We are not the prophets or even watchmen of this revolution but its missionaries, at a time when many organizations' reengineering–process redesign initiatives have floundered because leaders and managers lacked the appropriate redesign knowledge and artistry for crafting teams. Our text develops a framework for action, using teams as the building blocks crucial to accruing redesign's promised benefits. We describe how horizontal teams transform themselves into stewardships, thereby becoming the means to achieve sustainable process change and maintain organizational effectiveness. Drawing upon our actual experiences with hundreds of self-directed work teams and scores of horizontal initiatives, we show why some horizontal initiatives achieve success while others are still bumping up against their entrenched bureaucracies. We take a candid look at the challenges involved and provide hard-hitting practical suggestions and a prescriptive design for maturing individuals, teams, managers, and the organization as a whole through the four stages of the horizontal revolution: pioneering, settling-in, tilting, and transforming. Table I.1 outlines these stages and the characteristics you will see in each one. Table I.2 outlines the agendas of the horizontal revolution, describing goals in the areas of change, strategies, operations, policies, training, impact, challenges, benefits, and ownership.

   We take a process view of horizontal functioning. That all work is part of a process is a fundamental principle of quality improvement. A process is a set of interrelated work activities characterized by specific inputs and value-added tasks that produce specific outputs. Processes range from how employees perform their daily work to end-to-end processes for developing, producing, and distributing products and services. They can be internal and/or external and/or cross-organizational. Management and the continuous improvement of processes is owned by teams that do not just make and do things but are skilled in handling whole tasks and processes. They are mini-enterprises or small business units that can range from order fulfillment to product development.

✳   Reengineering, according to Hammer and Champy (1993, p. 32), is the fundamental rethinking and radical redesign of business processes to achieve dramatic improvements in critical, contemporary measures of performance, such as cost, quality, service, and speed. As we stated in the preface, the relationship between reengineering and horizontal teaming is analogous to both going on a diet *and* keeping the weight off. Someone on a starvation diet may reach ideal leanness within a very short time. Yet, unless the dieter undergoes a fundamental change in behavior, all of that weight, and perhaps more, may return. The horizontal teaming workout program that we propose here comes with a distinctive mind-set, approach, and tool kit for keeping corporate weight off once the firm is in organizational trim.

Horizontal teaming describes an organizational condition in which work teams have been transformed into horizontal stewardships entrusted with processes, a set of procedures for shared power and self-governance, a commitment to render service over the pursuit of self-interest, and a willingness to exercise long-term accountability for ensuring that processes meet customer requirements and for managing the improvement of team performance. Teaming challenges the traditional division of workplaces into two worlds: the patriarchal world of managers/supervisors and the subordinate world of workers/employees; the world of company and the world of community; the world of haves and the world of have-nots. These us-them worlds have been costly and are long overdue for redesign or retirement. The concept of horizontal teaming radically challenges all areas of organizational governance and control, establishing a new business mind-set and skill-set for the next generation of companies, which will employ work team partnerships for dramatic gains in productivity. Individuals and teams who will see themselves as stewards in this new order will accept ownership for the larger institution while surrendering the need to predict and control others.

With the reengineering of work into wider skill-sets around whole processes, the classic us-them icon of business, the pyramid-shaped organizational chart, is turned on its side—tilted, not inverted—to increase the capacity of individuals and teams to think more broadly, thrive on change, work across boundaries, and respond to the customer's definition of quality.

Horizontal teams are created from units that naturally fall together to complete a whole piece of work, a process. Members of these teams must be informed, constantly trained, and multi-skilled. Leaders must know how to support teams by listening, coordinating, coaching, counseling, training, removing barriers,

Table I.1. Stages of the Horizontal Revolution

Stage		Individual	Team	Management	Organization
					Arena
1. Pioneering Proactive		New team roles/goals, procedures and relationships clarified. Start-up sites identified and reengineered.	Orientation/awareness given. Team leaders, facilitators, and coaches selected and trained.	Supports teaming process and monitors results. Provides vision and mission.	Commitment to unfreezing of traditional culture occurs. Conceptual buy-in occurs.
	Reactive	Fears, confusion, alienation, and concerns about job security and new roles appear. Cautious affiliation appears.	No or little commitment to team or sense of shared ownership present. Us-them issues and cynicism appear.	Feelings of threat and resentment occur. Overwhelmed by support needs and transformation issues.	Economic, control, and competitive pressures felt. Productivity dips.
2. Settling-in Proactive		Problem solving and team leadership skills acquired. Conversion to team behavior occurs.	Whole work processes established across departments/work units. Harmonious cohesiveness and accountability for measurable performance goals appear.	Participatively shares more decision-making operations and authority. Makes process a priority.	Teams organized around business processes formed. Productivity and quality begin to improve.
	Reactive	Unresolved control and power issues appear. Distraction and political behavior appear.	Unresolved interpersonal conflicts and impatience appear. Cliques and factions competing for influence form.	Resists new management roles and shifts in power bases. Feels displaced.	Overwhelmed by increased training needs. Control versus letting go issues felt.

Stage				
3. Tilting	High degree of interdependence and integration with the sense of belonging occur. Communication channels open and mutual trust deepens.	Strong commitment to and support for the good of all team members develops. Individual performance and team progress on goals aligned.	Sustains vision, guidelines, and resources. Participates in team building and workouts.	Customer expectations for quality and service exceeded. Organizationwide commitment, support, appraisal, and rewards established.
4. Transforming	Competence in multiple tasks and adding value appears. High-performance, self-directed skills for collaborating, support, conflict resolution, innovation, and coaching are formed.	Leadership for cross-functional coordination, cooperation, and collaborative teamwork appears. Team stewardships throughout the organization and ownership of work outcomes appear.	Offers responsive leadership for strong team-based culture and norm. Coordinates, coaches, and facilitates boundary issues, cross-training, and celebrations.	Highly responsive, flexible, adaptive, and boundaryless system established. Perpetual improvement and renewal occur.

Table I.2. Agendas for the Horizontal Revolution

Characteristic	Individual	Team	Management	Organization
Change	Expect trust & new learning.	Require process ownership.	Incorporate new roles and reallocate resources.	Organize around processes not tasks/functions.
Strategies	Add value & contribution.	Reengineer mission and work.	Identify strategic objectives.	Flatten hierarchy & diminish boundaries.
Operations	Perform work where it makes sense.	Run processes & let customers drive performance.	Allow teams to manage.	Adjust norms & rewards.
Policies	Secure multiple skills over specialized know-how.	Challenge "whys" of everything.	Establish teaming benchmarks for goals.	Align new roles with budgeting system & structure.
Training	Link to involvement skills & customer satisfaction.	Increase skills for cross-sectional needs & team maturity.	Require coaching, facilitation, & leadership skills.	Foster behavioral learning.

Impact	Recommit to job security.	Make accountable for measurable performance & customer contact.	Eliminate all activities that fail to add value or contribute to teaming objectives.	Open the system & abolish corporate secrecy.
Challenges	Handle tight collaboration & peer pressure.	Become building blocks of organization.	Provide team support, resources, & compensation.	Use technology & information related to teams.
Benefits	Achieve greater control over work & personal development.	Accomplish more well-being, innovation, & multi-functional work.	Realize leapfrogging of ideas & improvements through the organization.	Sustain improved workmanship & revenues, & reduced bureaucracy & labor costs.
Ownership	Overcome barriers of denial, defensiveness, blame, & rationalizing.	Integrate support & sustain the next stop.	Move from storekeepers to revolutionists.	Transition into a culture of continous learning and renewal.

and resourcefully supporting. They must know how to empower teams by passing on business information; providing time and money for training; giving authority over to those who carry out decisions; and rewarding team performance. Executives must function as leaders who can influence and reinforce teams' values and beliefs by their words and actions. When teams are allowed to self-manage their day-to-day work, CEOs and top management are freed for such tasks as designing processes that ensure teams can do the job required.

The formal structure of an organization is a critical component in determining the information, knowledge, power, and rewards present at all levels. As a general rule, self-governing teams will compress work vertically as well as horizontally, resulting in fewer delays, lower overhead cost, better customer response, and greater self-fulfillment for workers. But the horizontal transformation required to make them self-governing represents no less than a bone-deep redistribution of power as teams make decisions once reserved for upper management. In the final stages of the horizontal revolution, teams have to be flexible enough to drive out the unnecessary work and adjust to changing market conditions, lean enough to beat any competitor's price, innovative enough to keep products and services technologically fresh, and dedicated enough to deliver maximum quality and customer services. Teams will have to pull diverse performance ethics and personalities together into work groups committed to a common vision and purpose, continuous learning and training, planning and communication, measuring and monitoring, successes and celebrations.

As long as teaming is in planning, most will declare their faith in it and think it is wonderful. The true struggle comes after the roll-out process begins. As pressure and confusion build, sacrifice, commitment, and artistry in fostering team work must replace self-interest, dependency, and vertical control. We guide you through the major structural and behavioral barriers so that your work teams can rise above inflexibility, unresponsiveness, the absence of customer focus and innovativeness, an obsession with activity rather than results, and bureaucratic paralysis. In this change, initially, many managers will experience a loss of power, feeling uprooted and unsupported. Senior leadership must create a new culture that is supportive and reassuring for these managers as the power dynamics of the system change. There will be many highly personal reactions by everyone in the work force, and we provide tips for dealing with them. Because systemwide acceptance and trust are difficult to achieve in the early stages of implementation, the revolution is fraught with additional costs of training and implementation to help workers develop "we" attitudes, share leadership, and enjoy social interaction.

We are the first to admit that undertaking the horizontal revolution is tough. Our analogy for the kind of toughness and persistence that is required is the American Revolution. The Revolutionary War was only a part of the struggle on the new states' road to becoming a modern nation, not the end. In 1783, after the war, this country entered a period of unstable commercial and political conditions. States acted like independent countries, running their affairs as they saw fit, with no concern for the broad purposes of the republic. They circulated their own currencies, which became inflated to a point where they had practically no value. State legislatures refused to pay the debts they had assumed during the Revolutionary War. Worst of all, some people began to think once again of taking up arms in order to solve their internal problems. George Washington and other leaders began to wonder whether the colonies had rebelled in vain. They felt it was time to end these troubles and bring peace and order by forming a new national government, but the task of creating that government was not easily accomplished. On several occasions, arguments over one point of dispute nearly wrecked the Constitutional Convention. Finally, there was partial approval of a direction to take.

We see a similar pattern every time the horizontal revolution is begun. So far as we know, there are no completed horizontal revolutions to serve as paradigms. What we do have, though, are some valid substantiations of the revolution's effects as it progresses. One of our client firms calculated its return on investment after it made its entire operation horizontal. By its own accounting, it put $1 million into teams and got a $6.5 million return on its investment. Productivity was up 45 percent; the scrap rate was reduced from 16 percent to 7 percent; total plant labor realization increased from 77 percent to 122 percent; and quality improvements, process innovations, customer satisfaction, and employee morale improved significantly with teams. We are believers!

Nevertheless, every step in any organization's horizontal revolution is a comma, not a period. There is always a next step. Frustrations and conflicts have to be the tools for growing and change. Challenge has to be a contribution to growth, not an adversary. The major lesson for all employees will be how to really serve each other. Unfortunately, a deep cynicism that is built upon anger and resentment is the greatest barrier. People's experience is that organizations and upper management are not able to listen to feedback and to change, that they cannot break out of their illusion that what they are doing now is essential. Cynicism makes getting a footing for change an awkward process. There is much skidding about during the revolution.

Some basic guidelines that we have found useful for people as they go through the stages of the horizontal revolution that follow are: put your initial effort on a localized central part of the organization involving a cross-section of middle management; coach these people in teaming until they are prepared to involve other key people who have the makings of commitment and are restless for change; provide inspired leadership and coaching for all the key people; and do not concentrate on the whole organization all at once or on high-powered selling, but ignite and guide each step as those involved take ownership for the process in a stimulating, forceful, and rewarding adventure at work!

Part One

_____

Staging the Revolution

Chapter One

Stage One: Pioneering: A Manager's Guide to Teams

> Most of us require a certain amount of
> independence and predictability in our lives.
> Change, particularly major change, may threaten
> our undeniable experience and convictions about
> individual responsibility and the risks involved in
> trusting other people. We may resist the change
> and cling to old views, ways, and habits. At those
> moments when our organization most needs to
> unleash [its] employee potential, our natural immune
> systems are screaming "control." We remember, only
> too well, the old days when our managers tightened
> everything down when things got bad. All this is
> only our natural reaction to fear.
>
> —*Line manager in a*
> *large service-directed organization*

A new, radical breed of high-performance work design and practice is propelling organizations into the next century. It is based on unleashing employees' potential through collective action and local accountability rather than control, so that committed employees at all levels are responsibly motivated to innovate and achieve together in self-directed teams, to face fierce competition, and to take on unprecedented challenges to serve customers. This new breed of work design empowers work teams to be builders and movers within horizontal structures. As management goes across, not up and down, teams develop the capacity to perpetually learn, improve, and innovate.

We cannot promise that the transformation of traditional teams into horizontal stewardships will be a joyful journey. This change is no quick, simple, and painless fix. On the contrary, it entails a smart implementation strategy followed by difficult, strenuous work. It requires that teams learn to run companies and learn how to reinvent and change themselves, replacing their old practices with entirely new ones, as each team, with its own independent personality, learns to manage a business process, a service, a geographic area, a function, or a core competence in a specific technology or service.

This chapter describes the first of four stages through which organizations can make teaming takeovers happen. A methodology for initiating horizontal functioning through teaming, the identification of resistance, and tactics for dealing with the most common implementation problems are key elements of this stage.

Overview of Stage One: Pioneering

The horizontal revolution in any organization begins with a pioneering stage, or exploration period. This stage is a time for seeing a new horizon beyond the ongoing functions of the organization, a time for searching out and blazing new trails for horizontal functioning and a time to issue a wake-up call to the work force.

Organizational leaders should expect this stage to take six months to two years. The time depends partly upon top management's willingness to put themselves at risk and enter the revolution. But it also depends on the amount of damage done by the war stories that will begin circulating and the depth of people's hidden agendas and their cynicism about the organization's ability to change. Old-line organizations will have sunk many resources into the status quo, and organizational members generally will not support the horizontal revolution unless compelling reasons convince them to do so. There will be several generations of workers who have never known anything but top-down hierarchy. They do not like this hierarchy, but liberation has frightening aspects for them also. They know what happened to those who followed Moses out of bondage across the Red Sea. Some would rather have predictable captivity than the aimless wandering that might result from freedom. Some question whether they can learn to function effectively in teams and to achieve benefits within a horizontal structure. Others question the validity of leaders' past decisions in order to assess the probable validity of this one. Moreover, at this stage, the organization's culture still promotes conformity to existing values and norms.

Our experience with revolutionary start-ups confirms that people will resist moving from the known to the unknown until they start meeting together in teams, gain an understanding of the nature of the change, legitimize their fears and concerns by discussing them openly, and then become active participants in the revolution's subsequent stages. In this early stage, people have concerns about how and where they will fit into a team, their individual and collective ability to accomplish the tasks ahead; and the team's ability to cope with problems and conflicts within the team itself. During this stage, attachment to teams is guarded and tentative. Team members are busy assessing each other's trustworthiness and acceptability and trying to become emotionally comfortable with each other. Power, influence, and authority issues will emerge if strong personalities attempt to dominate team agendas.

At this stage, expect few accomplishments and low productivity. However, once team members establish a comfort level of mutual trust and acceptance, they will begin to focus their attention on the work of the team.

Up-Front Involvement

Most horizontal team-based rollouts shake up virtually all aspects of a company. Up-front involvement by management is the key in identifying us-them conditions and increasing commitment to horizontal functioning. Managers who get involved in the nature of their changing roles gradually unfreeze their perceptions, broaden their thinking, and seriously consider the alternatives. Up-front involvement does carry risk. Whenever executives involve employees in the design and implementation process, they risk losing control. And if one cannot know at the outset of the horizontal revolution exactly what will happen, they wonder if the risk is worth taking? Most, however, find that it is. On one occasion, for example, we met with a branch manager who was concerned about her people's inability to gel into a self-directed team. But most of this fledgling team's frustration, lack of trust, and lack of confidence about making changes could be traced back to the manager's controlling and sometimes abusive management style. Team members openly expressed concerns about their ability to cope with problems and conflicts involving management. After listening to the group's concerns, we decided to involve the manager with the team in solving the problem of developing a relationship of trust. The employees, with the manager, came up with appropriate ideas and actions. Once involved, the manager felt responsible, and her responsive involvement contributed greatly to the success of the team.

Steering and Design Teams

At the outset of the horizontal revolution, organizations must create steering and design teams. The steering team is a policymaking body that oversees and guides the horizontal revolution, sets priorities, establishes task forces to address specific changes and make recommendations, makes final decisions on changes, and monitors processes. It establishes throughout the organization a spirit of self-diagnosis and self-redesign of workplaces around processes. This team is important in the initial stages, but its function will diminish as teams mature.

A design or "reengineering" team is a select, cross-sectional/functional group of eight to fifteen people—key managers supervisors/team leaders and key functional people with technical expertise. It is supported by the steering team and it researches staffing and operational issues that must be answered prior to start-up during the four phases of the horizontal revolution. Both these teams will be discussed in greater detail in Chapter Four, but it is important to remember that they must be present from the beginning of the process.

Intervening with Revolutionary Initiatives

What makes horizontal initiatives so difficult is that many try to achieve them with methods springing from the very systems that they intend to reform. Change efforts fail when the revolutionary process is not congruent with its intent. If management's intention is to create ownership, self-directedness, and responsibility among frontline people, they must transform the distribution of power, purpose, and ownership. Following are four intervention steps we have found to facilitate the process of change.

Formulate a Vision Together. Creating a vision of the desired future state is a major task of leadership at all levels of the organization. This task will be heavily driven by people's values and their beliefs about what horizontal functioning should look like and how it should function. When the process of stating a vision is worked out with subordinates and others who have a stake in the changes, it will energize commitment, provide a valued common challenge, and create a means to guide and assess both the implementation of change and team members.

Vision statements should include the organization's major strategic purpose or reason for existing; the specific performance and human outcomes the organization would like to achieve; a statement about what the organization should look like to achieve the valued outcomes; and the desirable organizational conditions that will occur between the current state and the desired future state. Such a vision statement, properly prepared in an environment of horizontal action, will be a blueprint for the revolution, providing a view of a place individuals, teams, managers, and the organization have never been before.

Recently, an executive stood before an assembly of his company's managers and supervisors and declared the following vision:

> This is the message of the horizontal revolution that has to come forth from those responsible for the entire organization.
>
> 1. This is not a top-down thing driven by a bunch of VPs. It is based upon each person in the organization being the starting point.
>
> 2. We must change the way we do business or we will be out of business. We have to do it. We can't just talk about doing it.
>
> 3. We have to be open to change like we have never been open to change. Our success in the past has little to do with our need for success in the future. What has happened to once great organizations that are now fallen should be incentive enough for us to change. There are footsteps behind us.
>
> 4. We will find a way to deal with those who are not team players.
>
> 5. This is going to be tough, and we have to deal with frustrations, blockages, and problems that come along.
>
> 6. We have to work smarter, not harder. We have to get our people to find ways to really enjoy their jobs.
>
> 7. This is a time for internal reassessment. We are too bureaucratic. We are too slow. Internal barriers are holding us back. Politics and hidden agendas play far too great a role in our organization. There is a lack of cooperation and coordination here. Risk taking is discouraged. There is a fundamental resistance to change. Communication is top-down and people don't get the message right. We don't listen.
>
> 8. I am committed to making this change happen. This is a call to action. This is not a short-term thing; a one-way-only method;

a series of cost-cutting measures; or a program. This is a new way of thinking and a process-journey.

9. From now on, we are coaches, not bosses. We communicate frequently at all levels. We get and use feedback. We encourage risk taking. We promote values of teamwork. We energize those around us through involvement and commitment building. There will be new leadership training and management development. We will change the evaluation process to one of 360-degree assessment. We will launch succession planning. We will develop vehicles for facilitation. Management will spend more time communicating with staff.

10. We must start the revolution by identifying barriers. Management will be held accountable for strategies and initiatives. Some of you think your bosses won't get this. Those who don't get it will have an uncomfortable time here. It's priority! We have to resort what we are doing and deal with conflicting priorities. Behaviors have to change. We will assess our change on a six-month interval.

This executive has the message of the horizontal revolution; he is seeing before saying. He realizes that the top-down hierarchy is being tilted on its side and that all processes are now done through teams. As the tilted hierarchy becomes more multidimensional, it also becomes more substantive by eliminating waste and work that do not add value. Much of the unproductive work of this manager's organization existed due to boundaries and fragmentation of tasks within its bureaucracy. Now, people are spending more time doing real work. They have examined and abandoned long-established procedures and looked afresh at what processes are needed to make a better product or service and deliver added value to the customer. They have taken tasks that were performed by individuals or groups that had no responsibility for, or knowledge of, the entire process, and integrated them into the work of a team. These teams are not only producing new wine, they are pouring it into new bottles, producing their own commitments and quality and in turn creating climates for customer responsiveness.

Create Readiness for Change. When people become dissatisfied with organizational pyramids and fragmentation, they are ready to try new ways of behaving. We design orientation sessions that lower people's thresholds of awareness and that sensitize people to the pressures for change, reveal discrepancies between current and desired states, and convey credible positive expectations of change. One of our most fundamental axioms is that people's readiness for change depends on management's creating a felt need and that people's willingness to act on that need must involve a commitment for change.

As the hierarchy tilts, work groups need opportunities to break down old rigid patterns that hinder innovation and competitiveness. Have team members generate a list of barriers and work through approaches to eliminate them. Following is a typical list, compiled by a pioneering team in a client organization:

- Jobs have become routine.
- We have been beaten down so much and so long we are cynical.
- We believe those above us need to be open to change without being threatened.
- Our ideas have been squelched.
- We are inbred and closed to new ways of doing things.
- [We] believe if we express an opinion there will be negative ramifications.
- Intimidation prevents risk taking.
- We get no thanks, just criticism.
- There is fear of management.
- Teams have been formed, but with cautious people because of concern for who gets credit.
- We do not have the resources needed to deal with our problems.

- There is too little positive reinforcement for doing a good job.
- We need to find our special niche and way to create, contribute—but we need the time/priority.
- Ideas are territorial.
- We are apprehensively excited—we have to get beyond this to what is holding us back.
- We have position-to-position relationships—not person-to-person.
- We need personal recognition, appreciation, respect.
- Management are too corporate.

Once this work group had worked through and resolved most of its list, it was ready to blaze ahead.

Create a Commitment for Change. To help people make the mental transition into horizontalizing and be committed to carry out their new responsibilities, we suggest that managers use a four-step commitment pattern of one-on-one preparing, inviting, following up, and resolving concerns. This pattern guides people from where they are to where they need to go.

Prepare. Begin by building interaction with all concerned and affected employees. Present the vision and redesigned plans and take time to find out how employees feel about the vision and plans.

Invite. Have key executives and consultants/coaches share their understandings and convictions about horizontal systems with employees. Then ask them to study the literature on horizontal organizations and participate in clarification sessions.

Follow up. Arrange interviews between coaches and employees to see if individual employees have questions about horizontal structures.

Resolve concerns. In the interviews, help employees resolve concerns by identifying their problems, asking them to describe more about the problems, and explaining whatever will assist them to find solutions.

Before managers are asked to develop commitment patterns with their employees, they need to work out their own concerns about coaching. Listen in to selected comments as this horizontally inclined group of managers discusses how group members see their need to prepare, invite, follow up, and resolve concerns:

"We need to become a center of learning, and particular individuals need to break off for team building and coaching. It's time to resolve our conflicts. It's time to identify our leaders of the future. We have a problem learning from our mistakes. We don't like to face ourselves."

"Managers don't know how to be coaches."

"Managers need to get experience in coaching. We have to continue moving forward. We are a lot more open today than we were a year ago."

"We aren't going to make it by coming to this meeting expecting to be spoon-fed."

"We have to learn from each other and share our experiences in the field. We need to come to this group and identify something we have tried that hasn't worked. Then, we need to get help."

"Our problems are with each other, so we can't get help from each other."

"Coaching is putting aside the way we have been doing things for many years. This is new leadership."

"My twelve-year-old son would respond to coaching the same way we do. He would vote against it, for the same reason that he hates math, English, and other hard subjects."

"The most important thing we can do is to be accountable to each other in our relationships."

"Issues are, one, What are teams and what is coaching? Two, What do we do as managers?"

"The larger the group, the more diversity of the agendas."

"We need skill development for everyone, whatever group [he or she belongs] to."

"We are at a pivotal point. We are at a crossroads."

"When we meet, we have to have a purpose. Just meeting won't do it. We have to create a team to solve problems."

"We can't appropriately address problems unless we have gone through team building. With team building, we conflict but aren't left with baggage."

"Are there any other ideas? We have only heard from a few. Participation is expanding, but many haven't said anything—and this really bothers me that some of you never say anything."

"It is expected that we are all strong technically. We will be looked at in the future for the leadership we provide and the way our behavior contributes to our goals and pursuits."

At this meeting, these managers said things to each other and about each other that they had never said before. They broke a new path leading from manager to coach. Managers are required to walk this path or be consumed by the horizontal revolution.

Create a Climate for Dealing with Resistance. Change can generate deep resistances in people, making it difficult, if not impossible, for some to be part of horizontal organizations. A proposed change can arouse considerable anxiety about letting go of the known and moving to an uncertain future. Individuals may have significant questions about whether they can learn to function effectively and to achieve benefits in the new situation. Specific forms of resistance that people will engage in are:

- Showing fears, confusion, and alienation
- Expressing concerns about job security and new roles
- Resisting coaching and teaming activities

- Continuing a business-as-usual attitude
- Bringing up many issues of control versus letting go
- Endlessly grumbling about others behind the scenes
- Playing intensive political games

Methods for dealing with such resistance should include at least the three following strategies.

Respect and empathy. Identify those who are having trouble accepting change, the nature of their resistance, and possible ways to overcome it. Respect and empathy demand active listening—a willingness to suspend judgment and see the situation from the other person's perspective. People respond to the offer of a more open relationship by being less defensive, more willing to share their concerns and fears, and more committed to do the joint problem solving needed to overcome barriers to change.

Communication. Lack of effective communication leads to distortion and gossip and adds to the apprehension generally associated with change. Effective communication begins when people increase each other's capacity to confront personal ideas and face unsurfaced assumptions and fears. Individuals can advocate their own position but combine that advocacy with inquiry and self-reflection. It is important for people to encourage others to say what they know yet fear to say and to minimize thoughts subject to distortion and cover-up. Each party should advocate his or her beliefs in a way that invites inquiry into those beliefs and encourages other people to be open about their beliefs

Participation and involvement. Involving employees directly in planning and implementing change is one of the most effective strategies for overcoming resistance. During the pioneering stage, there are many hidden agendas. While there will be talk aplenty about the desirability of moving away from a hierarchical pattern, most of this talk is not to be believed. At this stage, espoused theory is not believable. Behavior, or theory-in-action, is believable. The behaviors to be looked for are those that indicate ownership: taking on new team roles and goals, learning to be coaches, clarifying new procedures and relationships in groups, and identifying new agendas and action items.

Work groups indicate that they have taken ownership when they engage in team building, show new awareness for work group relationships, are driven by team leadership, and select and train team facilitators.

Managers indicate that they have taken ownership when they become new champions of teaming and coaching, provide directions and discipline for teamwork, appropriately monitor results, and learn new management and coaching skills.

An organization indicates that it has taken ownership when it walks its talk, unfreezes from the traditional ways of doing things, shows conceptual buy-in, and clarifies expectations.

How Do Organizations Tilt the Pyramid?

How do organizations tilt the organizational pyramid with minimal resistance? How do they redistribute the power, authority, and responsibility so that the employees closest to the customer, the product, or the end result have the power to do what needs to be done in order to meet constantly changing customer demands? When work is designed around whole processes and process management responsibilities are established with teams, much of the need for supervisors to coordinate work and motivate individuals vanishes. When the need for managerial and support staff functions diminishes, the organizational pyramid begins to tilt. When self-directed, process-oriented teams produce most of the products or services, the organizational pyramid begins to tilt. Acting within the agreed upon boundaries of accountability—that is, desired outcomes, quality standards, deadlines, and so on—teams determine how and when work is going to be done. If they wait for supervisory direction, the organizational pyramid will not tilt.

Once some horizontal functioning is in place, leadership must be willing to let go of even more control in order to provide teams with sufficient authority and the resources necessary for increased team self-management. As teams become operational, they can do what needs to be done to identify and satisfy customer requirements. They can look for problems to be solved: How can costs be lowered? How can waste and bureaucracy be eliminated? How can things be done faster, better, and smarter? As one new team leader stated: "We have to give our work teams some structure. They have to define their responsibility. We have to help them categorize their responsibility into similar functions and give each category a title. Elect members to fill each position and rotate positions. . . . Our teams have to mature. We may want to use the word partnership more than team. Each team needs a mission statement, philosophy, and a set of values. We have to spend more time with the teams to be sure our philosophy and values are together."

A lack of good grounding is a common design implementation problem in the pioneering stage. A client in a religiously affiliated organization explained how they had enthusiastically started creating teams but how, after a year, they had "lost the faith." Their voluntary teams had become "peripheral to" or "stuck on to" their old structure, or could not be found on the organization chart at all. One insightful individual in this organization then observed that their experience was reminiscent of the parable of the sower, who went out to sow his seeds, and some fell by the wayside, some fell upon rocks, others fell among thorns—and they either were trodden down, devoured, withered away because they lacked moisture, or were choked among the thorns. Similarly this organization's teams had been sown with hope but had fallen on such poor soil as lack of organizationwide ownership and commitment, ineffective planning, inadequate skills, and an infrastructure unsupportive of the team concept.

In this stage, it is key to remember that restructuring needs good soil. That soil is prepared by a design exercise in which those closest to the job participate; they are often in the best position to recommend design changes. In addition, most successful horizontal implementations involve people at all levels of the old hierarchy. The more all the stakeholders are involved in the design and implementation process, the more likely it will be that a balance can be realized between short-term performance and longer-term institution building. Often, workers closest to the job, especially at lower organizational levels, are not accustomed to having significant input in decision making. Part of the pioneering stage is helping them realize, through the strategies suggested in this chapter, that their contribution is part of the product, that outcomes are only as good as the number of contributions made, and that only when healthy conflict and consensus decision making translate into new norms will the team culture bear fruit.

Internal Barriers

Initially, management must pay attention to features of us-them conditions that increase the potential for embarrassment or threat to managers and employees. Managers, for example, may find the revolutionary initiative that is unleashed difficult to control. Feeling threatened, they may revert to the old practice of unilateral control. The resistant manager typically fits this profile:

- Is fairly new in his or her current position and wants to make all the right moves.
- Has done the same things the same way for twenty years.
- Is a linear thinker and has an arrogant attitude.
- Makes changes through restructuring, not behavioral change.
- Is responsible for twenty to thirty managers and/or supervisors who are working hard but not getting desired results.
- Employs a formal, but awkwardly used, form of performance appraisal.

- May appear to work hard to get others to take ownership but has specific productivity objectives.
- Conducts formal staff meetings and knows little about coaching, facilitation, or involvement.
- Defends against all new ideas by saying, "I'm already doing that!"

Many a manager will view proposed changes as threatening to his or her power and importance. When such managers see the revolution coming, they cry out that top management are turning the institution over to the inmates. They see any reduction in the old hierarchy as a total abdication. But the horizontal transformation should not be viewed as a change from dictatorship to anarchy. Pioneering the revolution is a process of finding a balance between all-inclusive hierarchy and no hierarchy. Us-them barriers that can restrain the change process crop up in issues involving management role changes, return-on-investment, redistribution of power, egos and arrogance, creative types, old-timers and turf, increased workload and stress, trust, lack of accountability, feelings of being overwhelmed with quality control issues, perceptions of unequal work, and consensus seeking. Barriers thrown up by these issues should be addressed concurrently with any checklist for implementation. The following sections address each issue separately to help implementers work through the barriers.

Management Role Changes

Suspicion, uncertainty, discomfort, and resistance to any new way of acting or thinking are natural and inevitable. Because managers, especially first-line supervisors, enjoy the status and money that the hierarchy gives them, they may feel robbed or cheated as their power apparently slips away, and they may resist and sabotage the revolution, even though the employees may love it. It is important for top management to realize that first-line supervisors are the key to making the revolution work, and yet they have the most to lose. Therefore, if possible, they should be assured that, while their roles will change, they will still have jobs.

However, sometimes, it is sometimes easier to change *people* than it is to *change* people. One manager at a client organization forthrightly stated: "I believed that my actions were perfectly aligned with the organization's vision of coaching, when in reality I am overly directive. It feels awkward to let people have a say. I know the solution, and it's tough to give them control. There are things they don't know about the situation, and they don't need to know them either. Why should I show any inclination to change when I see no need? I guess that I'm supposed to have some feedback. If I don't get it—or if I do get it but don't accept it and act on it—I'll continue as I am. I'm pretty set in my ways." We appreciated his personal awareness and frankness, but our response was, "Did you ever find a tiny fly in a great big bowl of soup? What was your reaction? One thing is certain: all of the soup was spoiled."

There is a flip side to the situation just described. In their effort to change, some managers will model the desired participative leadership style but overcompensate and fail to be directive when direction is needed. In the pioneering stage, new teams are often highly motivated but do not know what to do. They need direction. Leaders need to exercise the right balance, allowing young teams to act but also telling them what they need to do when necessary.

Maturing teams will gradually assume most of their supervisor's responsibilities. First-line supervisors will have to let go of titles and authority and let teams make decisions for themselves. As mentioned, some will be wondering if they are even going to have a job when the change is in place and others will be left with an inadequate understanding of their new roles and feel frustrated and insecure. Their apprehension about being caught in the middle should be unfounded, since people should still be needed in creative roles, and supervisors can often move into advisory, coaching, and facilitator roles and work across teams as leaders of change. Some will become senior technical experts or just team members. Others may move into higher management. And, indeed, some may choose to bail out—a 5 to 10 percent turnover among supervisors is common unless a dramatic restructuring initiative or middle management "meltdown" is the order of the day. However, the supervisor who learns the business of the emerging organization, who is well informed of his or her new responsibilities, who is willing to share power and become a leader of change, and who gains new skills as a bureaucracy-busting team player will feel more assured of the future and will offer less resistance to the organization's change to horizontal functioning.

After the transition to horizontal work teams, managers must assist workers to take on their new roles of leading themselves. They must learn to coach rather than order, to allow teams to go through the sometimes arduous process of decision making. For most managers, leading this change and later functioning in the new environment that results from change will be as difficult as anything they have ever undertaken, and it is helpful to know the typical concerns voiced by managers reluctant to accept the horizontal concept:

- We'll lose power and control of outcomes.
- What we're doing was "not invented here."
- Don't rock the boat; or, if it's working, don't mess with it.
- The work force is not able to solve problems.
- The change interferes with budget policies.
- The unions may threaten to intervene.
- Unions will feel threatened by the team process.
- Teams will generate overloads in work changes (especially in engineering and maintenance organizations).
- There will be too much additional work to be done.

- We will lose our recognized authority (ego) as we become "associates."
- The seniority in the system is threatened.
- Changes in the us-them relationship will affect valued class distinctions in pay and perks.
- Job duties and responsibilities will shift.
- Responsibility will be pushed down.
- We will have to share information that has not been shared before.
- We will be subject to performance tracking systems.
- We may lose quarterly profits.
- We do not know when we will see the payback.
- We will face mandatory participation in the process.

Top management must be strong enough and clear enough to withstand the ups and downs that characterize the pioneering stage of development. By becoming aware of the depth of people's concerns early on, top management can determine if horizontal functioning is appropriate for the organization and/or what precautions or preparations to take. If top-level managers promise middle managers that the change will be deeply rewarding, they should state what, exactly, will be so rewarding about it. Finally, managers, like first-line supervisors, should know that seasoned managers need not be discharged as the organization proceeds with change. They can add far more value as internal consultants or trainers or as internal software developers than they ever could as managers.

Return on Investment

Like any major undertaking, the shift to horizontal teams involves an up-front financial investment. However, horizontal development happens over time and does not follow a straight path as teams move along the evolutionary continuum toward high-performance. Therefore, start-up costs and the patience to implement a team culture will likely be challenged up-front. A return on investment may not be apparent for at least a year or so. However, our experience affirms that horizontal organizations have always been the ones with the best people, training and developing what they have and recruiting the best they can get from the labor pool. Over time, horizontal teams will provide a definite edge.

Nevertheless, since most companies' measurement indicators are centered around profit, it is difficult for the typical manager to look at the team process and not be skeptical, and the greatest concern usually comes from the accounting areas. Moreover, sharing information with the work force about profits, costs, and feedback from customers has not been the order of the day. After giving up total control, management may focus on who will be responsible for loss in profit. Who will be held accountable in monthly cost analysis meetings? When will we see the returns, or reap the benefits of this process? Some may even demand measurable success a month after implementation!

✻   Long-term commitment is required of a leadership hoping to establish a horizontal culture. The CEO must be overtly committed, with visible support from the staff. This is not to say that the change process goes unmonitored, but that a long-range plan established to measure success must be based on years, not months or quarters. In some cases, it can take up to six months for a team to overcome the difficulties of working as a group, initially showing nothing on the books.

Moreover, as teams do start contributing, reward systems and policies will need to be changed. Matured teams can increase productivity by 30 to 40 percent, and it is guaranteed that team members will then be asking a valid question, "What's in it for us? We're making the company all this extra money, creating innovations and making improvements, and so on, and we are still drawing the same old wage." Management must be prepared with team-based compensation plans in which as much as one-third of a team member's wages are determined by individual and team performance.

Redistribution of Power

When managers come to realize that their repertoire of management skills, often developed over years of experience and struggle, will become at least in part obsolete, they worry that they will not successfully master new coaching and facilitating skills. As discussed earlier, considerable time should be spent helping supervisors and managers understand their new roles, and some will not be able to make the transition.

Supervisors and managers in new roles may mask their fears with the concerns listed earlier about union intervention or poor decisions and sharing information. These people may be unsympathetic to team decision making, for this is an area in which their special skill was the basis of their reputation and influence. Singular expertise owned by such loners can be disruptive to teamwork and result in ploys and power moves designed to upset the process of team development. Genuine equality becomes a reality only when all team members are equally talented (cross-trained), or equally ✶ ignorant.

Redistribution barriers like salaried benefits, reserved parking, executive lunchrooms, differential sick leave, comp time, and so on will surface early. These should be quickly addressed and modified as the team culture transforms the organization. The best approach is a long-range training program that initiates management into the participative style and gives them the tools they need to work successfully in their new associate roles in the participative culture. In some instances, managers may require individual counseling. When members of the leadership begin to understand their roles as coordinators, coaches, and facilitators, they will realize successes and dismiss the threats they initially feared. It is up to the leadership team to work on this problem together and to talk openly and honestly in workout sessions about the difficulties each one faces.

Egos and Arrogance

Aside from the fear that participative teamwork will take power and authority away from management, there is the issue of the ego (self-esteem) bruising that comes with the advent of work teams. The manager who took twenty years getting to the top expects some sort of recognition, respect, and authority with the investment. When a team comes up with a good idea never thought of by management, this manager perceives that action to be a put-down of his or her managerial skills. Subsequently, the manager may view the idea of teamwork as something not invented by management, but imported and imposed, and reject it believing that it will not work here. Whatever the reasoning, and no matter how trivial it may seem, it is his or her perception of the situation. If the change process is to see the light of success in all areas of the company, this manager's concerns should be addressed. Such attention to individuals' concerns may make implementing the team concept tedious at times, but since the benefits and growth potential are limitless if the leadership team is on board and has a mission statement to direct it, this attention is well worth the time it takes.

The toughest part of the horizontal revolution is getting big egos off their high horses. However, big egos should diminish as the passion for change moves even executive spirits. As one executive who made this move from ego to passion stated, "When you see everyone benefit and all being winners, you have to go for it. It's amazing what goes on. It works! It really works!" The horizontal revolution works, but passion, not ego is its driving force.

Look at the history of those organizations that have crumbled, or are crumbling. From all accounts, they have been ego- and arrogance-bitten. Almost without exception, this drive to fulfill management egos has meant that the leaders of these organizations failed utterly to adjust to the new realities of fast-moving technology and less loyal customers; played out a tragedy in which their passion for the company inspired but ultimately blinded them; developed an arrogance that could not contemplate change, let alone failure; created a culture that was paralyzingly closed and conformist; endlessly debated but did not decide; were rewarded for presenting ideas, not implementing them; and practiced a form of "organizational fascism" in which they kept an iron grip on employees.

Creative Types

What about those people who stand alone, the entrepreneurial and highly skilled craftsperson who exhibits an irreverence toward the new norm, which may render him or her an effective generator of ideas but a lousy team player? As team members, these creative people can be critical naysayers of others and thereby block team requests for resources, information, people, and permissions; be alienated from others by their intensity, personal project focus, and idiosyncrasies; be segregated and misunderstood; be perceived as indifferent, self-serving, and disruptive to the team's way of doing things; and suffer from feelings of abandonment. A typical reaction to maverick personalities is to pull them out of the team to work alone. This is a legitimate response, and one that some feel will circumvent the time-consuming effort of getting mavericks to become high-performance team players and the tendency of large teams with several mavericks to split into smaller interest groups.

Some companies are starting to hire only people who are team players, but they are denying themselves potential sources of innovation. Creative thinkers should not be discarded but taught team skills so that their brilliant ideas will not be rejected. Working in a team may never be their forte, but they can learn enough skills to get along. Conversely, team members can be helped to develop tolerance of creative thinkers.

Old-Timers and Turf

Older workers, in particular, may be distrustful of change. Partic-ipative management practices have, by and large, not been central to their work experience. Some old-timers do not want added responsibility, do not want to change, and may fault teams as abusers of the freedom in the system. They may think that the orga-nization should go back to the "old school," in which managers had control and, they think, it was easier to get things done. Change takes them out of their comfort zones and their expert/specialty roles, and they may also feel that they are not receiving as much preference and training as some of their more eager and younger colleagues.

Often, there is a wide chasm of misunderstanding that must be bridged, and it is important that team leaders and managers be aware of how older workers feel and find ways to venerate and inte-grate their expertise. Teams can employ their most senior members as expert trainers by allowing them a few minutes during team meetings to train the team. All team members learn how to do their jobs better, and the older worker feels useful and a part of the new culture. Management can be supportive by openly encouraging such strategies and by privately counseling individuals pessimistic about the process.

Increased Workload and Stress

It should come as no surprise that, when there is talk of a horizon-tal initiative on the drawing board, the first question that arises is, How are we going to give an hour or two a week to a team meet-ing when we are already behind schedule and pushed for time? This question is usually asked by first-line supervisors, and for a good reason. As the ones who interact with the front line directly, they will be much more intimate with the work teams than will middle and upper levels of management. At first, they perceive this new interaction as bringing them more work and do not see their changing role as one of making teams function.

Support areas ask, If teams begin to make changes, will they impact on the workload of our departments? The answer is a definite yes! Initial items that teams address are usually maintenance related. They are such things as building or work-area layouts, process or assembly steps, logistical and vendor-related parts problems, and so forth. This creates an additional workload on the support areas. It is up to cross-functional teams to aid in the work-flow process, remove obstacles from a team's path, and help the implementation penetrate support staff.

Capital expenditure issues will also have to be dealt with by leaders. One suggestion is that the organization use a streamlined *improvement account* with a discretionary fund so that approved suggestions from teams can be implemented without having to go through the capital expenditure approval process. This will do two things: expedite the implementation of cost-saving ideas and create trust that management are truly committed to the team process.

Finally, teaming does not function well in organizations experiencing high levels of uncertainty. A launch can be impaired significantly if implemented during the periods of rapid growth or decline, merger rumors, change in top management, or retrofitting operations. As one team member in this situation put it, instead of desired self-directedness, "we're getting new responsibilities that we never wanted."

Lack of Trust

Trust is one of the prime catalysts for increasing productivity and quality in any organization. Managers and supervisors need to trust that, given time, employees will actively support the extensive changes necessary for success. Employees need to trust that this is not a new approach to get more work out of fewer people, that management are sober and committed about wanting people to make decisions and take risks. Those who continue to compete among themselves, rather than pulling together to better compete against outside competitors, will never see the horizontal revolution. As one manager we know said to his peers, "The biggest thing is for us to get defensiveness down and get self-satisfaction and personal results up in the process of institutionalizing change. . . . The world of work is changing and it's not about control anymore." And so many times, we have heard managers say, "All of us have a mindset for doing good, but we put up with all this B.S. We butt heads and have this 'I'm right and you're wrong' attitude." Managers must have credibility to be accepted. They will not gain credibility until they show trust, of each other as well as of workers.

Generally, work teams' reactions depend on the quality of the organization's past relationship with all its employees. Workers will be asking of management, "Can we trust them? Or is this another way of getting rid of people?" If trust is not in place, people will withhold sharing their ideas and disengage themselves from horizontal functioning. It is necessary then, to communicate the total intent of the horizontal teaming process to the whole work force, even though all of them will not enter into the process at once. This communication of intent is meant to get beyond "read my lips" declarations to a companywide agreement of "let's trust each other." By going public with their intent, management are taken more seriously about that intent. Organizational surveys have found that workers in companies undergoing change state that the problems are caused by management not walking their talk, management declining a team suggestion without explaining why the idea would not be used, management sending mixed signals about the cultural shift, and management not helping to remove those obstacles that hindered team development (Beer, Eisenstat, and Spector, 1990, p. 161). Thus, one of the best ways to show management support for the horizontal revolution is to launch work teams of managers first or to include management in the initial cluster of teams. In addition, to encourage an atmosphere of trust, a special task group, made up of the most positive and desirable players in the organization, should be given the task of monitoring the progress, problems, and concerns of the teams. They can accomplish this by meeting the facilitators weekly and discussing issues that have come up in team meetings, and helping to curb problems by showing positive support of the team process and a commitment to the participative approach.

Lack of Accountability

We have found that, because they have less fear of personal punishment, individuals in a group tend to make riskier decisions than individuals who are solely responsible for an outcome. Group members are willing to take risks because the whole group will absorb the consequences. Moreover, groups usually are not held as accountable for their work as individuals. Conversely, group members may not put forth extra effort to bring about good decisions because they feel they will not get recognition for their sacrifices.

However, as horizontal functioning introduces the process of continuous improvement and groups become work teams, all the organizational accountability factors change. Everyone is expected to work on improving quality, timeliness, safety, and other measures by eliminating waste, rework, non–value-added time, unnecessary paperwork, bureaucratic rules and procedures, interruptions, and so forth. It is a never-ending journey because there is no limit to the potential of a team of accountable people working constantly on improving things. Accountability is enhanced when teams establish their own ground rules, mutually agreed, on ways of conducting themselves.

There are lessons to be learned from companies involved with Quality Circles in the 1970s and 1980s. In some cases, circle activity became nothing more than a lame suggestion system—circles made recommendations that their managers would consider and accept or reject. Circle members were asked to come up with solutions, but they rarely had the power and authority to transform their ideas into actions. The process also became stifled by the inability of circle members to cross over into other areas for input and implementation. Managers, too, were told to keep out of circle activities and assist only when invited. In other words, managers were to support circle decisions at their discretion and take responsibility for a circle's outcome—but not interfere. This estranged relationship created feelings of frustration and resentment and led to the demise of many circles. It became obvious that a successful partnership between managers and work groups required accountability from both groups in the sharing of goals, resources, communication, and problem solving.

Managers of horizontal functioning become accountable partners with team members by creating their departmental goals with and through each of their teams. The idea of goal alignment with teams is not a new concept. Creating departmental goals through teams is new. The logic here is fundamental. First, the process allows for straightforward communication to each member of each team. Second, it makes the manager more accessible to team members and develops a level of trust and accountability that otherwise might be lacking. Third, an awareness of the business system is available to each team on an assigned basis, creating better understanding of how the firm functions overall.

Feeling Overwhelmed with Quality Control and Team Issues

Our observation of numerous total management control (TMC)/ self-directed work team initiatives across the United States has revealed a common barrier that must be dealt with at the outset of any joint implementations. Employees can get very uptight about "instant quality" imperatives. For many employees, the concept of quality control relates strongly to feelings of both success and failure, both self-esteem and meeting somebody else's expectations.

It is one thing to empower workers to decide questions of cost, quality, vendor relations, and administrative practices. It is quite another thing to replace capital equipment, introduce a statistical process control system, or train everyone in customer service. Organizationwide quality initiatives may collaterally discourage teaming initiatives by presenting quality strictly as a matter of standards, specifications, control, zero defects standards, and "doing it right the first time." A directive that starts out as simply as, "Get those teams up to speed on statistical process control," can elicit mixed reactions from team members. The emotional question often asked is, What does this quality stuff mean to me? or, What's going to happen to me? As employees look for answers, attempting to create meaning and stability in their new work world, there will be some organizational upheaval and a tendency to retreat to business as usual.

The quality paradigm for horizontal functioning, however, is not so much one of immediate results as it is one of processes; it is a journey that takes many steps (small successes) and ultimately adds up to larger successes. Emotional reactions are to be expected but can be minimized if visions, goals, processes, and benefits to the employee and company are communicated up front. Good implementation designs will integrate and project quality and team priorities down the road one to three years. Set goals and timetables, but let teams figure out the work reorganization on their own.

Unequal Work

A newly created multifunctional team is often carried by a minority while a majority get by on minimal or no work at all. If this situation continues, soon the members in the minority will get disheartened and lower their quality of work. A lack of incentives and recognition, caused by an ineffective system of measuring individual effort and contribution, will soon result in the decline of productive members' output. Multifunctional teams do not usually have peer assessments until the team has been together for a period of time. When teams do begin to use peer reviews certain assumptions can be made about the benefits of peer assessment over traditional forms of appraisal: peers know each other better than outsiders can;

each peer can really see—both technically and as a team player—how the others work; peers have most to gain, or lose, by providing fair, accurate feedback; peers will provide fairer assessments by several raters, not just one opinion; and peer pressure will be a powerful motivator to resolve the problem of unequal work.

Consensus Seeking

Many of the actions taken by teams are driven by consensus decisions that the majority favors, and that the minority, after being heard and having had ample time to persuade and influence the majority, agrees to implement. However, this participative process is time-consuming and may not promise the best, or even a workable conclusion in all cases. Simply put, even when most agree, it does not mean that the best answer has been found. Even in a truly horizontal organization, it is scarcely conceivable that all decisions can or should be made in a highly participatory manner. Often time is short, so the decision needs to be made by an informed individual without widespread consensus.

Reaching the point where everyone on the team can agree often drives the common denominator so low that all the controversial items have to be put on hold to be dealt with later. A team may get so involved in the process of achieving consensus that its main goal will soon become that of reaching team agreement rather than obtaining the best decision through the agreement of a knowledgeable few and moving on. Moreover, cliques are often formed within teams, with the goal of presenting creative arguments merely in order to win the debate rather than to work toward the best decision. Discussions can become competitive rather than a collaboration of ideas, knowledge, and perspectives. Good decisions are often not realized because individuals or cliques remain stubbornly attached to their ideas rather than working to rise above their narrow self-interest and arrive at the decision that is best for the organization as a whole.

A team leader's or coach's aim must be to provide time for their team to meet and to help the team talk through the issue until an agreement is reached that everyone can support. Simply voting on every issue is not recommended. By voting, the team assumes that the minority may give only token support. Thus, when a crisis arises, the team may fall apart because of the lack of collective support. Consensus may not mean that team members are in 100 percent agreement, but they have been heard and will be more inclined to support the team's decision. (Sometimes voting will be required to overcome a gridlock. In such a case, closed-ballot voting is recommended to preserve individual choices and minimize group pressures.)

Skills with which team leaders and/or facilitators can intervene when the team demonstrates its inability to manage agreement are critical here. It is important that every team member hears out the others and feels listened to in return. Each member should not give in just to reach agreement but should view conflict and difference of opinion as good. Team leaders and facilitators should establish a ground rule of openness and encourage each member to ask questions and make sure he or she understands everyone's opinion before making up his or her mind.

Why So Much Resistance?

The concept of self-regulating teams, according to some historians, came to the United States from English coal mines, accompanied by a lot of skepticism. But the failure of the work team movement to catch on widely in the United States has little to do with the evidence of team performance all around us. When teaming works it shows impressive results. Why then are teams emotionally undervalued and openly questioned, and why do they experience so much resistance? Three reasons are apparent.

   Overall, we still believe in a scientific management that compartmentalizes work for individuals into narrow specialized tasks managed by the numbers, rather than in groups that self-manage whole, functional segments of work and do it better than individuals performing narrow tasks. Many are of the opinion that teams initiate more fuss and problems than they are worth, supposing that members waste time and resources in unproductive meetings and discussions and generate more complaints than constructive results.

U.S. employee's work experiences may not have prepared them to value working as a team. They fear or do not like working teams. Instead, they may have learned to focus primarily on what it takes to quietly get their own objectives accomplished. This attention to individual agendas, so important to the completion of many tasks, can inadvertently work against success. Those that take an evolutionary rather than a revolutionary approach to management, however, keep shooting themselves rather than outshooting the competition.

There is a reluctance to rationally and emotionally commit one's worklife fate into the hands of a team. This reluctance may develop out of a person's having more concern with internal organizational politics and personal security than with a commitment to a clear set of performance objectives that balances the expectations of the customers and stakeholders. This self-centered line of thinking undermines the mutual trust and openness by which teams mature. Minimizing the individual accountability systems that focus people on organizational politics and personal security, while enhancing the team's performance accountability, will be critical as teams become more important.

In addition, any team may have generic problems that may have to be addressed and surmounted. We commonly observe these problems:

- Incomplete/nonfunctional mission statement
- Breakdown in probing and listening
- Conflict within and between teams

- Lack of candor about what is really happening on the team
- Insufficient generation of ideas
- Pointless meetings
- Poor horizontal linkages
- People constantly cycling things up to the boss
- Impatience and discomfort with working through nonaction periods

Leaders of the pioneering stage will need to be skilled at forging collaboration and teamwork among a diversity of individuals with competing needs and issues, and moving teams through pockets of resistance. These leaders will help individual team members understand and support the overall goals and standards that their team's collective efforts can achieve. Specific roles and responsibilities for each team member will be clearly defined. The details of team coordination and follow-up plans will be established early. Members will be encouraged to find ways to dovetail tasks and to support each other. Finally, leaders will be models, leading by example as they bring teams to maturity.

As teams desire increasing levels of maturity and freedom, the three remaining transformational stages outlined in this book can be a framework to gauge readiness. Without well-defined goals and markers or guidelines along the way, anxious team members may fail to coordinate their activities, and leaders may fail to delegate certain responsibilities, unable to read team readiness and fearing that teams will botch them. Appropriate boundaries will also help shape the social norms and technical innovations of the teams.

The Heart of the Matter

All efforts to effect change must begin in the heart with a genuine caring about people. Working people will not have it any other way these days. The caring must extend into the statement of vision. Leaders, facilitators, and coaches must begin every work session with some reference to the organizational vision, which should center on humanistic values. A vision statement aligns people with the company's higher purpose. It tells how the organization feels about fostering teamwork, being innovative and profitable, growing and caring, and being supportive of one another and customers. Also emphasized should be improving the quality of life, providing the best possible service, being part of a winning team, and finding ways in which each individual can truly make a difference. Of course, the vision-giver must have credibility and be believable or the vision will be dead from the start.

The vision put forth by leaders of work groups must relate to the emotional and spiritual feelings of each individual. There is a strong parallel between the principles of life that affect an individual and the shared values that cause an organization to flourish.

Initial flourishing is always at the individual level. The following are measurements made by a leader in a client organization of the results of three months of coaching and teaming work in the horizontal pioneering:

Without horizontal coaching:
- Kevin would still be reading books, going to seminars, and watching videos—and wondering what to do to create change.

- Les would still be at his computer counting numbers—instead of enhancing his people to grow and do a better job.

- Brian would still be micro-managing and cutting people off at the pass—instead of creating stimulation and leadership for cooperation and empowerment.

- George would still be cutting people up and playing "spectator games" in meetings and work sessions—instead of becoming the major element for positive movement at the supervisory level.

- Dean would still be disgruntled and holding his potential to himself—instead of expanding and extending his capabilities, and moving toward becoming one of the organization's major leaders.

- Bob would still be a misfit and outcast in a grossly underutilized state—instead of qualifying himself for the "most valuable player" award.

- Rita would be a frustrated ball of energy without direction and focus—instead of becoming skilled and competent to lead and bring together people and tasks.

- Bev would still be the resident critic with lots of insight but little know-how—instead of being competent to get involved and move the organization forward.

- Billie would still be cynical, turned-off, and on-the-shelf— instead of being participative and enthusiastic toward the activities of change.

- Jackie would be a technical specialist buried in the isolation of her personality and craft—instead of coming out of her shell and giving her heart and soul to the work at hand.

- Earl would still be bitter and a negative force because of thirty years of disappointing experiences—instead of seeing new ways of doing things and developing a brighter future.

Passion has to drive insight, otherwise, there will be no change. Passion comes from the vision of newness and the willingness to see beyond the present boundaries of work. The vision of the horizontal revolution causes people to say things like, "This is a thoroughly supported effort with cheers for everyone," and, "Everyone is caught up in feeling and seeing the excitement." The horizontal revolution must impact our feeling and seeing.

Summary

During the pioneering stage of the horizontal revolution, the organization conceptually adopts a teaming system and completes a front-end assessment of its readiness to install work teams and make a management commitment. Champions of the work team concept have to surface. Organizational unfreezing begins through education and training, steering and design teams are organized, teams and leaders are selected, whole work segments are redefined, and support systems are established. During this stage, the pitfalls to avoid are overloading teams with too many responsibilities too soon, lacking meaningful measures and an information system to provide teams with ongoing feedback, and supplying inadequate management support and commitment.

Horizontal implementation is never easy. It usually involves the whole organization and extends over a period of years. Additionally, it demands radically new behaviors that can provoke strong resistance ranging from simple denial of the need for teams to outright sabotage. As horizontal functioning begins to become a solution to present and future organizational needs, it can initially be both disruptive and disorderly. Nevertheless, for the horizontal revolution to succeed in forming teams that act as stewardships, management will have to be committed. They will also have to be willing to give up having someone to blame, unquestioned authority, status and status symbols, and the apparent safety of hierarchical structures. They will have to surrender the notion that people need supervision to do good work or that, without a strong leader, teams are likely to dissolve into chaos. Not everyone can work in this new environment; thus, options should be available to everyone.

The price for teaming is the hard news to accept: long-term commitment and practice, practice, practice. The easy news to accept is that when a teaming transformation becomes mature, it will outperform other work designs and individuals. It is proven to help build sustainable competitive advantage in quality, innovation cost effectiveness, and customer service in an ever-changing global marketplace.

Chapter Two

Stage Two: Settling-In: Rewriting the Constitution for How Work Gets Done

Those executives who impetuously push us
employees into a teaming implementation without
an understanding of the forces of change and
resistance should expect the worst. If they don't
begin to legitimize and discuss our fears, we will
never have the courage to let go of our control needs
so that we can unleash our potential. Know this:
when things are really clicking for us, we seldom get
tired, and we can then accomplish many times the
work we previously did. Our fatigue is caused not by
work but by worry, frustration, and resentment.

*—Frontline worker in a
medium-sized industrial organization*

The old worldview of clear hierarchies and management by spreadsheet was easy to understand and easy to manage, but somewhere between Ozzie and Harriet, "9 To 5," and the Simpsons, things changed. Now, few organizations can sustain a structure where the average task is to do one thing well in a stable environment over a long period of time and where employees are motivated to do only a small piece of the total business process. As organizations are reengineered, supervisors and managers are replaced by coaches, and functional divisions by process groupings. Teams are structured around products, services, customers, or some combination of these three. These teams do everything possible to become small profit centers within their companies.

As organizations pass through the pioneering stage and then seek an approach for breaking themselves into mini-enterprises, they must go through a settling-in process. This settling-in is the second stage of the horizontal revolution, and it will take time—how much time depends on how settled into old ways people are and how willing they are to take on new learnings and behaviors. This chapter outlines the concept and practices of settling-in to a horizontal design that involves all levels of the organization.

Overview of Stage Two: Settling-In

In stage two of the revolution, work teams struggle to close the gap between expectations and reality, with some confusion, frustration, and anger. Some members grow impatient with the team's lack of progress and become pushy, before ultimately realizing that the team's job is different and more difficult than they had initially imagined. Team leaders or those vying for dominant positions are tested through confrontations that lead to blaming and defensiveness. With the help of team facilitators, teams will turn to the strong team members to take control of the team, deal with management, and resolve team issues. There is still some anxiety concerning redesigns, new roles, responsibilities, power shifts, and job security. Working relationships take a beating. While an increase of information sharing means management are able to push more decision making and operations down to teams, those teams will feel the urge to plateau by sticking to familiar tasks that bring guaranteed results in productivity, rather than going on to manage whole processes or taking risks on new, creative assignments.

Organizations that respond most ineffectually to horizontal initiatives in the settling-in stage are those steeped in bureaucratic or mechanistic systems with rigid hierarchies, high degrees of functional specialization, narrow and limited job descriptions, many written rules and procedures, and impersonal relationships. Conversely, structures that are adaptive and already require great commitment and use of people's talents will experience less resistance.

But in any organization, the settling-in of the horizontal revolution will produce some muddle. As the nature of work changes, supervisors and middle managers are still redefining the rules of the game while playing by at least some of the old rules. The process can feel like trying to shoe a horse while riding it, and the typical disruption is well exemplified in a feedback report from a manager who had been involved in a horizontal changeover during a six-month period:

1. Over the past two decades, there has been an aggressive erosion of employee confidence in management in this organization.

2. When anxiety is high, cynicism rises and morale sinks; and resentment, apathy, and mistrust constantly break out within our ranks.

3. Beyond lip service, most of our supervisors find it terribly hard to push down responsibility and authority.

4. Our supervisors see themselves as the ones who need to be decisive and all-knowing with their troops, and they still do not have all the tools and skills to become coaches rather than field marshals.

5. Our supervisors really want to work as hard and well as they can while struggling with the anxiety of recognizing that their life isn't going to be like it was ever again. They are having trouble learning to view this new reality as an ally and not an enemy, whom they can work with rather than resist.

6. Each manager needs to set realistic, achievable, short-term goals for his/her respective supervisors, so they can gain a sense of accomplishment for their coaching efforts.

7. We still have hidden agendas and mixed messages destroying our trust; and we have a lot of them being used regularly.

During the settling-in stage there is an admitted lack of trust among both teams and management. As one team member declared,

"We all have the same goals; we're just screwing each other." Most feel that communication has improved but that there are still some barriers. Many teams will feel directly responsible for saving the company money but see nothing in it for themselves. Some will think this unfair and may begin to pull back from active participation. Conflicts may still exist over tasks, goals, priorities, direction, and teamwork. For the most part, however, a sense of shared responsibility develops during stage two.

Getting a Reading on Where You Are

After awareness orientations and before team rollout, the steering team formed in the pioneering stage should oversee a survey and/or interviews that will identify supporting and restraining forces. How committed to the horizontal teaming concept are your employees? What are their concerns or fears? A people audit administered by the human resource staff or an outside consulting group can provide this needed information. Or you can use focus groups, bringing various combinations of employees together in small groups to discuss relevant issues. Focus groups can be formed on one or many different organizational levels, and they can be asked to generate lists of cultural norms, that is, designs and rules for getting things done and getting along in the organization. Inhibitors to productivity and communication and a host of other us-them issues can be gleaned from the resulting data. To start, ask focus groups, What is it like to work here? or, Give me one word that best describes this organization. From these answers, they can make as-is agendas, with corresponding consequences, and then to-be agendas (these agendas are discussed in more detail in Chapter Seven).

A typical list from a production group contained these perceptions of current organizational attitudes:

- No one listens to our suggestions.
- Women don't get into top management positions.

- Management doesn't tolerate complaints.
- Human resources is a disciplinary function in the company.
- Other departments do not work with us.
- Management cares only about production, not people.
- Screw up and you get zapped.
- Don't enjoy the work or they give you more.
- Certain people get away with [poor behavior] because they can do no wrong.
- Look busy, even if you are not.
- Don't tell jokes or smile because people will think you are messing around.
- Complain about your job in secret or outside work, or you'll pay a high price.
- Don't share your success.
- Self-directed work teams are just another management fad that will pass like all the others.

Although, at first glance, this appears to be a list of employees' complaints, not an examination of how the company operates on shared perceptions and assumptions, these items represent why a horizontal revolution comes from within, rather than being externally imposed. Although most employees never receive formal instruction on how to survive in an organization, they encounter a course in corporate values and assumptions every time they come to work. It is important to realize that "complaints" reflect these assumptions and are operating factors that influence how people work with each other. These factors will directly affect the success or failure of a team initiative. Usually individuals in focus group exercises are amazed to see how they have contributed to the counterproductivity of their areas when acting in accordance with the unwritten rules of the culture.

After management discuss the implications of employee as-is perceptions, a discussion about what should or must be should take place, to establish where individuals want to go with the team process and what obstacles lie in their way. Specific areas to discuss include management styles/perceptions, attitudes/trust about teams, departmental/interdepartmental cooperation, and interpersonal skills. The discussion of management styles will invariably end up in an analysis of what these styles mean to "what we are trying to do here." It is understandable that real change requires an alteration of management styles and the removal of obstacles that the present styles reinforce. If a minor alignment is all that is necessary, then a management role model can be discussed and implemented. Training is recommended if a more sensitive shift is needed to mold management styles to fit the team atmosphere.

It is essential that the top management understand this process by which cultural norms are changed, thereby making the horizontal process an inside-out, interrelated, organizationwide implementation. Image the changing organization as a greenhouse full of small plant cultivations. Each plant represents a team. To ensure maximum growth, these new plants must be transplanted to better soils. Some individuals will find it difficult to switch soils, to switch from a product volume focus to a customer focus or from a traditional supervisory method to self-directed units. Some transplants will not take to the new ground and will choose to leave. Both teams and management become gardeners in this change, and they must exhibit a clear and positive layout for the new garden. Start developing new directions by asking: What should our ideal organization look like? What would encourage an increase in the level of trust in the organization? or, What changes would foster the growth of interaction between departments within the organization?

Departments need to be committed early in a team launch, and networked into the planning. In many cases, area or section managers are given direct responsibility to shepherd transitions or transplantings. To function well, they will need a clear under-standing of what their role is throughout the implementation and the opportunities and benefits work teams can bring them. Because section managers given these additional responsibilities may feel overworked and under-recognized, they should be treated with special care from the beginning. It is important that they receive awareness training, coaching, team leadership, and transitional skills before anyone else. These managers need not become obstacles. They can do a number of things to facilitate the new plants' sprouting process and they can serve as positive role models as they create their own work teams.

The only drawback to implementing the process from the department level down is that networking is limited to the area of the supporting manager's control. Nevertheless, by beginning the horizontal revolution in an area that wants the process and letting the other area managers see its successes, the process can sell itself. ➤

The Training Focus

The training focus in this stage concerns helping team members understand how a whole process can be managed by a team that has become a small business unit. Strategic planning, customer skills, problem solving, and work performance measurement techniques are the subjects of training at the team level. Interpersonal skills training is conducted at all levels. Effective facilitators will conduct role-playing exercises with team leaders and encourage teams to evaluate themselves by giving both positive and constructive feedback within the team. Clearly, one of the bigger issues during the settling-in stage is to help teams "skill-up" enough to overcome their cynicism and negativism toward change.

Middle managers begin to move into roles of analysts, barrier busters, coaches, and mentors of teams. They should be prepared to model the behavior that builds trust and empowers teams; workers will insist on it. However, even though employees at all levels will expect or demand to see model behavior from their bosses, nobody should use the excuse that "my manager doesn't manage me that way" as a cop-out. It is unrealistic at this stage for employees to expect their bosses to fully live up to employee expectations.

Managers who feel threatened and refuse to "debrick their chimneys," or to think outside their functional specialties, need training. For teams to form and work, "nonfunctional chimneys" must be dismantled and managers persuaded to lend their time, people, and resources to other functions, supporting them in their efforts to successfully redesign work and teams around entire cross-functional business processes. Moreover, for each step forward that teams take toward managing themselves, managers must take one step back. If this does not happen, toes will be stepped on and the credibility of the whole idea of horizontal structures and teams will suffer. Employees will ask, Are management committed to teams or not?

Horizontal Design: From Buffalo to Geese

At the settling-in stage, we often use two analogies from the animal kingdom to communicate that *different structural designs will produce different behaviors and different outcomes.*

Traditionally, employees may follow their patriarchal managers the way buffalo blindly follow their leaders. Unfortunately, that kind of management almost led to the buffalo's extinction. Buffalo hunters used to slaughter whole herds by finding and killing the leader. Once the leader was dead, the rest of the herd stood around waiting for instructions that never came, and the hunters (the competition) could exterminate them one by one.

In contrast, a horizontal high-performance team is like a flock of geese on the wing. They do not look like the functional organizational chart but, instead, form a V of individuals who are aligned to the common goal, take turns leading, and adjust their structure to the task at hand. These geese fly in a wedge, but land in waves.

Most importantly, each individual goose is responsible for its own performance to the team.

Clearly, our flock of geese, or the horizontally oriented structure, will not fit all organizational strategies and situations. It fits strategies that organize profit centers around customers, making it easier for the organization to align employees with the external customer who gives feedback and who makes purchasing decisions. A really "goosey" design must be guided by detailed specifications of the types of behaviors. It is not enough to simply require high-quality flying, speed, and low maintenance. Each goose in the flock or member of the team must be clear about what is meant by quality flying, what kinds of variations are acceptable, and just how fast and how long they need to go to realize their competitive missions. Specifically, both the team and the organization need to look at which kinds of behaviors are likely to produce high-quality flying and speed of delivery and then custom design themselves into the V structure.

Key Settling-In Concepts

In creating a settling-in experience for all employees, management should answer the following four questions:

1. How do we design lean teaming structures around integrated processes?
2. What are we to understand about people and participation?
3. What do management need to know about creating partnerships with team structures?
4. How are teams to structure their work sessions around process-based work?

The remainder of this chapter focuses on issues raised by these questions, suggesting the behavior and results management should expect to see as teams settle-in and specific techniques for fostering settling-in.

Design Lean Teaming Structures
Around Integrated Processes

Teaming designs must mesh with today's need for value-added analysis and lean structures. Teams should contain little or no fat. Each team's self-design should include a responsibility chart that shows how the team will, over time, take over with fewer people the tasks performed by staff and supervisors. Teams should learn to deal with cost and revenue and identify their competitors. They should receive feedback on how their business processes are doing, and gain a sense of the entrepreneurial and business environment in which the organization operates.

Assumptions about structure and behavior usually focus on two central dimensions of organizational design: first, that organizations divide work by creating a variety of specialized roles, functions, and units, and second, that they must then tie all those elements back together by means of both vertical and horizontal methods of integration. For example, a company selling computer services offers its customers software services, maintenance services, hardware, and an array of consulting services. The customer expects and wants the service processes to be integrated, not fragmented. Improvements in a system do not come about by attending to narrowly defined tasks and working within predefined organizational boundaries. Each business process should be an entire process, one that cuts across typical organizational boundaries and integrates functions. Integrated processes then give rise to multidimensional jobs that are best organized into teaming structures. The competitive marketplace is then in the position of controlling team performance, making most hierarchical controls unnecessary.

The need to run flat out for flat and lean structures goes further. Every individual in the organization represents a double cost: the cost of employing that individual and the cost associated with the work that the individual creates for others to do. Every activity carried out by any employee must be subjected to a value-added analysis that looks at the employee's work and asks whether its total cost is offset by a comparable benefit. While some staff activities will turn out to be justified, others will be best be done by line employees and yet others by outside contractors. Moreover, value-added analysis should not be a one-time activity. Only by constantly asking and re-asking value-added questions can an organization keep its groups or teams at an appropriate size and position.

Another factor driving the move toward lean staffing levels in all areas is the cost competition that most organizations face today. In the high-wage U.S. work force, labor costs are a major expense, which is by itself a strong argument for limiting the number of staff who do not directly add value to the product or to the services of their organization.

Responsible Autonomy

Mature workers value participation and involvement. When responsibility for and control of task performance is located with the people directly engaged in the task, then productivity, motivation, and satisfaction will increase. Under these circumstances of responsible autonomy, teams can take on a responsible role in the design and implementation of the production system, not the peripheral supporting role envisioned in old hierarchy.

Responsible autonomy is further enhanced by:

- Clear purposes and objectives that are well understood and accepted by members
- Maximum energies focused on performing tasks basic to the achievement of these purposes and objectives
- Cultures that reflect a high value placed on satisfying interests and needs of individual members
- An emphasis on producing products and services that are value adding to customers and clients

- Leadership actions that induce widespread clarity and con-sensus about—and commitment to—an organization's basic purposes and objectives
- Technologies that permit the efficient use of human, physical, financial, material, and information resources
- Enough stability to take maximum advantage of the effi-ciencies that technologies offer, coupled with enough flexibil-ity to respond quickly and effectively to changing conditions, demands, and opportunities
- An emphasis on individual and organizational learning and development
- High levels of congruence, or fit, between team design elements and organizational purposes and objectives, and between the organization and the demands and expectations of horizontal environments
- Enough diversity to encourage innovation and creativity in finding new solutions that allow for more informed choice

Teams that realize these conditions most effectively will con-centrate on end-to-end designs that create value for customers and will continually modify the various ways their people work together to support those designs.

Healthy Dispositions in Horizontal Teams

Our work with clients has especially helped us to understand why some teams will flounder or get sidetracked while others steadily thrive in a world of customers, competition, and change. We have discovered the common threads or dispositions among effective teams that managers need to know as they design team structures around entire processes. These dispositions are team attributes and entitlements that profoundly reverse the deterioration of competi-tive advantage (Figure 2.1). They are vital signs, which do not

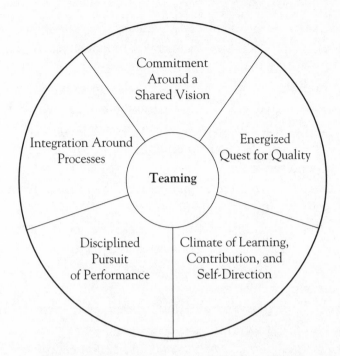

Figure 2.1. Dispositions of Effective Teams.

reverse aging but are crucially prescriptive of effective horizontal teaming activity.

A commitment around a shared vision. In successful teams, members rally around a vision; they have shared purposes, values, attitudes, guiding principles, and responsibilities. They are personally committed and intrinsically motivated, not compliant. Once the vision of teaming is established, team members are in a good position to identify and provide solutions to organizational concerns effectively and speedily.

An energized quest for quality. The team releases its enthusiasm and energy through continually improving products and services that will meet and even exceed customer expectations. Quality is a team effort. Effective communication and team skills help teams rethink their everyday activities and interactions within a quality context.

An integration around processes. The team is coordinated around processes, the products or services flow, as opposed to functions. The team becomes the best means to integrate processes across functional boundaries, and it can both design and energize core processes. A high degree of diligence and mutual accountability for each other's betterment enables team members to develop interchangeable as well as complementary skills and hence greater flexibility around processes.

A climate of learning, contribution, and self-direction. Team members sustain a caring climate of support for the growth of others, sharing the leadership; fostering feedback; and coordinating efforts without restricting self-direction, creativity, a sense of fun, and a willingness to learn. When everyone has input as to how he or she can best support the team's goals and strategies, performance improves. This climate ensures that the team not only becomes but remains an integrative learning, renewing unit.

A disciplined pursuit of performance. To realize performance goals and meet customer expectations, the team uses its unique qualities to explore territory where no one else has ventured. Team members meet weekly (the norm) and exercise the courage and tough self-discipline to directly confront problems or barriers in order to achieve optimal outcomes and results that they can live by. The team takes its own development course, constantly reviewing its vision, the actual progress it makes toward its achievement, and the adequacy of the skills and resources that are in place among its members.

People and Participation

The us-them conditions that occur during pioneering can continue during settling-in. A common perception that team members and managers share with us is that they see some people in the organization thwarting the goals of teaming and participation through their need to control everything. When us-them lines are drawn, the majority of employees are usually found to be trustworthy, motivated, and willing to participate in change, yet some old-timers and controlling managers remain uncommitted, distrustful, and autocratic.

In some organizations, these two camps are referred to as the * "good" people and the "wicked" people, and the good have little tolerance for those who are different. Yet, obviously, labeling people as either "participative" or "autocratic" dangerously oversimplifies reality, ignoring the vast diversity among people and the variety of constraints, often unknown to others, under which each person operates. Labeling, therefore, detracts from dialogue, openness, and trust. It closes rather than opens doors to communication and understanding at a time when, as one executive observed, "We're going to have to be able to listen to other people's point of view without saying, 'You're wrong.'"

Management and teams must ask questions, listen to the answers, and learn people's views. They must listen to the way individuals craft their views, evaluations, and attributions. Does the person illustrate his or her views? Does the person encourage testing of his or her views? The answers to such questions provide important information about the strength of us-them conditions and defensive behaviors.

There are a number of ways management can work to close the gaps between us and them and between expectations and reality. It is important to understand human nature, human relationships, people's perceptions of the environment and their motivation, and the integration of team roles. To replace the traditional tools of control and caretaking, horizontal structures offer partnership and choice to their employees as well as their customers. Companies cannot attempt this shift without the following assumption about human nature: *people can change in order to make the new structure a success.* In fact, the clear purpose of a team-oriented structure is to empower employees to make business decisions and process improvements. Team members are given authority and trusted to use it wisely in the best interests of all stakeholders. Trustworthiness and goodness must be dominant themes from the outset. Published mission statements should refer to the value of employees and the need to push decision making down as far as possible. Training programs should stress autonomy, the need to work without supervision, and even the importance of self-esteem. The theme

✳ should be: *employees can be trusted, and they should feel good about themselves*. Participation and the sharing of power are the ultimate bases for human relationship in organizations. Management's patriarchal assumptions will be an obvious dark thread in a structural fabric bright with the colors of participation and the sharing of power. Much of the us-them frustration that teams express results from the perception that managers are running "our" team. As one team member said, "The manager won't let us do anything on our own. Our team meetings are a waste because nobody thinks it would do any good to come up with any ideas."

We find useful perceptions about existing human relations can be generated by simply asking team participants one basic question: What's it like to work here? In response to this question, a cross-sectional team we call a Next Step Team found they were critical of each other, politically driven, had conflicting work ethics, had a caste system, lacked balance, had too many demands on their time, and focused on facade as opposed to substance. The identified characteristics became targets for horizontal shifting and eventually generated a blueprint for total teaming throughout the organization. Obviously, perceptions and attributions will always differ somewhat from one person to the next; however, teams should identify which differences are due to unrealistic expectations and which to variance in cultural backgrounds and influences. Unrealistic expectations, in particular, frustrate people and cause distrust. As one team member said, "We thought that perhaps things aren't as bad as they seem and the only problem is that the 'ultimate' vision isn't coming to fruition fast enough." The hype surrounding participation may cause expectations that are much different from what can actually happen. The gap between the expected and the actual autonomy may result in dissatisfaction among employees and a loss of trust in management.

The relationship with the environment is often another us-them case. If employees perceive a significant long-term decline in company business due to management's ineptness in dealing with external factors, they may work less efficiently in order to protect their jobs. This will limit the organization's ability to bid on new opportunities and further reduce the level of business. However, employees can also view the business environment in a more positive manner. Work teams, especially, should be given considerable data about the environment to help them avoid the temptation to assign blame. The tendency to view situations as the result of something we or they did misses the complexity of most situations. If work teams persist in labeling and do not understand complexity, the downward cycle of human relationships will continue. However, if dialogues about the environment can be opened between management and teams, so that the latter can understand that management's actions are not based on wicked motives, work teams will be enabled to discuss issues rationally and move ahead on recommendations. Overall, effective reciprocity between teams and the environment requires creative management-team partnerships that carefully think and work through plans to implement effective strategies. The team implementation process is basically one of preparing people to embrace the organizational ideal and quality of worklife. Managers and team members need to feel that they have a partnership in the change process and that their interests will be protected.

Horizontal structures can increase employee motivation, helping employees satisfy their basic needs for security as they become multiskilled and constantly learn and improve. Horizontal teams place substantial demands on employees in terms of their ability to solve problems, contribute to group discussion, and perform a wide array of technical activities. Since teams stress continuous development and improvement, the organization will need individuals who are willing and able to continue to learn and develop. Human resource systems should try to determine the kinds of people who will fit into the horizontal structure and what training is needed to help them adequately perform their jobs, tasks, and processes. Ultimately, it is paramount that the organization has employees who possess the right talents, motives, and orientations to make the teaming structure work effectively.

A horizontal work team redesign will integrate specialized and different roles within the team. Everyone knows the frustration of trying to get help from someone who says, "That's not my responsibility." In addition to finding the right division of labor and tasks, a team must develop a reliable method of linking individual efforts into a unified whole so people accept a broad responsibility. Horizontal teams require employees to do what management did in the past—make decisions about goals, duties, productivity, and quality. They operate on the conviction that properly fitted and trained employees are the best ones to make important decisions about how the whole team does its job. Team members must be able to justify how their proposed changes will improve quality and support the organization's vision and mission as well as have a positive impact on other employees and systems.

Those involved in horizontal work teams must accept accountability for themselves before they look to what is required of others. An effective way to get team members to look first at themselves is to ask them: What can you communicate about yourself without using a hidden agenda? Responses might be: "I need to raise my confidence level and the confidence others have in my ability"; or, "I stifle creativity by having the answer for everyone. I control and encourage people to find my answer." Once unhidden, such agendas indicate what each person on the team must do to construct a foundation for ownership and action. Through this process, each person handles his or her personal change as well as assisting to create new life-styles for other team members.

Management's Role in Creating Partnerships

Managers need to take a number of initiatives and precautions if they are to foster partnerships with team structures.

Perform a self-examination. Initially, managers need to take an honest, hard look at themselves in terms of their real strengths. If their strengths lie in hands-on work, they should keep themselves up-to-date and move toward overseeing reengineered processes. The challenge is to get and keep a performance edge. If their strengths lie in leadership, they should develop their people-nurturing skills and become employee coaches.

Ensure time and expenses needed. Before initiating teams, management must assess whether a high-level participative structure can stay in place long enough for employees and managers to take on self-directive styles and feel worthwhile and safe. Risks are substantially reduced if there is strong systemwide support for the change at the outset. Managers of change need to be recognized and backed with time and adequate resources.

Clarify the team role. Teams should be viewed as structures that develop ever-wider skill sets in order to bridge the space between long-range corporate strategies and the day-to-day reality of continuous quality improvement. By clarifying the role teams play, management help teams translate concepts and directives into localized team initiatives. Self-directed work teams should become the critical link between the executive vision for quality and the concrete daily behaviors. The most common traps that hinder the work of a new team are lack of focus, lack of information about the problem at hand, lack of an agenda, and lack of trust.

Focus on specific opportunities. Management will need to learn how to focus teams on specific opportunities consistent with the organization's quality improvement strategy. More specifically managers should:

- Outline the details of an organizationwide quality effort
- Encourage teams to identify, meet, and exceed internal and external customer needs
- Prepare teams to attend quality skills training
- Stimulate team members' ideas about improving quality
- Resolve feelings of resistance to teams: feelings of being overworked, doubtful about the organization's seriousness, or skeptical of the need to change

Share information and knowledge. The communication flow within an organization is critical to any organization. The more work teams make decisions designed to support organizational goals, the more they will want and need operational information, including financial data. Information must flow to employees at all levels. In general, management need to share with the teams valid data about production, quality, service levels, business plans, and the work unit's performance and directions. The latter is critical, because without a sense of where the organization is going, teams will have trouble identifying with and contributing to its success. Each team must understand and be empowered to act on financial and accounting information. In addition, with proper coaching, horizontal work teams will usually do an excellent job of charting the future course for management. A typical technique we use is to ask the team to compose a to-do list for horizontal leadership. This invariably produces such action items as remove roadblocks, get the best from our people, look at our differences, and commit to constant never-ending improvement.

A capability for horizontal communication among teams and individuals at all levels in the organization is also often critical. Specifically, teams need any information, from whatever direction, that directly affects their work. For example, in team work sessions, members of staff teams and senior managers can be invited in to share information about customers/suppliers and the future direction of the organization. The visiting manager should, of course, be familiar with concerns of the work team before attending. Besides promoting the downward and horizontal flow of information, managers also need to promote the upward flow. It is critical that managers regularly and systematically ask team leaders and facilitators how they are doing. Whether this information is conveyed through memos, meetings, electronic mail, videotapes, or the telephone is not critical. Occasionally, a manager may want to collect relevant information through a short attitude survey. Summarized results can then be shared and discussed during a team meeting and/or a management team meeting or team steering group. Managers should take responsibility to make sure the feedback is communicated to and acted upon by upper management. In addition, teams should receive broad instruction in the operation of their work areas. Management should also exchange information about projects and procedures relative to each team.

Value employee contributions. When a team approach fails, it is often because a department manager neglected to build a strong branch network of supportive collaborators that included top management people. This neglect usually happens because a greater value has been placed on technical aspects of the work as opposed to personnel aspects. But to be successful, a department manager must be a strong advocate for his or her team's significant contributions. Team members can then become enthusiastic and the excitement is contagious. You will hear comments such as, "It's great not to have someone breathing down your neck at work!" or testimonials about the positive effects on people's private lives of the roles they learn on the job. Most striking is the team member pride when, for example, they sit on a panel in grubby workclothes, speaking as peers to visitors in suits and ties about the benefits of work teams.

Pay attention to conflicting emotions. Hidden concerns and general apprehensiveness among new team members are not to be overlooked. Members of cross-functional teams are often beset by conflicting emotions: excitement and anxiety about being on the team, loyalty to their function, nervous anticipation about a project's success. Left unattended, these undercurrents can inhibit a young team's chance of becoming an effective team. Such interpersonal concerns need to be quickly resolved by skilled managers, team leaders, and facilitators.

Maintain backing and support. Without the strong backing, artistic coaching, and skilled support of human resources, managers of team initiatives may be constantly in conflict with personnel and other staffing systems that make it difficult to share information, knowledge, power, and rewards with teams. When these conflicts surface, many managers may conclude that high-level involvement and performance are unrealistic and that the team effort is doomed to fail, while the teams themselves report "stonewalling" or "lip service only" by management. Furthermore, when teams must obtain permission through various channels to implement changes, this red tape can leave them feeling powerless to improve quality.

Focus on results over activities. Activities include training, teams formed, meetings held, and ideas submitted. Results are actual improvements in quality itself. The best way to stay focused on results at all levels of the organization is to organize the organization around processes, or around products, services, or customers or some combination of these three.

Monitor replacements. Finally, in company after company, managers have successfully built team structures within organizations only to see them wither and die when they leave. Unless team structures are supported systemwide, they can be endangered by incoming managers who are not active team disciples. As a result, employees who have supported teams may become critical and cynical about management. Worse yet, any attempts by the new management to introduce another employee involvement program may be met with bitter resistance.

Successful Management Styles and Practices

Interestingly, experiences with successful work team structures are well represented in organizations facing crises, where both workers and management were motivated to act in order to save their company, themselves, or both, and to do so quickly. Their actions during these crises enabled them to overcome or bypass obstacles common to traditional team implementations. Failed work team structures had one characteristic in common—team members felt that teams were really an imperative from management.

What is the lesson of these organizations? Clearly, the most important condition for the success of a partnership is that both groups be willing to go more than halfway to make teaming work. Managers must be willing to risk a complex and costly organizational innovation, which could affect their futures. Employees must trade their traditional jobs for less certain and more demanding roles as team members.

Management support can only be perceived and interpreted through a demonstration of commitment to change in several noticeable areas: in organizational structure, in work design, in information and measurement systems, and in the recognition and reward system (see Chapter Seven). Those who are managing from the top should follow these cultural guidelines:

- Company values must be defined and articulated by senior management.

- Company values must be enforced through exhibited practice by all levels of management.

- The appropriate climate must be established and reinforced continuously: for example, everyone should be treated with dignity and respect.

- Innovation should be encouraged, risks taken, and failure tolerated in order to grow, improve, and prosper.

- Provisions must be made to remove ineffective team leaders.

Agenda for Work Group Work Sessions

A sample agenda for managers conducting work group work sessions at the beginning of the settling-in stage is shown in Exhibit 2.1.

Exhibit 2.1. Work Group Work Session Agenda.

Purpose:

1. To identify new ideas and new agendas for horizontal functioning.
2. To learn some techniques for coaching and teamwork.
3. To become horizontal revolution missionaries.

Participants: (list team members plus any additional personnel needed)

Schedule: (initial time and date to be determined prior to the session; continuous work sessions to be determined by the group)

Goals:

1. To identify and work through agendas and action plans for continuous improvement.
2. To accept ownership for ourselves and the process of horizontal work.
3. To provide some basic leadership training in coaching and teamwork.
4. To develop a work plan for the extension and perpetuation of coaching and teaming.

Process:

1. *Warm-up and clarification:* exchanging perceptions of the as-is condition.

2. *Mapping your personal organization:* the route to greater success.

3. *Teaming and coaching:* experience in interpersonal relationships.

4. *Horizontal empowering and impact:* learning new work-related processes.

5. *Leadership characteristics:* changing roles and new responsibilities.

6. *Behavioral blockages:* dealing with whatever is blocking us and others from being more effective.

Outline:

1. *New look:* Where are we and where do we want to be?

2. *New direction:* What do our leaders need to do?

3. *New responsibility:* What do we need to understand and do?

4. *New skills and capabilities:* What do we need to learn?

5. *New preparations:* What is our blueprint for training and development?

6. *New results:* What are our objectives and expectations for coaching and teaming?

7. *New Pursuits:* Who needs to meet with whom, and for what purpose, to do what needs to be done?

8. *New Commitments:* Who is committed to what?

Resources:

Assorted handouts and learning materials.

Theme:

Employees choose not to exchange critically important feedback with others when they predict that the other person(s) will be defensive and will not listen and that the endeavor will be a waste of time. Either way, they waste time.

A successful transition into horizontal teams requires a flexible, adaptable plan, with many employees recognizing how well the plan is being adapted along the way. All levels of the organization are affected by the creation of teams and everyone will need information from management about what is happening, why, and when. Team structures sometimes become root-bound and fail to thrive; some plants, however, bloom best when they are somewhat root-bound. There are many instances in which both regular fertilization and occasional repotting are required for really vibrant blossoms. This analogy between structure and growing plants translates into three sets of team member needs: a factor that motivates excellence; orientation (especially for new employees) and celebration; and concentrated planning, ongoing evaluation, formal performance reviews, and ongoing coaching efforts.

Will the team structure work in support areas, management areas, or with vendors? The answer to all these questions is yes; however, it may require a slightly different structure or format to make it work well. How do we approach this problem? By the use of trial and error. Find out what is best for the team by allowing the team to struggle and discover their own best method of functioning. Trial and error activity in the early stages of teams is very important. It sets development patterns for success in the future. Discovering what works and what doesn't is a continuous process in team development. The debriefing that should be done after each experiment allows team members to discuss with the team leader both the strong and the ineffective aspects of the activity.

Work Sessions for Process-Based Work

Much of what happens in team work sessions is discussed in detail in Chapter Five when workouts are described. In the settling-in stage, managers should be aware that work sessions can be like "garbage cans," into which all problems are dumped, or they can be one of the most efficient ways to get everyone involved, committed, and responsible for things that need to be done. Team work sessions should be regularly scheduled times when teams coordinate activities, solve problems, schedule work, keep productivity levels high, share new ideas and suggestions, plan for the future, and discuss matters relevant to everyone on the team. So it is disappointing to both team leaders and members when they soak up time and energy, as people get bogged down in creating new myths and renegotiating old ones. Garbage cans are particularly likely to materialize when people discuss issues that are emotionally powerful and symbolically visible but technologically blurry. If unproductive work sessions occur regularly, teams come to feel ineffective, frustrated, and expect failure. In addition to their obvious purpose of getting work done, work sessions should also be the prime way that members experience being a team.

In essence, effective team work sessions rely on several steps, each complementing the other and supporting the overall outcome. The purpose is well planned; objectives, goals, and expected outcomes are identified; an agenda is prepared; necessary materials are gathered; members are notified of time, place, and assignments; and a plan is in place for follow-up on action items (see Exhibit 2.1, for example). A properly trained facilitator can assist the team to be effective by keeping members on task, quieting the talkative, drawing out the silent, keeping conflict constructive, keeping the group aware of its process (how it does things), clarifying, moving discussion forward, helping the group reach resolution, and directing the group toward accomplishing its objectives. Also necessary are good leadership skills involving appropriate eye contact; proper body language and voice inflection; and the ability to encourage involvement, inclusion, and participation. Organizations can hire full-time facilitators, train in-house people from various units, have teams appoint their own facilitators, or rotate the facilitator responsibility among all team members.

Can you determine a work session's productivity by the close of the session? Not always. If action items were decided in the work session, the proof of productivity is in the follow-through. Productive work sessions will meet these criteria: work session objectives were accomplished; they were accomplished in a time-efficient manner; and team members were satisfied with the results.

Measuring Team Growth

Companies invested in growth are willing to listen and adjust to what their work force is telling them. Their people become interested, dedicated, and committed to change in direct proportion to the degree they are involved. Work groups give employees a say in what is happening and can reveal needed areas for change. They answer the question, How well are we doing? And their existence gives everyone the opportunity to be open, candid, and confident in the process of evaluations and improvement.

When a Next Step Team at a client organization measured its growth after settling-in, it began a presentation to top management about its new focus, learning, and improvements in this way:

> The purpose of today's presentation by the Next Step Team is to do just that—present the next step. During the two months our cross-divisional, multilevel team has been meeting, we have had the opportunity to grow from a work group into what we feel is a bona fide team. The goal of the next step is to: "Create the Experience."
>
> By creating the experience we hope to transform our company into one that provides an atmosphere in which people are valued and teaming is a way of life. Our team has identified eight critical areas which we must address now, in order for us to flourish in the future. Through our continued learning we hope to move toward a more balanced and profitable business experience.
>
> Our expectations for this presentation are to show you the work which we have already accomplished and to give you our strategic

blueprint for the next steps. This will include our proposed work plan, the specifics of our eight critical areas of development, and ways we feel are appropriate to measure and validate the success of these initiatives.

The eight areas are: (1) new leadership skills, (2) ownership, (3) interdependency, (4) quality of life, (5) communication, (6) innovation, (7) job satisfaction, and (8) passion.

Summary

A gap between expectations and reality occurs among team members during the settling-in stage. Members grow impatient with the team's lack of progress in self-managing. Subgroups may form, with factions competing for influence. Actively working on the issues of mission, goals, processes/tasks, roles, and responsibilities, teams make some progress accomplishing their objectives. Specifically, each team must make decisions about what its work is and how to accomplish that work. This second stage continues in earnest the planning and decision making that usually surface first during the pioneering stage.

Teams should be introduced to the strategies that pertain to a company's plan of action, causing it to allocate its scarce resources over time to get from where it is to where it wants to go. During stage two, teams become more aware of horizontal structuring; how the separate teaming entities of the organization are tied together for effectiveness. The horizontal structure should make sense to everyone as a means of breaking the organization into smaller, stand-alone, more self-manageable units or teams of multifunctional employees responsible for doing a whole job (an entire piece of work or a process) and accountable for producing specified end results.

The forms on organizational charts for horizontal structures should look flatter, to show that no one dominates another; we have seen such graphics used as pepperoni pizzas, starbursts, or wild shamrocks. The white space around these forms is where collaborative interaction is expected to occur. Work sessions enable teams to solve problems, schedule work, share new ideas and suggestions, plan for the future, and discuss matters relevant to everyone. In doing its work, each unit or team is reinforced by a structure that internalizes a set of interlocking values, linking managers, other teams, and stakeholders into partnerships for getting to where they want to go together.

Chapter Three

Stage Three: Tilting:
Moving from "That's Not My Job" to
"How Are We Going To Do This?"

We won't embrace a new system until we are willing
to individually let go of our old one. Unless we drop
unwarranted assumptions and feelings about the new
system, we shouldn't be expected to bring about
lasting improvements in our organization.

—*Executive in a
well-established entertainment organization*

There is an old story about three men of the cloth fishing on a small
lake—a Protestant minister, a Catholic priest, and a Jewish rabbi.
The priest watches in astonishment as his companions, one after
the other, climb out of the rowboat and walk across the water to the
concession stand. Assuring himself that his faith is as great as theirs,
he steps from the boat and promptly sinks. The minister turns to
the rabbi and says, "Do you suppose we should have shown him
where the rocks are?"

Overview of Stage Three: Tilting the Axis

The process of transforming a traditional hierarchical organization
into a horizontal company has received such favorable publicity of
late that the process might well be viewed from the shore as a
simple matter of stepping out of the old rowboat and strolling
across the water and into a glorious by-and-by. But, as many organizations can already attest, you will have much better success if
you know where the rocks are. At the outset of this chapter, we
present a few nautical cautions we have learned from organizations
that have braved the attempt.

All boats and water conditions are not the same; do not be too quick to jump overboard. Attempting to replicate exactly some other organization's endeavor may not work. We, too, find that what worked with one client system will not work exactly the same way with others. People and cultures are different from company to company. Even divisions or departments at the same site can differ significantly. Because environmental conditions (that is, the water one is going to walk on) are in a constant state of change, there are problems associated with focusing too much on team structures (the supporting rocks) themselves. First, people can begin to believe that the rocks that bear them up are the end instead of the means to an end. Teaming is a method for dramatically improving results, not a substitution for results. Organizations can lose sight of getting to the shore, focusing instead on the care and maintenance of the crews ("Sorry—our customers aren't getting the best service because everyone is in a team meeting right now"). Second, overemphasizing the stewardship of teams can lead people over the side of the boat in search of their own rocks. In fact, newly formed teams do not have stewardship, nor will they have it for some time—possibly two to three years. Team development is evolutionary, does not follow a straight path, and will have ups and downs as it moves along the continuum toward stewardship and ultimately horizontal functioning. Describing fledgling teams as having stewardship establishes unrealistic expectations. At the start-up, call them task teams.

Recognize that not every person on board will easily qualify as a good crew member. In some respects, a work team is like a crew trained to handle a racing shell, consisting of rowers and a coxswain who steers the boat. Coxswains are like first-line supervisors. They are the key to keeping the crew working in unison and the whole thing going in the right direction. No single rower will be able to accomplish the team's objective alone. Each rower needs to understand his or her role and the role of each of the other rowers. On each maneuver that is set up and executed, each rower must know what the others will be doing. If rowers identify problems, they work through solutions and try them out. Rowers depend on one another's motivation and skills to maneuver the boat properly. Trust between rowers and loyalty to the coxswain are vital to success. No single rower can perform well without others, no matter how hard he or she tries. Success and rewards are a product of team efforts. Getting to the level where your crew maneuvers the boat well requires considerable restructuring of current work practices, management policy, wage and hiring policies, and a whole host of other operating techniques.

Coxswains and rowers must operate under this nautical rule: "Know where the rocks are before venturing out." Organizations that launch into horizontal initiatives without intensive planning are probably headed for disaster. Without planning, initiatives are cast onto the water and sink. Teams may collect the wrong kind of data, invest in unnecessary tools, or ignore customer needs. They may end up with a process no better than at the start, an expensive investment that has done little good. Perhaps worst of all, these unsuccessful teams create a host of once-hopeful managers and operators who now conclude, "teaming doesn't float here."

Reduce horizontalizing to its essentials, and it comes down to not very many changes. A business must shift:

From	*To*
High specialization of jobs and fragmentation	Process focus around teams
Task work units	End-to-end activities that create value for customers
Narrow job focus	Cross-functional alignments
Elaborate controls	Decision making and self-managing
"It's not my job"	"How are we going to do this?"
Stable and predictable	Dynamic and learning

From	*To*
Hierarchy	Networks
Information control	Information exchange
Upward mobility	Horizontal mobility
Politics, status, and ego	Trustworthiness, equality, and creativity

Despite the brevity of the list, the actual process of shifting can be chaotic. At the outcome of the tilting stage, however, teams should have largely resolved their interpersonal and task issues. Previous warring factions mellow into harmonious team relationships. Competitive relationships become cooperative, close, and mutually supportive. Team members feel a sense of belonging and are proud to be associated with the team as communication channels open and feelings of mutual trust deepen. With the development of communal skills and the attention directed to self-motivation and the motivation of other team members for task accomplishment, the quantity and quality of work slowly increase.

The emphasis during this motivational and commitment stage of team development is on execution and achievement, whether through a process of questioning and prodding or through evaluative feedback and process improvements. Team members horizontalize when they initiate activity and ensure that the work of the team really gets moving; establish standards to use in evaluating team performance and members; and support, encourage, and recognize the contributions of their teammates. The mind-set for horizontal functioning should be one that emphasizes process over specific content and recognizes organizational change as a team-by-team learning process rather than a series of companywide programs or quick fixes.

If, at this stage, the CEO and his or her management team do not apply to themselves what they have been encouraging their managers and supervisors to do, then the whole process can break down. Managers must make a determined effort to adopt the teaming behavior, attitudes, and skills that they have demanded of others in the earlier stages of change. Their struggle to change will help sustain horizontalizing in several ways. It will promote the attitudes and behavior needed to coordinate teaming efforts throughout the company and it will lend credibility to senior management's continued espousal of a horizontal work force.

Some leadership, of course, just cannot or will not change, despite all the direction and nurturance in the world. Stage three is the appropriate time to replace those managers who arrogantly will not or simply cannot adapt to horizontal functioning, even after they have had opportunities over time to prove themselves. Sometimes those who have difficulty working within a horizontal structure have extremely valuable specialized skills. Replacing them earlier than stage three or before they have worked in the new culture would be unfair, likely demoralizing to others, and disruptive of the transformation process. Moreover, the understanding of the kind of management and worker roles the new horizontal organization demands matures slowly and only from the experience of observing some succeed and others fail.

The remainder of this chapter focuses on the new roles and responsibilities needed to distribute ownership and responsibility to work teams and on the training required to sustain necessary role changes. Helping supervisors and managers make successful role transitions from patriarchal caretaking to shared governance and partnerships is one of the most challenging endeavors in the horizontal revolution. Organizations should ensure that their managers have clear expectations about their new roles, as well as the necessary training in the various coaching tools. They should also expect change to occur slowly, allowing team leaders and managers the time they need to learn and practice their new stewardships. In the following sections, we look closely at the roles of top managers, middle managers, supervisors, team members, facilitators, team leaders, and recorders, and at the functions carried out by steering teams and design teams.

Role of Top Managers

Developing a task-aligned vision that places a premium on distributing power horizontally and giving up the need to control and take care of others is no small feat. No teaming implementation should ever be undertaken without buy-in and support from the box at the top of the old organization chart. Upper management must be sold on the whole investment and be in a position to allocate funds commensurate to the growing needs of a new culture. New roles and responsibilities must be defined before functions are redesigned or funds committed to properly train employees. Managers must understand up front that participating in this change, and later transitioning from directing action to ensuring that teams self-manage processes, will be as difficult as anything they have ever undertaken. Indeed, the toughest part of the work team equation is the changing role of the manager. Change in direction from high control, centralization, and economic constraints is best implemented by top managers themselves. Typically, social changes start in the middle of an organization and spread outward. The top will need to pick up on these social changes, supporting efforts after they are under way and showing promise.

Managers should be prepared to model the behavior that nurtures the social changes. Some managers are like cowboy actors in an old Western movie set, sitting on stationary wooden horses, elbows flapping, pistols smoking, in front of the camera. As we have emphasized before, employees are quick to read managers who pay lip service to the "Great Team Scheme" but do not lead by action and example. These managers can cause more damage than those who are honest enough to oppose change openly. Subordinates will be quick to notice that nothing is really changing and will conclude that all "team-building stuff" is just another training program. Credibility, once shattered, is doubly hard to rebuild.

With only several layers of operations now reporting upward, general managers and chief executive officers must master methods of networking and redesigning the workplace around customer requirements. They must address how to create procedures that make it easy for core workers to take ownership and responsibility for meeting customer requirements. They must learn how to lead a large system by establishing subsystems that push authority and responsibility considerably below their own positions in the organizational structure. In other words, general managers will be measured by how well the system of work teams functions and how well it achieves its goals.

Redesigning the organization into horizontal functions is not an added task for managers in this stage—it is their only task. What else is there that is more critical to survival? Top management must continue to steer teaming efforts with their own hands and demonstrate their faith in the ability of teams to direct themselves. For example, a seven-person business management team composed of the general manager and his staff at an artificial diamond manufacturing company became the organizational vehicle for redesign, coming up with a horizontal model in which multifunctional teams would accomplish all work, particularly new product development, and ultimately eliminate several layers of management. The business management team would set strategic direction and review the work of lower-level teams. Business-area teams would develop plans for specific markets. Product development teams would manage new products from initial design to production. Production process teams composed of engineers and production workers would identify and solve quality and cost problems. And engineering process teams would examine engineering methods and equipment. Within less than a year, the teams became their own champions of improvement, eliminating functional and hierarchical barriers to sharing information and solving problems.

In another setting, before the redesign and change were conceived and implemented, we asked workers to take a machine as a metaphor for their organization and to identify the machine's strengths and weaknesses. They compiled this list:

Strengths of this "Machine"

1. Decent reputation

2. Human and financial resources

3. Efficient operation

4. Multifaceted

5. Reactive

6. Gigantic

7. Continues to operate

8. Provides security

9. Interchangeable

Weaknesses of this "Machine"

1. Outdated

2. Resources not always allocated properly

3. Breaks down occasionally

4. Task-driven

5. Repetitive

6. Lack of creativity

7. Intimidates and runs over folks

8. Needs refueling

9. Interchangeable

10. Disposable parts

11. Not user friendly

The horizontalizing of an organization gets under way as top executives realize that the organization over which they preside is no longer user friendly. Working people will no longer put out for an organization in which hierarchy has rubbed out most user-friendly characteristics. This is when strong leadership from top management is crucial. Regretfully, in most cases, commitment to change is uneven. Some top managers will be enthusiastic; others neutral or even antagonistic. The CEO should offer support to those who want to help him or her horizontalize; to those who will not, he or she should offer outplacement and counseling.

Role of Middle Managers

When teams take on more responsibility, the new roles of middle managers and a wide variety of traditional support functions will definitely change in the transformation. Change to what, no one may be sure. Telling middle managers that they are going to be coordinators, facilitators, boundary managers, and coaches is not giving them anything that is concrete. The more appropriate response is that they are going to have to figure out where and for what they are needed. In most cases, managers who made a living planning, organizing, and controlling will become unnecessary as teams perform almost all supervisory duties and regulate their own operations. Most mature teams operate without direct supervision, because supervisory tasks have been analyzed and reassigned to where they can best be performed. However, any regulating and coordinating that teams still require will be performed by middle managers.

To realize successful role transitions, middle managers should compile a list of existing or proposed supervisory functions and activities and then sort them into one of four categories:

- Must be performed by a supervisor/manager because (a specific reason is stated).

- Could be performed effectively within a team.
- Is best accomplished by establishing a procedure or process.
- Is not important and need not be done by anyone.

In our experience, the majority of activities will fall into the latter three categories. Surprisingly, to some managers, mature teams will absorb many tasks traditionally assigned to such support groups as human resources, maintenance, quality, and accounting.

Most individuals will need to experience a defining moment before they are really equipped to deal with the horizontal revolution. When middle managers really get involved in the nature of their changing roles, they gradually loosen up, unfreeze their perceptions, broaden their thinking, and seriously consider effective actions. Besides being able to step back effectively as teams step forward, middle managers should be effective in using personal power and influence to create a receptive environment for teams. This requires that the manager achieves a balance between setting limits (so that teams do not go too far afield) and removing barriers so that teams can accomplish their work. In addition, the manager should collaboratively develop a flexible charter with each team. Once charters are established, managers can continue to be available to teams as coaching resources, as needed.

Another task is to develop team leaders (often first-line supervisors), professionals, and team members, enabling them to assume substantial amounts of authority and shared responsibility for the actual operation of the business. The middle manager is also responsible for the actual operation of the business and for helping integrate the entire organizational system. Hence, these managers are measured by how well their people work as teams to accomplish daily, weekly, quarterly, and yearly objectives. In this area, managers can work with teams to establish criteria for evaluating team and individual performance effectiveness. In a horizontal environment, this involves getting useful and timely performance feedback to teams, feedback that carries a sense of equity and fairness. Ultimately, middle managers have the responsibility for coordinating their teams' activities and for keeping productivity levels high.

General and middle managers need to develop patterns of interaction that are team compatible in such areas as the following:

Planning:	Participative with active analysis; reaching out to involve
Goal setting:	Stretch, vision, and pursuit; set jointly
Organizing:	Emphasizing collaboration, access to data, involvement
Control:	Understanding, self-awareness, clear expectations
Delegation:	Articulate, collaborative, encouraging, supportive
Communication:	Active listening, feedback, ideas held-in-common
Leading:	Mission-oriented, guiding, problem-solution driven, mentoring
Conflict:	Constructive, reaching closure, healthy
Openness:	Leveling, candor, trust, unhidden agendas
Meetings:	Lively; well-prepared; have purpose, agendas, actions
Interaction:	Between equals, person-to-person, active interplay, give and take
Decision making:	Optimal responsibility, understanding, analysis, discussion
Climate:	Spontaneous, participative, fun, exploratory
Values:	Positive, achievement-oriented, stress authenticity and credibility
Responsibility:	Develop people, be flexible, coordinate with others

In a technical sense, team supervision is making sure you have got the right people in the right place, and that the environment the team is working in is conducive to making processes and teams work well.

Role of First-Line Supervisors

It is crucial that an organization thoughtfully help its first-line supervisors with a new set of roles and functions. Success will depend, to a considerable degree, upon how effectively first-line supervisors give teams strong encouragement and direction at the outset and then allow team members to learn and take on many of the responsibilities that were previously reserved for supervisors. This adjustment is quite painful for some, and many organizations employ grief counselors to help troubled employees deal with change and the reactions from their families and friends.

Unfortunately, first-line supervisors often get in the way of horizontal implementation. In a sense, they have the most to lose. They are to work themselves out of an old job by wholly changing their roles and functions beyond all recognition and putting their own futures on the line. Some will find themselves in a Catch-22 situation: they must serve as coaches to help teams work effectively, but a successful team implementation could threaten the security of their supervisory jobs. The baffled supervisor may ask, "What's left for me to do?" Reducing the number of supervisors is not the only option. But whatever the options, top management, steering teams, or design teams should be prepared to respond clearly to typical questions first-line supervisors will ask: "How will I be involved in the teaming design effort? If the technicians do all that, then what do I do? Will I lose my job? Will my pay structure change? Will I be blamed if things don't work out?" It is to be hoped that, at the outset, the organization can affirm to its first-line supervisors that their roles will change but that they will still have jobs.

In addition, two conditions are critically important in the institutionalizing stages of the horizontal revolution. First, make it understood that with a flatter structure, it will be difficult to tell what is up and what is down in terms of ranking. Becoming a team member is not necessarily a demotion for a supervisor unless pay rates are adjusted down. And second, encourage supervisors to find roles that are best for them and best for the organization. Indeed, encourage supervisors to examine their own backgrounds, interests, abilities, and career plans and then make their own decisions. A supervisor might become:

- Planner, organizer, and facilitator for a larger population of activity
- Administrative liaison with higher level in sending and receiving communications of an administrative nature
- Monitor and advisor of legal requirements of affirmative action and other employment law issues
- Facilitator, counselor, advisor/consultant, and coach of interpersonal relationships within the teams
- An obstacle remover, to ease the path to goals, including protecting the team from unwarranted interference and organizational bottlenecks, and clarifying understandings to higher levels
- Assessor of overall team effectiveness

In time, the traditional distance between first-line supervisor and employee roles will become less evident. Benefits, job meaning, empowering others, challenges, and recognition become the new order for those who make the transition.

Role of Team Members

In the long run, team maturity depends on each member's accepting the collective team purpose and goals as his or her own. Teaming carries with it an obligation that team members commit themselves. Without a commitment and definition of shared power, people will too often just recreate the patriarchy they have grown up with. Rather than pursuing effective change, they will pursue better us-them practices. The responsible role of the team member requires an emotional investment to act now, to live with consequences, and with failure. The commitment has to be to the team within the workplace, not just to one's self-interest or one's career. Not everyone will welcome the horizontal effort. Some will not want more responsibility on the job than they already have. Also, it will not take long for team members to realize that the fruits of their labor often translate to the need for fewer workers. The challenge for leadership—and the most dangerous potential barrier— is to get people to stay committed to improving their process when they know they may be working themselves out of a job.

Team members need to understand the reasons a horizontal approach was established, what function it has, and what its success represents to the organization and the clients it serves. To function effectively, team members will need:

- A compellingly articulated vision of the company's future
- A clear picture of the overall horizontal purpose
- Clarification of and focus on the team's role and responsibilities
- An understanding of processes and required standards
- A knowledge of and respect for each other's jobs or roles
- A common knowledge of how things are supposed to work
- Skills to create strong mutual respect between all members
- Skills to reduce potential conflict with members of other teams

Members must be aware at the outset that they must go through a team building process to begin to function as effective teams (Exhibit 3.1). In time, they will become frontline innovators and be a reservoir of creativity and knowledge from which the team will draw many of its ideas and data. Members participate in brainstorming, information gathering, problem analysis, diagramming and charting, and finally, suggesting and making improvements in the quality of the product or service performed. With team maturity, they will take on additional responsibilities such as cross-functional training, data gathering, leadership, monitoring, and self-correction. They should thrive on autonomy, develop a sense of pride, self-respect, dignity, and a strong bond among themselves.

Exhibit 3.1. Team Building Process.

Purpose:

To draw on the reservoir of diverse resources and creativity.

Concern:

If teams do not develop and nurture a creative, problem-solving climate, innovative thinking and quality improvements may not be available when critically needed.

Definition:

Task groups are to be productive work teams made up of a diversified composition of individuals. Members must work out personal and stylistic differences by finding strengths on which to build and by balancing commitments to one another to improve service, performance, and quality against the demands of everyday work. Dealing with individual needs and differences in the team is as important as performing tasks. Many team initiatives stall because attention is not given to process, or how well the team is working together.

Steps:

1. Deal with identity issues.

    Do I belong? Do I want to belong?

    Who will have the most influence? Will I have influence?

    How will I get along with other members? Will we be cooperative?

    Will I be open or guarded in what I say?

    Will others put up with me?

2. Prepare members for collaborative action.

    Be constructively focused.

    Provide necessary facts and information.

    Encourage balanced participation.

    Avoid group think.

    Respect all views.

    View each other as colleagues.

    Allow for informal socialization time.

    Identify coaching, facilitation, and leadership needs.

3. Engage in team building.

    Clarify purpose and objectives.

    Identify procedural and interpersonal blockages.

    Drill in skills for involvement.

    Train in dealing with behaviors.

    Handle wasted energy and wheel-spinning.

    Prevent from getting sidetracked and unproductive.

    Identify expected results and negotiate for collaboration.

4. Provide follow-up coaching.

    Sustain the commitment.

    Align the energy and skills necessary to ensure perpetual performance.

Create new awareness of roles and performance of team members.

Contribute to a positive climate of support, flexibility, coordination, and encouragement to achieve better ways of doing things.

Guide others' skill and courage to tackle problems and obstacles to being more supportive of each other.

Assist in gaining greater recognition and ownership of team purposes, goals, and achievements.

Intensive team building is typically a three-day activity conducted by a competent coach. During these three consecutive days, team members learn how to deal consistently and usefully with each other, learn new communication tools, develop cross-functional agendas and action items, make commitments for change, and involve themselves in coaching. "My take on team building," said one member of a team-building group, "is that we walk our talk, become authentic, value what each other thinks, and act human to each other." Another member observed, "Openness and trust can no longer be a penalty around here. We have to keep this credibility with each other. We have to combine this work climate awareness along with our task drive."

Employees throughout the organization must see themselves as part of both a corporate process and an autonomous team supporting that process, understanding that their collective role is, first, to lead the entire organization and, second, to lead their respective teams within the system. The most effective organizations make certain that team members ultimately possess all the authority, skill, knowledge, competence, and commitment required to do their jobs.

Role of Facilitators

The facilitator brings together the necessary tools, information, and resources for the team to get the job done, and facilitates team efforts. Two questions that commonly surface for team facilitators are, What is the appropriate role of the facilitator when a team is supposed to lead itself? and, What behaviors empower teams toward greater effectiveness?

The primary role of facilitators is to manage group dynamics and engage in observation, evaluation, and feedback. The facilitator enables others to act efficiently and productively instead of directing them and delegating to them. Team leaders who are facilitators will employ skills that:

- Involve team members, build consensus, and get commitment.
- Lead others to participate in what was once the domain of management.
- Draw fully on the expertise, knowledge, and experience of team members.
- Help team members solve problems and make decisions.
- Help team members use group processes to run effective meetings and maximize participation, productivity, and satisfaction.

Facilitating means managing through people. The underlying function of the facilitator is to foster both interdependence and self-reliance. Therefore, the facilitator does not give direct instructions, but observes and asks questions relevant to customers, processes, adding value, key results, basic structure and constraints, guiding principles, and difficult issues. The facilitator knows how to conduct role-play and involvement exercises to improve work sessions and member effectiveness, and continually encourages and stimulates problem solving. Team facilitators understand that most team problems result from a lack of awareness rather than a desire to subvert the operation. Facilitators also understand that motivation is internally generated, that they can allow people to be productive but cannot make them productive. Hence the title facilitator rather than leader.

We found these measurable results from facilitation when we asked work group members, "What's happened in the last three months that you are aware of?" They said:

"I feel it has been the chance to speak openly about issues that bother me at work. I am now seen as a major part of a group instead of a small function in the paper process."

"I am more aware of being able to recognize communications from others through becoming more attentive and a better listener."

"In the community spirit of self-improvement, I feel I have been, and others have been, more open and accepting of change."

"I have greater confidence in how people work and relate with me."

Role of Team Leaders

Team supervision is provided by a team leader who may be appointed or who may emerge from the group. That person is to lead, coach, counsel, and team build with members; make sure that the team has the needed support and resources; and to encourage it to make its own decisions on a wide variety of current as well as future operating problems. A broad team leader job description might read:

- Ensures resources are available for the team to produce on-time, quality products and/or services.
- Develops the team toward horizontal maturity (coach and counsel).
- Represents the team in organizationwide activities.
- Trains and leads team in problem solving and decision making.
- Unleashes team energy and enthusiasm to achieve goals.
- Assumes responsibility for indirect tasks.

Additional team leader responsibilities may include providing overall direction for the team, analyzing business information, recognizing team contributions, coordinating and problem solving between teams, coordinating with support groups, training, providing technical expertise, managing conflict, evaluating team members' performance, championing innovative ideas, facilitating work sessions, budgeting, and fostering quality and continuous improvement.

Obviously, leading horizontal teams requires some special perspectives and competencies: the team leader must be the *leading example* to others; the *people builder* who develops others' potential; the *barrier buster* who challenges the status quo and breaks down barriers to team performance; the *boundary manager* who performs tasks at the interface between the team and its environment; the *customer advocate* who develops and maintains good customer ties and keeps priorities focused on meeting and exceeding customer needs; and the *workout master* who develops action plans, agenda items, and action items.

Team leaders must be team members and not surrogate supervisors. As mentioned, provisions should be made for teams to remove ineffective leaders or have them select themselves out. Most teams rotate members through the leader position. Some will name several members who serve as leaders in different areas such as safety, quality and production, communication, and team development. Facilitators should work closely with team leaders until they fit comfortably into their new roles.

The characteristics that make an effective team leader are similar to those that make a good facilitator. Team leaders must be people who develop trust quickly with others, are responsible and competent, are eager to learn new skills, have a clear sense of propriety, give clear direction, and create an open and honest work environment.

Role of Recorders

Usually the recorder role is rotated among members. He or she records the action of the work session and may assist with flip chart writing during facilitated problem-solving sessions. Whoever does the recording must be able to accurately capture individual and collective ideas. He or she must listen attentively for the meaning of each idea and be careful not to leave out any pertinent ideas. It is important that the recorder take a subdued role in discussions and remain neutral except when his or her ideas are directly called for. In addition to accurately capturing each idea in a brief phrase, the most important function of recording is to keep track of all decisions and action items, noting key words or phrases and recording team consensus as much as possible. At times, the recorder will need to have important ideas or recommended actions restated in a few words.

Our recommendations for typed records are that organizations use the same format throughout the company, keep formats ✂ recorder and user friendly (one or two pages long), and make sure the records are typed and circulated before the next workout. Our teams prefer the format shown in Exhibit 3.2 at the top of the next page.

Role of the Steering Team

The membership of the five-to-eight-person steering team usually consists of top managers, union officials (if there is a union), and other key people from across the organization. That is, members should come from different functions and different levels of authority. Their personal qualifications should include open-mindedness, good communication skills, and candor. Go after the people who will say what they think and not those locked into the status quo.

As the body that guides the horizontal revolution and models self-diagnosis and self-redesign, the steering team should operate under the ground rule, "don't assume anything." Little will be gained from sociotechnical redesigns if teams are paralyzed by the old paradigm and are unwilling to consider new methods. However, the role of steering teams in some organizations does not end

---

Exhibit 3.2. Sample Format for Team Workout Record.

(Heading identifying team name, date, time, and place)
    Present:

    Absent:

    Purpose:

    Agenda:

    Item:

    Main Points:

    Action Items:

    Next Step:

    Item:

    Main Points:

    Action Items:

    Next Step:

    Action Plan:

    Summary:

---

there. Steering groups can indirectly assist teams to maximize their efforts by:

- Clarifying a team's function in the organization and the impact it has or is expected to have
- Clarifying why certain results and standards are required
- Clarifying cross-functional roles and responsibilities and providing collaborative networks within the organization
- Identifying procedures, resources, and assisting planning-to-action transitions for teams

- Sponsoring team development activity
- Orchestrating opportunities for team celebration for efforts and accomplishments
- Identifying managerial boundaries

A skillful coach/consultant can help steering team members build their team and be open and honest about thoughts and feelings concerning this new venture. Visiting other organizations together also builds team member insights and rapport.

The insight, vision, and articulation of the steering team is essential to organizational transformation during the horizontal revolution. However, team members are a hard group with whom to work because, as one steering team member put it, "We are scared like hell to hear the word 'horizontal.' We have to get out of control. I don't know anything but control. . . . It's going to be hard to break the control mind-set, but it has to be done. We're going to have to change our attitudes." With hard work, new awareness, and a deliberate breaking down of isolation and arrogance, a steering team can begin to function with purpose.

We find that steering teams make valuable use of the following printed observations about their role.

Purpose

People resist change because their feelings are ignored, they do not understand it fully, or they have no part in planning or implementing it. Resistance decreases as empathy, communication, and involvement increase.

Understanding the complete picture is crucial to accepting change. It is easier to confront real problems than vague fears and apprehensions.

Objectives

- To exchange relevant information regarding horizontal functioning.

- To identify performance and results expectations.
- To detail the roles and responsibilities of each individual.
- To define and plan the scope of work.
- To build mutual support and common vision for the horizontal movement.
- To develop an action plan for selection, preparation, and integration of coaches into the process.

Action Items

- Clarify the purpose, function, and role expectations for the design team.
- Resolve uncertainties of reporting relationships, business concerns, and work priorities.
- Begin some involvement and interaction as teams and coaches.
- Create an attitude of involvement that generates a high-level commitment to the horizontal approach.
- Work on issues of interpersonal relationships, communication skills, and definitions for success.
- Learn individual and organizational backgrounds, history, and values related to the horizontal approach.
- Prepare to introduce teaming and subsequent change to the organization.
- Detail and review the action required to accomplish objectives and new performance standards.
- Reinforce achievements and assist in problem solving to assure that targets are being met or modified if circumstances so indicate.
- Deal with differing expectations and perceptions.
- Intensify the collaboration and awareness of interdependence between all team members.
- Celebrate achievements and design new opportunities.
- Create an identity and mission statement as a steering team.

Expected Results

- We will have a detailed readiness for implementing and sustaining the horizontal concept.
- We will achieve closure on unresolved issues and mixed agendas regarding the horizontal moves.
- We will have coaches who are prepared and have a set of strategies for vision, clarity, definition, direction, communication, mission, performance, and goal achievement within their assigned teams.
- We will have all members of the organization seeing the vision and significance of the horizontal change and their roles in its implementation.
- We will have employees who will identify the nature of their team involvements, and the roles and relationships of all players.
- We will have everyone supplied with an agenda and action plan for his or her collective work in undertaking new assigned duties.
- We will have an organization in which there will be a new spirit and positive anticipation.
- We will have benchmarks and checkpoints to use as guidance in accomplishing new goals and measuring our performance.

The steering team can take pride in its work when task groups have been transformed into teams and the horizontal revolution is functioning across the organization.

Role of the Design Team

An eight-to-fifteen person design team, made of people with cross-functional responsibilities and technical expertise, can explore staffing and operational issues before teams are rolled out and in each stage of the horizontal revolution. Design teams look at such questions as: How will work teams be selected? How are people prepared for pioneering or launching teams? What processes or management systems are needed to ensure success of the initial teams? What needs to be in place at each stage of implementation to proceed successfully? What team boundaries need to be developed? What management boundaries need to be developed?

The design team also reviews the needs of outside customers, vendors, and others who exert an external influence on the organization, examining how the organization is meeting their needs. It also examines the current work design system (hiring, terminating, training, planning, scheduling, compensating, and so on), asking where the system must be redesigned to align with the philosophy and values that the new system will embody. The design team invests time and effort in reviewing literature, taking courses, talking and interviewing key people, and visiting and benchmarking other companies involved in teams.

The design team also makes periodic reports to the steering team and other groups on the status of its findings and proposals and receives feedback on work design proposals under consideration. Information sharing with the people who will be involved in the implementation in any way is crucial. Finally, the team drafts a redesign and implementation plan and submits it to the steering team, usually within a three-to-four month period. The proposal identifies volunteers for pilot and other groups, selected because they meet certain criteria and would have the best chance of succeeding. In general, design teams champion, diagnose existing processes, suggest new processes, monitor, and consult, without getting directly involved in work that teams are responsible for.

Since they have to develop their own identity and credibility, design teams must go through their own team building process and firsthand experience with change initiatives. They evolve from making recommendations of overall redesign for the transition of teams, conducting awareness training, and investigating operational details to keeping watch over the transition as a whole, and recommending corrective measures involving different sites, organizational levels, or functional areas. That is, as work teams gradually mature, the design team, correspondingly, becomes less intrusive and more supportive.

Because the design team is at the heart of the whole body of change, continuous, effective communication with the steering team and out to the system is paramount. Memos are not enough. Open communication, often lacking at the outset of a horizontal transformation, will build trust in the design team. (But be sure the communication is genuinely *open* and does not perpetuate war stories and gossip.) We recommend that the design team oversee a team newsletter and prepare videos on developments and activities for periodical circulation to all units.

Illustrative of the role and function of a design team is the work shown in Exhibit 3.3, which was accomplished by a client design team during the formative stage of its organization's horizontal revolution:

Exhibit 3.3. Sample Design Team Work.

Horizontal Functioning: Design Team Initiatives

Theme:

A new direction for life and learning at work.

Creed:

Our purpose is to: Enhance the quality of life by redefining the style of management, the vision and the values of the organization.

Philosophy:

We believe that we can achieve a new direction for life and learning at work through:

- A learning organization
- Trusting relationships
- Mutual respect
- Empowering through participation
- An encouraging environment
- Person-to-person communication
- Use of our diverse resources
- Personal accountability

Goals:

- To remain together as a team
- To be coaches
- To be missionaries and examples
- To keep learning and improving . . . continue the journey
- To fulfill leadership expectations
- To ensure that our vision is forward moving and that we evaluate the process
- To keep on the cutting edge of horizontal functioning
- To ensure that other groups begin the process
- To establish new methods of recognition for individuals who exemplify horizontal functioning behavior

Objectives (targets):

- To benchmark internal/external situations
- To be supportive of each other's specific teams
- To give feedback to the steering group
- To roll out horizontal functioning
- To evaluate and develop resources/paybacks (success measurement)
- To give natural feedback to all groups/levels

- To balance/improve the quality of life
- To bring all of our divisions together as a team
- To bring the whole organization together as a team

Commitments:

- To continue to be honest and supportive [and] to trust in each other
- To fit in priorities
- To be a team

This design team later reported that they had "gone from being a group of individuals to being a team and acting as agents of change." They further described their learning as "relearning how to learn." Their goal then became to continue to pass that learning and enthusiasm on to others in order to improve the whole organization. Some specific results they reported were reduced labor cost, less time spent coping, managers interested in becoming coaches, less distrust of those "above" in the organization, more open communication and ownership, improved quality of service, and increased revenues and cost savings.

Role Clarification in All Teams

If there is an increasing amount of disruption or mishandled tasks due to overlapping or conflicting responsibilities within and around any of the teams we have described here, it is advisable for managers or facilitators to conduct a role clarification exercise with all players involved. It is likely that teams needing role clarification will also need to develop or redevelop a mission-and-purpose statement. A team rarely needs role clarification if it is heading in a unified direction.

What do you do with employees who cannot or will not adjust to team roles and direction? Our experience and counsel is that you have to have patience and make every effort to help them, but you also must be firm. While new team members are learning how to cope with new responsibilities, managers are learning how to guide work teams. Role clarifications are happening simultaneously, and everyone needs to exercise patience over time. But, sometimes, as with managers, you have to let team members who cannot participate go.

Training

The organization changes as its training changes. Our involvement with organizations has certainly borne this out. Without an effective training intervention, no successful team transition can ever be realized. Experience has shown that organizations that do not help employees understand why there is a need for change and do not lay a solid foundation of communication and problem-solving training prior to introducing teams find that team members are unable or unwilling to meet their new responsibilities. In addition, as teams are formed, the emphasis should shift from *training* to *learning*, putting choice in the hands of the learners as teams choose their own ways and places of learning.

We have found that most companies venturing into teaming tend to underestimate the need for new types of training, especially the heavy investment in technical training. Team leaders and members in their first two years of team operation can spend as much as 20 percent of their time in training activities in the areas of job skills (technical skills required for job performance), team/interaction skills (interpersonal and communication skills needed to function in a group), and quality/action skills (skills needed to identify problems and implement solutions).

Training works best when it is provided with continuity over time rather than in a lump sum. There is much to be learned, and coaches can prevent training overdoses by prescribing training on a just-in-time basis. Not only must team members learn one another's jobs—a massive cross-training effort in itself—they also must learn how to work as a team, adapting to new group processes and dynamics. Training is critically important for helping employees use these dynamics as tools instead of seeing them as hindrances.

Training should be a line/team responsibility, and concepts should be taught in a functional context. This ensures that the training is relevant to each unit's activities and the participants' specific needs and that it aligns with team culture. Training for many organizations usually begins with train-the-coach sessions for team leaders, who in turn conduct the training for team members. To become coaches, leaders need preparation in communication skills to facilitate individual and group interactions. They will also need skills for keeping schedules, maintaining records, and recording results. As part of their preparation, they should receive a workbook on effective coaching.

Who Should Do the Training?

When a team is started, the company's organization development specialist, trainer, or human resource manager usually starts the training process by training line managers. Trainers should examine their motives and self-interest: the team philosophy requires training line managers to train their people and training team members to train themselves, while trainers train themselves out of a job.

Most teams elect or designate the leader who will be the team trainer. This leader, if not the immediate area supervisor, is a regular team member who is also responsible for other team leadership responsibilities. In some cases, this team leader is responsible for recognizing areas of concern for training, and in other cases, team members collectively decide what type of training is needed. Team members are also free to design their own training but are usually given ample resources to draw on. Job skills training, too, can be handled by the team members themselves. One at a time, employees can learn to master one skill or service from their co-workers. (This training can, in many cases, be bolstered by computer-based training programs.) Team leaders/trainers can monitor the many skills of their peers and design, refine, and deliver training programs in all skill areas, using themselves or technical experts, human resource trainers, or even supervisors transitioning into teams as instructors.

Training Task Force

Some companies have a training task force made up of team members, team leaders, facilitators, managers, and executives. These people discuss a team's progress and areas of difficulty, select appropriate training, and offer it to the team. Members of the training task force are often also the people who deliver the training, although they can also select instructors. A training task force can provide a necessary link between the developing work team and the organization, keeping the work team on track. A training task force might commission and train teams to work on improving top-ranked processes. The approach would be to start out with one team in one functional area and then build on that team's successes by training additional functional and cross-functional teams. By concentrating resources on the start-up of just one or two teams working on a major organizationwide process, impressive results can be realized in short periods of time.

Interpersonal Skills Training

Team members often refer to interpersonal skills training as the "glue that holds the team together." The early phase of team development is frustrating because members must confront one another, not a manager, when they have a problem. As teams evolve, members need additional training in group communication, conflict resolution, and problem-solving skills. One effective strategy is to offer the teams training only after the members request it. With this strategy, team members have an immediate application for the training.

Multiskilling and Cross-Training

Technical skills needed to perform a variety of specific work tasks and interpersonal skills are two of the most obvious areas where training is needed. Team members should also be multiskilled to perform all the functions of self-management. As teams become increasingly interdependent, their relationship to other parts of the business necessitates business skills. Adequate skills in interface systems and feedback channels for outputs and results help teams access various departmental and organizational supports. Writing skills are important, as are skills that revolve around knowledge about the customer, sales, safety, and salaries and benefits.

The healthy development of autonomous work teams is usually associated with these multiskilling requirements and cross-training. Team members are more likely to help one another and have more innovative ideas if they have more skills. Teams themselves can identify all the skills required of their members and monitor the degree of proficiency in each skill for each member. Many teams prominently post *skill charts* that allow team members to identify their team's experts on specific subjects and, therefore, the assistance they need. Programs like pay-for-knowledge also encourage cross-training.

When organizational systems are phased out, multiskilled employees in these systems can be farmed out to other areas to avoid layoffs. Cross-training then becomes more important because the life of a system is much shorter than in the past.

Training Sequence

Team members should be taught to tackle tasks and utilize group dynamics efficiently and effectively. A basic training sequence for new teams could include these items:

- The vision of the transformed horizontal workplace and why there is a need to change

- Awareness building and ventilation of trainee anxieties
- Orientation with specific directions and clear models of behavior
- Team role clarification with each team creating its own mission statement, goals, and guiding principles to realize its objectives
- Establishment of procedures for business processes and continuous improvement of processes

Skills taught in this initial training should be presented in this sequence:

- Feedback and interpersonal communication skills
- Group relationship and becoming-a-team skills that establish intragroup procedures
- Intergroup processes, such as scheduling, coordination, and planning skills
- Technical and cross-training skills
- Self-monitoring and take-charge skills
- Problem-solving and decision-making skills
- Supervisory and self-management skills
- Additional job and cross-training skills
- Quality/action skills and skills that allow power to be transferred to teams

Notice that problem-solving skills fall toward the end of the sequence because teams typically must learn to get along together before they can problem solve effectively together.

Launching Training

The design team has responsibility for designing, organizing, and implementing training. The way to head off potential resistance in team implementations is to involve people in an awareness process of understanding where and why changes are needed and what is to be accomplished through a transformation to teams. Awareness training will help the organization develop a vision of what competitive output will look like with teams in place. It will vary in content and format for each level of anticipated involvement within the company; however, in all cases, the process should guide employees to think about how they will motivate themselves to achieve the vision. After awareness training is complete, the steering committee in conjunction with the design team should prepare executives, managers, and employees for the shift to teams.

Our observation is that leaders of teams use a combination of self-managing behaviors to prepare and develop their people: self-observation, self-evaluation, self-expectation, rehearsal, self-criticism, and self-reinforcement. The most essential behaviors we identified were encouraging self-observation and encouraging self-evaluation. Some specific means leaders use to coach these behaviors are:

- Conducting role-play and situation-replay exercises
- Giving both positive and negative feedback within the team
- Interacting to encourage group problem solving
- Encouraging the team to set performance goals
- Aiding the team to "think through" an activity before starting
- Assisting intragroup communication
- Working alongside team members

Team Member Development

Teams must learn the group process. Teams unskilled in the group process will lack understanding of the way a work group functions effectively, will be unable to move efficiently beyond analyzing problems to determining ultimate solutions, will experience a slow-down in their effectiveness after a few months of operation, will make decisions by default, and will find their energies sapped by unresolved issues.

After a time, team members may feel stale from using the same group discussion method to solve every problem. Effective team training should introduce options for facilitating the group process. There are many tools available to enhance team skills in identifying and defining problems, exploring possible solutions, and implementing solutions. Effective group process tools get team members to go beyond their normal way of handling information by offering fresh perspectives on dealing with information and issues. Whatever the approach, group processes benefit from shared input and healthy team interaction. Some key aspects of healthy teams are discussed in the following sections.

Responsibilities

The responsibilities of the team in running their own unit like a business typically need to be clarified for team members. In one training session, for example, a director of teams asked trainees what participative management meant. They gave such responses as, "participative management is when management listens"; and, "participative management is when management provides resources." Of course, participative management is much more than that. It means that the employees accept more responsibility and take more initiative, while also working toward the organizational mission and avoiding self-sufficiency.

As teams progress through their evolutionary stages, the roles of members become more responsible as managers and coaches become more indirect in their involvement, while remaining responsive. During this evolution, it is important to provide managers and coaches with new responsibilities to replace those that have shifted to the team. They might be assigned more teams and/or take on some of the responsibilities formerly held by higher management or resource people.

Recommended in the early stages of a team initiative are fre-quent role-clarifying sessions, as described earlier. Similarly, respon-sibility charting allows supervisors and team members to work together to list their responsibilities and then decide who handles each one by assigning codes to each item or checking off items on the chart. This method works best when teams are learning to handle more leadership responsibility.

Team Well-Being

Experience shows that the level of well-being of successful groups is significantly higher than that of unsuccessful groups. Self-doubt, lack of credibility, and lower creative input and improvement are consequences of lower team well-being. Training should enhance teams' belief that they have the ability to do what is required of them. Successful teams believe that "we can be effective." However, this attitude is difficult to develop in many teams because older workers often do not believe that the team can accomplish any-thing significant.

In one instance, a group of team members wanted to increase their responsibility, but every time the topic came up among the entire team, one of the three older workers would discourage any optimism, saying, "We are not capable of this"; and, "It's not worth the effort, management won't really deliver." As a way to confront statements like this, encourage ventilation sessions in which teams and supervisors openly share issues, concerns, and fears about their role changes. Beyond such airing sessions, training should teach new skills so that the positive attitudes that complement those skills can work to break down those years of preconceived assumptions about effective leadership.

Interpersonal Feedback Skills

In many team initiatives, a lack of effective interpersonal skills impedes progress. When it is clear that poor relationships are preventing team effectiveness, feedback skills need to be built into the training. Participants can learn to give and receive feedback in a constructive manner, work through issues and concerns in work relationships, and better understand the wants and needs of other team members. Feedback training should be constructive, showing people how to focus on tasks, issues, the job, and behavior; be objective; be specific; be open and honest; and use tact and consideration.

We teach people the following seven-step approach for giving feedback:

1. Explain the situation the way you see it.
2. Describe how it is affecting performance.
3. Ask for the other viewpoint to be explained.
4. Agree on the problem.
5. Explore and discuss possible solutions.
6. Agree on what each person will do to solve the problem.
7. Set a follow-up date.

Rather than training just the individuals with the greatest difficulties, it is better to train the entire team, enabling all team members to reinforce one another in using the skills.

Feedback training also serves as a catalyst to increase cohesiveness and the necessary team bonds for advancing change and innovations in the face of resistance. Problems associated with cohesiveness can be minimized by teaching team members how feedback can be used constructively beyond the team: for example, when work team members rotate to cross-functional teams or have contact with customers and with other companies in the industry.

Feedback is the lifeblood of team functioning. Feedback is a key ingredient of change. There will be no horizontalizing without it.

Customer and Supplier Interaction Skills

In addition to interpersonal and feedback training, team members also need training about products and services and about interacting with external and internal customers, clients, and suppliers on a regular basis. Teams that rely on others to deal with customers and/ or vendors are less effective than teams that must perform their own boundary-spanning activities. An understanding of the technical feasibility of projects is essential for moving new technologies through a system. Contact with the environment can help teams be marketers and can be an important stimulus for innovation, but unless employees are taught the importance of such contact, they will not be motivated to perform these needed marketing and innovating activities.

Each team has customers. Although it is unrealistic to assume that every employee will have an opportunity to connect with his or her external customer, each employee is a supplier for the next person on the line. If these people can get together and talk about what the next person needs, their quality will improve. Sometimes, for example, a piece of work passes inspection but is made so poorly that it is a problem for the next person that works on it. An understanding that workers have a responsibility to the next person along the line can decrease such problems. Both external and internal customers can give feedback in these terms:

- Continue doing the following.
- Do the following more.
- Do the following less (or stop doing it).
- Start doing the following.

Responses in these four categories can build workable agendas for meeting customer expectations.

Measuring Training Effectiveness

Effective evaluation programs to measure improvements resulting from training are usually a combination of three approaches.

Pre- and postmeasures of team attitudes and behavioral changes. Teams and other members of the organization complete questionnaires both before and after training. The posttraining questionnaires are distributed two to six months after training is completed. The changes in responses between two surveys are analyzed.

Observational analysis. Members of the steering team monitor progress. To verify that attitudes and behavioral changes are the results of training and not caused by external factors, a control (untrained) team is observed and evaluated. A comparative evaluation of the trained and the control teams confirms whether or not the training was valid.

Measure outcomes. Outcomes like service quality, productivity, scrap rates, rework rates, safety rates, and attitude changes toward the implementation of horizontal teams are key indicators for measuring training effectiveness. Care should be exercised with validation, since there is a risk of measuring things that are not direct consequences of training.

Summary

Organizations that try to go horizontal without making the exigent role changes and investments in sufficient training will find their implementations problematic. Responsibility rests on top management to move or replace people who do not make the shift to the new way of working. These people may be transferred to parts of the company where technical expertise rather than teaming competency is the main requirement. When no alternatives exist, people must leave the organization, through early retirement for example. The act of moving people is stressful but can reinforce employees' commitment to go horizontal by visibly demonstrating the CEO's commitment to the new structure.

Stage three, tilting, is a period to build teams that, under the influence of appropriate leadership, grow healthier and stronger and more autonomous. Teams become not a thing to do but a way to do things. They reintegrate the managing of work with the doing of work.

By stage three, the role of the new team leader is embodied in the shift from controlling to distributing ownership and responsibility to others. Training managers on how to assume a leadership role in a horizontal organization is critical to success. Managers must learn how to coach and facilitate rather than direct. They must understand how teams develop and mature over time and how they can facilitate that growth, and they must forsake a fetish for maintaining control, predictability, and the pursuit of self-interest, in order to become core workers with a willingness to be accountable for the well-being of the larger organization. The inability to make this stage-three shift from an us-them view to a we-are-partners-in-service view is probably the single greatest reason for team failures. Those making this shift in roles will require considerable clarity about the new role, a personal need to change, organizational support, and healthy self-esteem.

Training for team skills, as well as technical and business skills, must be an ongoing activity among team members. The training focus is on learning how to work in multifunctional capacities, with training in building collaborative relationships, confronting issues with peers, winning team support, and fostering improvements. Depending on the setting, revised personnel policies and business systems may be essential to empower teams to take responsibility for peer reviews and grievances. As individual and team skills develop, the quantity and quality of work slowly increase.

Results-oriented training will not roll out prefabricated courses but will incorporate a just-in-time delivery approach on relevant subjects, helping team members learn by experience, with guidance from their managers and advisors. Organizing into horizontal functions requires a combination of planning, selecting the right team members and leaders, designing teams for success, training continuously, and carefully managing the shift of power and responsibilities from leaders to team members.

By stage three of the horizontal revolution, most indicators are up: productivity/service is higher, customer expectations for good quality and services are being met, there is organizationwide commitment and support, and management has become positive and resourceful. Teams develop a harmonious cohesiveness as previously competitive factions mellow into using normal, healthy interpersonal patterns. Animosity decreases significantly as leadership duties are rotated to all members. As teams begin to realize that many of their problems are entirely within their control, communication channels open, feelings of mutual trust deepen, and individuals discover that they are proud to be associated with the team.

Chapter Four

Stage Four: Transforming: Tools for Continuous Improvement and Success

> During one of our learning experiences, we related
> this organization to the metaphor of war. We
> discovered that top managers were like generals, and
> we were like troops in the trenches. It became
> obvious to us that, with all of this change, the
> "generals" were only risking their reputation, while
> we as "trench troops" were risking our lives.
>
> *—Supervisor in a large specialty*
> *organization having many deep traditions*

The four stages of teaming follow the natural stages of human development. The first concern of the newborn child is, "World, will you let me survive? Can I trust you?" Similarly, during the pioneering stage of team development, survival is on everyone's mind. The settling-in stage is analogous to the toddler's saying, "Can I control myself? Can I affiliate?" The third stage, tilting, parallels the adolescent phase of life in which individuals say, "I am what I can get to work. Can I get an identity?" Then, as young adults, individuals make a rather profound statement, "I will be significant, important, successful! World, I'm going to conquer you and be powerful enough to make you do my bidding!" And this is what people also sense in the fourth stage of the horizontal revolution.

Overview of Stage Four: Transforming

As team development moves into stage four, "parents" must make a commitment to their "new adults" and be transformed from

121

command and control managers into leaders who give self-managing teams responsibility, accountability, and authority to deliver first-class customer service. Letting go is difficult, as any parent will admit. Patiently explaining the external environment and boundaries for a decision and utilizing less-than-ideal team decisions as springboards for coaching do not come naturally for managers. Anything less than this, however, short-circuits the growth process and leads to regression to earlier stages. Healthy adults and teams will be motivated by choosing service over self-interest and by having pride in their accomplishments and a sense of ownership and belonging. It is to be hoped that the parenting style of most people will allow each team to discover its own talents on its way to becoming an adult.

Stage four is the time the horizontal approach becomes entrenched: the right people are in place and the team organization is up and running. Teams that are transforming push beyond obvious assumptions, gut feelings, and sloppy reasoning. They insist on data, relevant information, and information systems that they manage. They are confident and skilled in self-managing and performing multiple tasks, with a remarkable capacity for enthusiasm and motivation. Horizontal teaming is aligned to organizational goals, and members feel a sense of ownership and investiture with the organization as a whole. Resources are allocated around structured processes, through which teams make decisions about tasks and processes, diagnosing and solving (or anticipating and preventing) problems and choosing and implementing actions and changes. Team members freely contribute toward the collective efforts to make sound decisions.

In their quest for better quality and productivity by improving internal and external customer and supplier relationships, stage four teams need training in small business management, learning how to read financial reports and how to evaluate their productivity in terms of return on investments. Additional skilled activities teams demonstrate at this stage are experimenting with new approaches, learning from their own approaches and best practices of others, and transferring knowledge efficiently and effectively into action. Team members have a constant need for reflection and analysis, learning together what is inappropriate, erroneous, and counterproductive.

In this chapter, we present several best practices for transforming teams to use, including workouts—effective tools that assist teams to eliminate barriers that impede learning and effective progress.

Workouts

The idea behind workouts is similar to the Japanese idea of *kaizen*, or continuous improvement. An attempt to extend the benefits of freewheeling debate to the whole company, a workout program first gathers employees together, regardless of rank, for sessions (often off site) at which people air their gripes and make suggestions. Managers are required to take action on the issues workers raise. Later, the workout program organizes employees into carefully targeted teams with the authority to define solutions to business problems. We find the workout practice a meaningful way of communicating the idea of employee/team stewardship—employees and teams entrusted with the management of property, finances, or other affairs not their own. The workout program has six basic steps, which we list here without detailed descriptions to provide a general flow of activities for workout sessions:

1. Tying business imperatives to ineffective work practices
2. Enlisting involvement in the workout process
3. Overviewing wasteful work practices
4. Auditing by functional groups
5. Auditing by cross-functional groups
6. Contracting, recommending, and wrapping up

Several overarching traits permeate every workout session: team members emphasize continuous improvement, use customer satisfaction as the main gauge of performance, and focus on managing the process and tracking how things are produced rather than on how much people can produce.

The workout program has helped employees learn more complicated self-managing procedures; however, what we have found most interesting is that workouts begin to redefine the nature of management. Workouts make taking a certain amount of guff from subordinates a standard part of an executive's job description. That is healthy in any horizontal setting.

The tying of business imperatives to ineffective work practices, in part, should begin before the workout session itself. Team members can talk with customers to anticipate changing customer requirements, identify best practices or benchmarks, and begin to develop a process map or flowchart that shows the operational flows that convert inputs to outputs, including material/service flows, information flows, and decision points.

Process Mapping

Process mapping and benchmarking spot opportunities for improvement and their use is critical to effective horizontal leadership and to successful workouts. Benchmarking, as all managers know, is the activity of comparing something to an objective standard, such as comparing your organization's customer service to a competitor's customer service. Process mapping is a simple flowcharting technique used to display the steps of a work process and their interrelationships. It involves writing down every single step, no matter how tiny, in a particular task, on the premise that the root cause of many work problems lies in the fundamental way that work is carried out, that is, in the work system itself, the process.

Process mapping is helpful when a work team wants to improve the current way of doing things, two or more organizations want to improve their working relationships, or a new work system is being designed. The mapping provides a visual display of the work process to make it easy to understand how things are done (documenting); to identify bottlenecks, barriers, and outdated procedures that slow things down (troubleshooting); and to develop new ways to complete the work (strategizing or planning).

Ordinarily, the mapping of the as-is work process is begun in a team (we use a Post-It for each step, sticking the filled-out Post-Its on a wall in the team area). The goal usually is to produce improvements that will lead to a new process map, or the desired state. The process mapping session follows these basic steps.

1. Establish boundaries for the process to be mapped (clearly define the process and reach agreement on the beginning and end points).

2. Break the process into chunks (brainstorm the major stages of the process and arrange the Post-Its into the work-flow sequence).

3. Identify the inputs and outputs from the overall process (identify what you receive from the processes that come before yours, or upstream processes, and identify the outputs by examining what you provide to downstream processes or directly to the external customer).

4. Select the highest priority stage or piece of the process and break it down further (repeat step 2, defining the inputs and outputs for the selected stage).

5. Identify who performs each step and how long it takes.

6. Analyze the process-mapping information and brainstorm issues and problems that need to be resolved to make the process better (look for major delays, large blocks of time consumed, complex flow paths, communication flow disruptions, repeated processes).

7. Clarify, prioritize, and select a few issues or problems to resolve (pick an issue or problem that the team can influence to change and on which the team can win).

8. Identify a proposed solution or action for each issue or problem (be creative; strive for speed and simplicity; benchmark how others do it if appropriate).

9. Develop a who/what/when plan for implementing the desired state (identify what will be done, who will do it, and when it will be completed).

10. Present the team's proposed solutions and who/what/when plan to the sponsor for decision (the sponsor provides one of the following responses to each part of the proposal: "Yes, implement right away"; or, "No, and here is the reason why not").

Additional hints are to start with the "macros" of the job, use processes that are manageable, and concentrate on mapping the current process, delaying improvements until mapping is complete.

Working up a Workout

Typical U.S. work teams are usually a rich mix of ethnic, gender, and generational diversity. If they are to get anything done, members must resolve personal and stylistic differences, find strengths on which to build, and balance commitments to one another. Dealing with a kaleidoscope of individual needs and differences in a work team is the beginning of teaming. One way to lessen everyone's fear of differences is to provide information and invite participation in workouts. Once individuals and teams are ready to look at their own motivations, power bases, prejudices, and biases in an open and honest forum, they can move forward in creating a productive, healthy, and profitable environment. When a work team runs smoothly, members can concentrate on their primary purpose for existence—improving a process. In contrast, a work team that fails to build relationships among its members as they tackle issues and problems together will waste time and energy on struggles for control and endless discussions that lead nowhere.

✿   Members of a workout often face four sets of personal dilemmas:

1. Who am I in this team? Where do I fit in? Which of my many roles should I play, or how should I behave? What kind of membership is best suited for me? What obligations does working in this work team impose upon me? What are the rewards for doing something in this work team?

2. Whom can I influence? Who will support me in this work team? Whom will I support? Who is showing signs of aloofness? Who is not willing to listen to me? How much influence can I have? How much acceptance do I have? How can I gain more acceptance? What is the best way for me to make a contribution? Who is important to me?

3. Where is the leverage located? Who will control what we do in this work team? What will the results be? What is the value of what we are doing? What types of individuals seem to control the direction of this work team? How can we change anything?

4. How will my behavior be affected by participating in this workout? How much can I say? Why should I say anything? How much will I risk of myself in this workout? How will others respond to me? How much will they see of my real behavior? What are the dangers for me? How well am I equipped to get involved with some of those in this workout? Where is my respect for others and confidence in myself? What are others' expectations of me? How answerable am I prepared to be for myself?

Workouts need to include steps that will help team members work through these and other questions. Since workouts usually begin with an air of ambiguity and dependency, they should always begin by clarifying the purpose of the workout.

What's Our Purpose?

Without a well-stated purpose, workout participants usually develop projective behavior, that is, they move prematurely to discussing possible consequences of being involved and possible motivations for what others are doing. Therefore, workouts must move quickly to prevent anxiety over purpose and direction.

Once the purpose for the workout work is in hand, intensified behavior will often emerge, based upon past experiences. Team members may liken the situation to several other group activities that have not worked. These remarks will be indications that individuals are fighting against getting involved or are taking flight away from the work group agendas. There may be signs of pairing, in which two or more individuals seek support from one another at the expense of the total work team. Participants in a workout need to abandon their dependency on central figures or procedures and grow into taking ownership for the workout process. They must face up to the issue of their behavior in this unstructured situation.

What Are Our Boundaries?

The initial work of a workout is to establish the conditions for membership and the boundaries of behavior that are acceptable for membership. This is done by each member listening carefully to other workout members while all of them are establishing the rules for team behavior. A foundation of respectful behavior is essential to the function of the workout. Team members need to review with each other the value of exploring and accepting feedback. They need to discuss the concept of ownership and growth. They must identify the ways in which accountability can be taken. They must have examples of arrogance-based behavior, such as defending, rationalizing, and blaming.

Once the workout begins to function, that functioning will establish goals that can accommodate the needs of a variety of different individuals. The workout session invents procedures for moving the team from issues to action agendas. It works toward consensus. It attempts to get some agreement on that which is most accepted in most ways by most of the participants. It finds out where the team leadership is, determines what will be accepted and by whom, and looks for sources of continued motivation for any particular action item. A work team will also need to learn how to handle authority problems. It must determine how much power it has; how it can acquire more power; and what its relationship is to the power figures in the organization.

What Is Our Action Together?

The workout must move to action. Workouts must have as-is, to-be, and to-me agendas (discussed further in Chapter Seven). It is out of these agendas that action plans are developed. Workout members must also decide who is to be involved in what type of action. The biggest blockage to appropriate action resulting from a work team workout is the way in which the team communicates. Someone must guide the process of communication so that it is real and valid. It is use of the principles for behavior that makes workout communication real and valid, group members hearing what others are meaning as well as saying and giving appropriate feedback to each other.

Proper behavior will be determined by issues that develop in the workout. There will be situations in which individuals are unsure of what is happening and need help to explore possible behavior. There will be situations in which individuals are groping to find a place and need feedback on how they are perceived by others. There will be a heightened concern over the roles of central individuals, resulting in a need to develop more subgroups or coalitions and a need for members to accept responsibility for workout events. Workouts need to move constantly toward the removal of old behaviors. Team members must see that new behaviors are more exciting and profitable for them to use before they will use them. Therefore, energy needs to be expended on building the work team by clarifying purpose and agendas, identifying behavior principles and their application, and establishing work arrangements toward action.

These benchmarks can be used to measure interpersonal effectiveness in a workout:

- The workout atmosphere is informal, comfortable, and relaxed.

- The purpose, task, objectives, and goals of the workout are well understood and accepted. Team members will have freely discussed the purpose and objectives until they were formulated in such a way that people could commit to them.

- There is a lot of discussion in which virtually everyone participates, but the participation remains pertinent to the purpose and task of the workout.

- Team members listen to each other. Every idea is given a hearing. New behaviors are used. People are not put down. Defensiveness is not an issue. Ownership is taken. Blame is kept in check. Creativity prevails.

- There is disagreement. Disagreements are not suppressed or overridden by premature action. Workout members seek to resolve issues rather than to dominate those who have differing perceptions. Behavioral principles are employed so that all workout members find a new perspective. There is little evidence of personal attack, either open or hidden.

- When action is taken, clear assignments are made and accepted. The action also includes a procedure for follow-up and moving to the next step.

The workout's success will be in proportion to how well management and facilitators keep themselves flexible as the workout progresses, and the extent to which they keep track of how well it is functioning. Workout functioning is measured by its level of effectiveness and level of team member satisfaction.

Information Gathering

Ongoing problem solving in workouts involves a process of gathering relevant and valid data about a work group's performance and assisting the group through steps of data feedback, problem identification, and problem solutions. In gathering data, teams can explore underlying causes of problems by asking these questions:

- How are we performing together as a unit toward our objectives?
- What types of problems is the workout experiencing?
- What are the impacts of these problems?
- Why is the workout having these types of problems?
- What keeps workout members from being as productive as they would like to be?
- What do members like best about the team and how can these conditions be strengthened?
- What changes would improve the effectiveness of members and the workout as a whole?
- How could our unit work more effectively as a high-performance team?

One of the best ways of gathering data from work teams is interviewing. One-on-one interviews by team leaders with group members can be open, candid, and built on a rapport that allows underlying needs and feelings to be expressed. Interviewing, done effectively, will draw on the experiences and perspectives of all workout members and other potential information sources. Where there are time constraints, lists of issues and concerns can be written out in question form and given to responsible people to fill out before the interview. Confidentiality should be maintained, allowing team members to address sensitive team issues.

Another approach to information gathering is open data sharing, which collects data from the work team as a whole and allows clarification and discussion of people's statements. Issues or concerns are given to the team in outline form, and open-ended questions are helpful to expand subsequent discussions. Team members can be encouraged to ask each other to "say more about that." Such discussions should be facilitated to ensure that total participation occurs. After the team interview is completed, the data are summarized by the team leader or facilitator and presented back to the work group for further interpretation and for planning the next step toward solving an issue or problem.

An excellent technique we use for gathering and organizing information in workout settings involves the use of Post-It notes, the adhesive-backed slips of paper also used in process mapping. In a brainstorming session, work team members anonymously record problems, issues, ideas, or solutions (whichever is the goal of the brainstorming) on Post-Its (one statement or idea per note) until they have exhausted their ideas. All the notes are then gathered and scattered on a viewable wall in the room.

Next, two or three team members are selected to read all the notes, arrange them in clusters, and label the clusters according to common themes or factors. The entire team can then interact with the dimensions or patterns of information that emerge. This interaction with "the wall" should add to, delete, or modify clusters. Subsequently, the team orders or prioritizes clustered information or ideas by their importance to desired outcomes (tasks, timeliness, appropriate support, and necessary resources). Afterward the clusters are removed from the wall into information envelopes, to be referred to later for processing. The whole exercise develops, organizes, and displays ideas in a way that will increase work group information gathering, interaction, and problem-solving effectiveness.

For example, one of our workout sessions with a group of nurses involved a problem of high turnover. In the first meeting, with some thirty-five nurses, the nurses were given Post-Its and asked to write down, anonymously, all the problems they had about giving their best service, one per Post-It. They then scattered their Post-Its on a designated wall, and four nurses were invited to cluster and label the notes. We invited the medical director of the hospital to sit in and observe all this. One of the clusters absorbed 70 percent of the Post-Its, and before any of the four nurses were invited to explain their clusters, the doctor rose to his feet, leaped to the front, reviewed the largest cluster, turned back to the nurses and said, "Why haven't I known about this? This cluster represents two very arrogant doctors who apparently treat you nurses like lowly order-lies. And, paraphrasing your responses, you're doing a great job, you don't need this crap, and at first chance you're out of here for another hospital and doctors who treat you like partners, don't yell at you but give you dignity and respect." By the second meeting, a revival of hope and commitment marked the flow of the work as changes were initiated under the direction of the senior doctor toward solving the problem to the satisfaction of the nurses. The Post-It approach was a quick workout tool to do a reading on the group's needs and allow everyone to participate.

Key Problem-Solving Skills

Problem-tackling skills empower work teams to solve problems and take action. Getting everyone to use a similar problem-solving process is as important as getting everyone on the same computer system, so the design team must select a compatible process that everyone in the organization can learn and use. There are many problem-solving approaches to choose from. What is important is that the approach is suitable to your people and the needs of the organization. In any approach, these following four skills will be highly useful:

• The ability to gather in-depth and relevant information on issues and problems from others

- The ability to contribute ideas helpful for solving problems together and to get ideas across to others
- The ability to make effective decisions together through exploring options and evaluating alternatives toward an acceptable consensus
- The ability to contributing to successful outcomes through planning, assigning tasks, and making sure things that lead toward desired results are accomplished

Many workout initiatives stall because they do not pay enough attention to process. In addition to the team's focus on content, time is needed to manage the group process functions. Early symptoms of process problems include the group's drifting away from focus, issues, or goals; individual members' dominating discussions, and members' feeling uncomfortable with the actions of others. When these symptoms arise, it is well to stop and "process the process," so team members together can identify team problems and make necessary changes before they interfere with team effectiveness.

Four-Step Workout Problem-Solving Model

The problem-solving process must be the glue that holds diverse groups of individuals together in arriving at their best solutions. Workouts can get so mired in the *what* of a problem that they overlook the *how*, the process. However, with the right guidelines, teams can avoid potential pitfalls and make the most of their efforts together. The abbreviated model shown in Figure 4.1 is most effective for work teams because it easily assimilates to group processes and because it is linear, memorable, and uses a shared vocabulary. It has four steps and four key actions to guide the group through a complete problem-solving process.

Step 1: Describe Present and Preferred Situations. Team members begin the problem-solving process by openly sharing ideas,

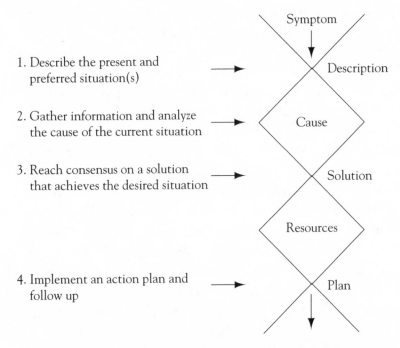

1. Describe the present and
   preferred situation(s)

2. Gather information and analyze
   the cause of the current situation

3. Reach consensus on a solution
   that achieves the desired situation

4. Implement an action plan and
   follow up

Figure 4.1. Workout Problem-Solving Model.

expectations, and feelings on work-related problems and opportunities for improvement. They treat each problem as unique, avoid early disagreement on the problem statement, and consider why they are solving the problem and what they need to reach the ideal solution. In most cases, problems are best identified through a gap analysis, or the differences between present and preferred situations. Problems should be clearly stated in terms of facts known, inferences drawn, and any assumptions made. Workout members should agree that any problem is worthy of their energy and time but that it is ineffective to focus thoughts and resources on solving a large number of problems at the same time. After questioning and elaborating the current situation, the team should selectively choose to work on only one to three problems.

Step 2: Gather Information and Analyze Causes. Questions stimulate information gathering and lead to an analysis of causes.

Asking, What? Who? Where? When? and, How much? can significantly assist the investigation. Gather all the relevant, accurate information that is needed, but no more. Do not become buried in details. Figure 4.2 illustrates a problem analysis cube that directs the user to ask what/who/where/when/how much questions about known information, comparative information, and differences/chances.

Once the questions are answered, consider how the verified what/who/where/when/how much information describes the problem and suggests probable causes. To make the specifics of a situation clear and useful, additional questions can be asked. If team members find they cannot appropriately describe the current situation, they may have to decide what critical information is missing or uncertain and then gather or confirm, where feasible, the necessary information to ensure that the problem is adequately detailed in terms of what it is and what it is not. To come up with potential causes of the problem being analyzed, the team members should brainstorm the probable causes from the identified criteria. Next, they should select two or three likely causes and determine what information will verify or disprove each likely cause.

In developing a list of possible causes, the team may follow this procedure:

1. Brainstorm for possible causes. Everything that comes to mind on the cause is recorded on a flip chart. Team members can use the following orderly process to contribute ideas:

   Each member is asked for ideas in rotation.

   Members offer only one idea per turn or pass.

   Members do not evaluate ideas at this stage.

   Good-natured humor and laughter should be encouraged.

   Exaggeration should be encouraged.

   If an idea needs to be edited to be written down, the originator of the idea must agree with what has been written down.

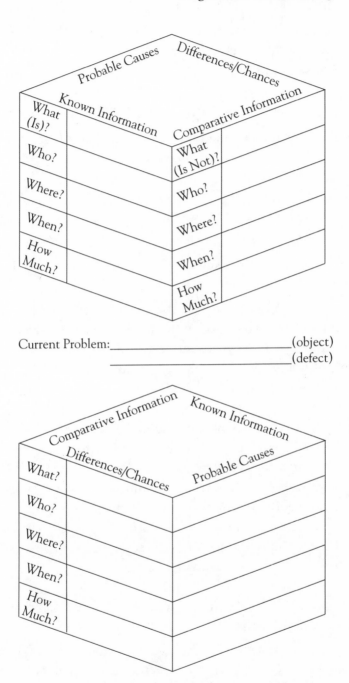

Current Problem:_____(object)
                _____(defect)

Figure 4.2. Problem Analysis Cube.

Brainstorming is completed when all ideas or possible causes have been exhausted.

Members numerically rank each idea to assist in identifying the best ideas.

2. Use cause classification, cause analysis, or process analysis. (Choosing the best method comes with experience. Workouts may want to start with cause classification because it is an easy way to begin.)

3. Discuss each cause and consider the possibility of its being the true cause. (Process analysis is helpful when individual causes are investigated, because it breaks the process into steps.)

4. Select one or more likely causes for investigation. Use consensus to rank order them.

5. Assign work team members to investigate causes. Make sure everyone is assigned and understands his or her assignment. Consider each member's interests and availability when making assignments. If possible, let workout members choose their own assignments.

Step 3: Reach Consensus on a Solution. To reach consensus on a solution, the work team determines whether the elimination or modification of the causal factors would be a solution to the problem. For example, in electronics manufacturing, the work team might consider whether changing the protective smocks on all machines on a regular basis would permanently do away with the problem of product contamination. Team members can follow this process to test their hypotheses.

1. Begin the data collection process on the most likely causes, selected in Step 2.

2. Determine the type of data needed, why it is needed, how it can be collected, who will collect it, when it can be collected, how it will be analyzed, and what will be done with the results.

3. Design check sheets to record the information.

4. Establish schedules that show when the data are required.

5. Review progress at each workout meeting.

6. Use questions to get specific facts.

7. During the investigation, consider:

> Degree of adherence to written procedures (if they exist)
>
> Similar operations
>
> Changes in methods, procedures, personnel, equipment, materials, management, or any aspect of the operation that could have caused the problem
>
> Anything unusual
>
> Questioning the managers and employees directly involved in the process or with the problem
>
> Experimenting, if necessary
>
> Developing a process flow chart and examining it carefully

8. If the causes selected for investigation are not the true causes, select other causes to investigate and repeat the process.

9. Ask for help from outside the work team, if necessary.

10. When the true cause is identified, confirm it.

At the completion of this process, the work team has identified the true cause of the problem and is ready to set appropriate goals and plans.

Step 4: Implement an Action Plan and Follow Up. During Step 4, the workout sets goals and establishes action plans to accomplish desired results. Consequences of taking different approaches should be thought through and discussed in advance. An action plan should specify the who, what, where, when, and how of putting the solution into operation. Plans should be concrete and measurable and should include a time period for completion and note any limiting factors. Action planning should also map out how the work team will proceed to obtain the support it will need to implement Step 3. Also, team members should develop contingency plans for any potential pitfalls that can be identified up front and anticipate what barriers might exist and how they may be overcome.

Action plan forms (Exhibit 4.1) are helpful to record steps/ actions, resources, persons responsible, and due dates. On the form, the team should list, chronologically, all the steps necessary for the solution to be successful. The team should also estimate the due date for each action. Due dates can be estimated by working backwards in time from the target date, using the length of time necessary for each step. Input from all individuals who are to be affected by implementation of the solution should be considered. The number of people involved should reflect the number of people who will have to change their attitudes and behaviors if the solution is implemented.

The likelihood that a problem can be solved and the means by which it should be solved are determined, in part, by the tools and techniques used. Past experience, in some cases, can be used as a guide. However, most problem solving can be greatly facilitated by a systematic approach such as the one shown here.

Problem-Solving Consensus

Bottlenecks can occur in problem solving when teams move from open to decision-oriented thinking (for example, when they move from brainstorming to focusing on key possibilities or from key possibilities to action plans). Although voting appears to be a quick solution, it often introduces a win-lose situation. Reaching consensus, on the other hand, is a win-win approach that pulls together diverse views for the good of all. Consensus helps the team move from individual to collaborative ideas. It works best when the following conditions are met:

Exhibit 4.1. Action Plan Form.

Action Plan

Change   From: To:

What Steps Are Needed to Accomplish the Change?	Resources Needed	Person Responsible	Due Date

- The work team is constructively focused.
- Ample time is provided for thought and discussion.
- Necessary facts and information are provided.
- Balance in participation is encouraged.
- Group think is avoided.
- All views are respected.

- Constructive contribution is reinforced.
- Participants are viewed as colleagues.
- An appropriate pace is maintained.
- Time to socialize informally is provided.
- Team leaders take charge when appropriate.
- The facilitator keeps the team focused and moving to successful resolution, helping to create an open communication environment and a structure for goal setting and problem solving.

A High-Priority Project Approach

Teams need successes on their projects. A high-priority project approach to workouts focuses on identifying imperative improvement opportunities and rapidly implementing solutions that are critical to the quality of the company's products or services. We suggest proceeding through the following phases to assist teams to realize successes with their projects:

1. Select an urgent, imperative, and compelling goal where success is vital and current performance is unacceptable.
2. Clearly communicate expectations, scope of empowerment, and parameters of the project to team members.
3. Analyze performance or quality improvement need and determine root causes.
4. Plan a solution to the causes, implement the plan, and ensure that it produces desired results in a prompt manner.
5. Expand or extend the process to achieve results in other areas.

Success is rewarding for those involved in improving quality. High-priority projects present to management and other representatives the lessons learned and successes achieved by work teams that can be applied throughout the organization. Any improvement effort gains momentum and commitment and increases in excitement as it spreads throughout the company as a result of causing actual results.

To communicate the results of a high-priority project, a *brief* written project summary, which is prepared with team input and on which team members have signed off, is presented to management by the team leader. (The team should also retain a copy for members' reference and use.) The summary should include the actual approach used, observations about the team process and accomplishments, specific decisions and results achieved, and recommendations for further extension of the current project or for expansion of improvement efforts.

Workouts for Early Success

Once teams are working together on goals and problem-solving agendas, it becomes imperative that they have early successes. After examining why team projects fail, we propose that the following four determinations be made before beginning any project to combat the common reasons for failure and to realize successes:

1. What are the expected outcomes of the project? Who will do the work? In what time frame is the work to be done? Determine precisely what the expected results are and specify the time frame in which they will be accomplished. Time should be short term; weeks instead of months.

2. What is the flow of the work? What is the location of the work? What resources are required? It is important to know clearly what the work team will and will not do in regard to implementing the solutions. There should be a clear understanding of what they have control to change.

3. Who is going to be responsible for what? How are the responsible parties to be empowered? Once the team has decided the goals, time frame, and scope of empowerment, teams and leaders will need to decide who is to be responsible for what. Some projects fail because of the it's-not-my-responsibility syndrome. Team members should be assigned to make sure each goal is carried out. However, putting two people in charge of the same goal is not advisable. Many members of the team may work on a goal, but only one person should ultimately be responsible. In addition to responsibility for a goal, each person should be assigned specific tasks. Next, people must get started. This sounds obvious, but many team projects with good intentions never get off the ground because they are postponed until this is ready or that is done. The key is to get started and make it work.

4. *What barriers, issues, and problems are anticipated along the way, and how are they to be resolved?* Team projects may stall when problems that arise are not addressed quickly. It is common for a team member to think that he or she should wait until the next meeting to discuss a problem that arises between meetings. But if a team member cannot accomplish a task, then other team members or the team leader as necessary should be consulted promptly. The organization should begin to establish a performance management system that supports the team concept, since teams that solve problems together gel very quickly.

Actions That Support Project Success

Regularly report status updates. Use the regular weekly meeting to follow up on the progress of project assignments.

Achieve expected results within time frames. It is important to achieve desired or expected results. Collect data to determine if what the team is doing is working, make course corrections, and achieve results. If at some point during the project, the team member or leader realizes that the goal was too ambitious or impossible, then the goal must be modified, making the change clear to everyone on the team.

Link to the future. When the project is completed, teams should report, as teams, to management. Surrogate reporting by a designated team member is not usually as effective. It is better for management to appoint one or two representatives to attend a team's report than the other way around.

Meet with management. Assuming knowledge of general goals or mission is shared by everyone, the following topics might be appropriate for the final project meeting with management: What are the immediate and long-term impacts for the customer? How do the current and the intended projects improve the quality of products or services? How does that improvement contribute to the mission and goals of the organization? How does the solution save money and increase profit in both the short and long term? How does everyone benefit by designing and implementing a solution throughout the whole system?

Workouts work when coaching works. Coaching is the key. One of our workout groups in a large industrial organization was able to make, and report, measurable change after only three months of regular work sessions. This is the report of this group:

Characteristics of Where We Were

1. *Who* was more important than what. That is, only if the boss proposed an idea did the idea get taken seriously.

2. Truth and honesty were hardly used, but people became accustomed to the deception.

3. There were mostly winners and losers. That is, people were building or losing their power.

4. There was authoritarianism, internal politics, and game playing. That is, who wanted what done predominated over what was right.

5. People were motivated by self-interests for survival and power. That is, everyone in some way automatically developed a highly political style.

Characteristics of Where We Are

1. Shared vision is taking root, but it is still having difficulty with those steeped in the habits of game playing and politics.

2. People are being encouraged to participate in openness by speaking out, and to engage in reflective openness by looking inward.

3. Skills are more important than just good intentions.

4. Some people are finding themselves troubled because they are having difficulty relating to new expectations.

5. Some people still believe that the boss is paid, and is in a position, to have all the answers.

6. The organization is being liberated in a remarkable way because more and more people are realizing nobody has the answers but everybody has the responsibility for learning.

7. There is a new spirit of openness that is being built into relationships along with a change of spirit and with a new set of skills and practices.

8. There is an irony to the new freedom of action to some because new freedoms have caused them to become more helpless, trapped, and impotent.

Summary

The tools for horizontal teams to workout are no less valuable than the team's ability to work through its own diversity and destiny. Without good tools, not much will be realized, and the team will soon be out of the game. As a formal mechanism for sustaining a horizontal functioning—and for transferring real power to employees—workouts are unsurpassed. Happier people come up with a flow of better ideas. Great things happen when people search for intelligent improvements, work out their own change strategies, and control their destiny.

Effective teams focus first on external issues, such as customer service or quality, where they can have immediate and meaningful success. Team successes build self-esteem and confidence, boosting team members to excel and deal with interpersonal problems that may arise. A lessening of boundaries, or organizational fluidity, is the goal. Boundaries inhibit information flow; they keep individuals and teams isolated and reinforce preconceptions. Opening boundaries by linking teams with their customers and suppliers ensures a fresh flow of ideas and the chance to consider competing perspectives. Team workouts that open boundaries become the learning forums and vehicles for change.

Workouts bring together groups of essentially coequal people operating with self-directedness and guidance by a few managers/coaches. Workout sessions link together team members, jobs, managers/coaches, and values. The ways in which work is performed determine the nature of team processes and how the teams who perform those processes are grouped and organized. In some settings, a whole process involves various steps in different locations. In those instances, a company needs cross-functional workouts, each member managing steps in the process.

The centerpiece of the workout approach is the recognition that creating new developments and solutions to problems is not simply a matter of processing objective information. Rather, it depends on tapping the talents and often the highly subjective insights, intuitions, and hunches of team members and making those insights available for testing and use by the organization as a whole.

Part Two

Leading the Team-Powered Organization

Chapter Five

The Horizontal Leader: Making the Commitment and Building Your Skills

This organization is built upon creative ideas. The
old organization is getting in the way of the new
organization.

*—Team leader with a large service organization
in transition from a 1950s style to a 1990s style*

Besides teaming, we have discovered that we enjoy the popular U.S.
comic strip "Calvin and Hobbes." Its hero, six-year-old Calvin,
assures his mother that Hobbes, his stuffed Bengal tiger (who talks
to Calvin), will eat her if she tries to put him to bed before nine.
When his parents send him to bed without dinner, he sneaks back
downstairs, imagining he is the fearless spaceman Spiff, "descending toward the mysterious planet below. . . . Crouching behind a
boulder, our hero hears alien voices, talking about him: 'Blork,
gablork, Spiff! Ha Ha!' Spiff burst into the open, death ray blaster
blasting! 'I'll give you something to talk about!'" he yells. The next
two frames go back to reality: in the first, the parents and another
couple have obviously been hit with suction darts from Calvin's dart
gun, and in the second, the mother runs after a fleet-footed Calvin.
In the final frame, Calvin and Hobbes are in bed. Calvin is Spiff
once again, thinking, "Back in the darkness of outer space, Spiff
reflects on his one miscalculation. Our hero resolves to revisit the
planet, this time with more ammo." The final comment comes from
Hobbes, "No sleep tonight, I see." If you read "Calvin and Hobbes"
often enough, you come to realize that Calvin's parents are in constant danger of losing the battle for control: his father muses about
calling the orphanage, while his mother wishes that she had been

blessed with a girl. Likewise, our experience affirms that most supervisors at all levels of organizations today operate from the control
rather than the commitment paradigm, perceiving their role as one
of controlling employees through policies and punishment. It
should not be surprising when employees behave like Calvin.

Behavioral Leadership

A team leader's starting point must be a fundamental shift in perception that allows him or her to embrace the commitment paradigm, rather than adhering to the strict control paradigm because
his or her authority seems to depend on it. If the team leader does
not embrace the commitment paradigm, his or her team might do
some paper studies or even come up with new process designs, but
no horizontal functioning will actually happen. Even if the process
of horizontalizing gets started, a controlling effort on the part of
the team leader will cause the team to run out of gas or hit a wall
by the time it is in position to make the organization the best in
the business. This is of particular danger for team leaders who come
from the managerial or supervisory ranks. The latter should bring
vision, conviction, and enthusiasm to their team leader role and
should inspire in others a sense of mission and self-directedness.
Leading means walking the high wire between rigidity and spine-
lessness. We believe that the best team leaders create and sustain
a tension-filled balance between two extremes. They combine core
values of commitment with elastic strategies to get performance
results. They get things done without being done in by any Calvins
on the team. They know what they expect of a horizontal team,
they communicate their expectations with clarity and purpose, and
they get commitments.

Team leaders also know that they must respond to the complex
array of forces that pushes and pulls teams in so many different
directions. They begin with ends in mind and think creatively
about how to make things happen. Their primary responsibility

becomes one of engendering the commitment of team members
rather than eliciting their compliance. Team leaders get commitment through coaching and by example, leading team members to
accept great self-control, which will replace the externally imposed
controls of traditional supervision. Furthermore, leaders will work
with the team to develop strategies with enough elasticity to
respond to fast take-offs and stops, to the twists, turns, and pot-
holes that the team will need to negotiate along the way to horizontal functioning. In this chapter, we will present some of the
challenges we have found that team leaders commonly face and
the skills they will need to create a horizontal unit out of a diverse
bunch of individuals.

The workplaces where we coach are characterized by team leaders who increase the number of employees who take ownership, and
function as though each were "president" of his or her own job. We
coach team leaders to build more self-management, responsiveness,
proactivity, initiative, collaboration, self-reliance, and personal
responsibility within their various projects and team functions.
Team leaders soon learn that the more people the organization has
making a difference, adding value, challenging the process, and
learning from mistakes, the more marketable the process of change
becomes. We see amazement as team leaders receive evidence that
their work is causing others to become more open, interesting, curi-
ous, bold, and able to use their own smarts. One team leader
reported that it was a miracle to see fewer people basing their rep-
utations on politics, information hoarding, back stabbing, intimi-
dating, and building turf and territory.

Effective team leaders set goals to have ever larger numbers
from all parts of the organization volunteering to work hard with
each other to build networks, create partnerships, earn trust, and
develop more workable relationships. We also usually ask team
leaders to keep accounts on how many fewer people are complaining, sulking, withdrawing, griping about unfairness, and/or getting
even with someone who has given distasteful feedback.

Calvins Are Out

Meaningless and monotonous work, abusive and controlling treatment has produced a work force prone to tardiness, absenteeism, and disability claims. There is an increasing trend for Calvins in the workplace to resort to sabotage as a means of expression against the control paradigm or the negative effects of having to "go without dinner." Sabotage has become the way a worker can take control over a situation in which he or she feels powerless. Those who perceive that they are powerfully controlled are finding any way they can to show their bosses that they will not conform. Many workers suggest that most supervisors at all levels of the organization today operate from the control rather than the commitment paradigm. What does that mean? Calvins are popping out everywhere with their dart guns.

Like Calvin, many of today's supervisors grew up in families where their parents were bosses who set rules, made the decisions for the family, determined chores, allocated resources, and executed punishments. They went to schools where teachers and administrators were bosses who made the rules, gave assignments, structured the requirements, determined the grades, and decided when you could see the school nurse if you felt sick. In the military, they had bosses who, because of rank, demanded compliance or else. They joined communities where city, county, state, and federal governments established and regulated rules and laws through control. They went into work settings where a hierarchy with multiple levels imposed a clear line chart and a chain of command. The organization came equipped with laws, rules, regulations, contracts, and procedures.

If you are a supervisor over people, is it any wonder that you see your role as controlling them? The whole superior-subordinate mentality permeates every facet of U.S. culture, including management thinking. In many situations, control may be entirely appropriate. However, as the following contrasting lists illustrate, there are fundamental differences between the two management paradigms of control and commitment and where each may lead.

Control Paradigm	*Commitment Paradigm*
Elicits compliance.	Engenders commitment.
Believes supervision is necessary.	Believes education is necessary.
Focuses on hierarchy.	Focuses on customers.
Has bias for functional organizations.	Has bias for cross-functional organizations.
Manages by policy.	Manages by principle.
Favors audit and enforcement.	Favors learning processes.
Believes in selective information.	Believes in open information.
Believes bosses should make decisions.	Believes workers should make decisions.
Emphasizes ends justifying the means.	Emphasizes compatibility of ends and means.
Encourages hard work.	Encourages balance between work and personal life.
Rewards compliance and loyalty.	Rewards innovation and personal growth.

The control paradigm is alive and well in our workplaces. Authority, roles, pay structures, and communication lines are clearly delineated on pyramidal charts. Selective information sharing usually follows hierarchical lines because senior managers "need to know" while others apparently do not need to know. Ironically, the people who must implement something often do not have the need to know or access to the information necessary for effective implementation. This is just one example of how what one manager we know has called "man-in-control management" will severely inhibit a leader's success in a work force that should be horizontally functioning.

Commitment and Horizontal Lifestyle

One of the reasons that the role of leading horizontal teams or people is difficult to clarify is that it is something more than just actions and activities. It includes the way leaders think and the values they are committed to act on. A person's thinking affects his or her behavior and that behavior affects others. What we have discovered is that a commitment to excellence can be boiled down to a simple declaration about how people are to view one another and how they are to lead by example: "In our commitment to excellence, we welcome and expect the leaders of our organization to set an example for us as we work together."

What the customer needs from leadership is an organization fully committed to demonstrate its values, to provide the finest quality services to them as guests. What employees need from leadership is respect, responsibility, recognition, and flexibility in their work. Put into practice, leadership means giving employees at all levels the knowledge, confidence, and authority to use their own judgment to make important decisions. And that means leaders need to be in the business of strengthening their employees' beliefs in the values to which leaders are committed and in their own sense of effectiveness.

In essence, then, horizontal functioning for organizational leaders is not simply a set of external actions, it is a process of changing the internal values and beliefs of their people about effectiveness. When individuals feel that the power to be effective is within them, then they will be in a better state of mind to adequately serve the guest or cope with the environmental demands, situations, events, and people they confront. They feel powerless when they are unable to cope with these demands. Good management practice, be it among managers or team leaders, increases a sense of self-determination in others to assist in delivering, as one organization puts it, "magical and memorable experiences which create a sense of joy and wonderment for our customers and consistently exceed their expectations."

Leaders must expect their people to manage themselves and their own work in collaboration with their teams and co-workers. Through horizontal functioning, all members become customers to their leaders, and the job of the customer is to teach the supplier how to do business. If it is the task of teams to teach teaming and service to those above them, it is the task of those above them to give teams focus, to give them an aim in the marketplace. Leaders have a wider, longer, and more experienced view and should spend time thinking about the next two years while a team may think mostly about the next two days. Teams need leaders who can interpret the marketplace and the environment to them and give them boundaries within which they can create strong teamwork.

Horizontal functioning is an idea whose time has come. However, for many leaders newly meshed in teams, horizontal functioning is considerably more difficult than they expected and they often face a whole new challenge of learning to do things differently. In what follows, we discuss doing things differently in terms of the leadership process; leadership principles; and coaching, artistry, and power; and we describe the tools and key actions for leading teams.

Principles of Behavior

As we are learning together with our clients, horizontal functioning is not built upon motivational hype but upon expanding the work content and involvement of employees. It is also built upon sustaining employees as they go beyond their current level of performance and beyond whatever was previously considered possible. Expanded performance requires that the quality of communication and production be enhanced. Too many workplaces today do not extend training beyond the delivery of information and knowledge. Horizontal functioning requires the use of new behaviors in on-line situations. This new behavior is accomplished through team leaders, or coaches, who can coach behavior without being psychological.

Establishing two principles for behavior creates a process for horizontal functioning that is simple and functional. These principles can be instantly understood and everlastingly remembered. They remove the need for hype, emotion, quick-fix motivation, and psychological treatment as a means of self-improvement and personal growth. They are the ingredients of personal change and self-directed learning. And they fortify accountability and continuity, the two essential elements for horizontal functioning.

The principles for behavior upon which horizontal functioning is developed are *service to others* and *accountability for self*.

Service to others is the conceptual aspect of horizontal functioning. It consists of a continuum of behaviors from submissiveness to arrogance. Respect for others and confidence in self are at the center point. The challenge in using this concept is to maintain a balance between self-confidence and respect without letting one's behavior move toward either end of the continuum.

All human interactions can be conceived of as exchanges of service. All relationships are good or bad depending upon the service given and received. We assess others' work based upon the way in which it serves our needs and expectations. Optimum service is achieved when all persons in a relationship display balanced behavior of self-confidence and respect. Optimum horizontal functioning is optimum service. Little service is achieved when one person exhibits arrogant behavior and the other is submissive or when both are arrogant or submissive.

Accountability for self is the action aspect of horizontal functioning. The action consists of being answerable for what one does and responding to the expectations of others. The challenge of accountability for self is in maintaining respectful behavior while exploring new information, handling feedback, taking ownership, and accepting continuity and at the same time resisting arrogant behavior, denying, blaming, and rationalizing.

The action of accountability is the work of horizontal functioning. Accountability produces the change in behavior that makes a person more responsible. Accountability provides the feedback a person needs to become self-correcting. Accountability creates involvement in personal perceptions, expectations, and perspectives, and in the pursuits of horizontal functioning. Accountability requires active listening and alternative behavior.

Accountability for self is the heartbeat of horizontal functioning. Without the action of accountability, the whole experience of horizontal functioning is just talk. With the action of accountability, there is self-generated responsibility for horizontal functioning.

Once the two principles for horizontal functioning are in place, the leadership process can acquire new skills and artistry.

Leadership Coaching

Horizontal functioning requires coaching; the behavioral principles require understanding and guidance. Just as a sports team requires a coach to help it assemble and integrate its power, so horizontal work teams require a coach for proper results. The coach's role is discussed in considerable detail in Chapter Seven. But it is appropriate for team leaders to take a moment here to think about what coaching means. In Greek mythology, Pygmalion was a sculptor who carved a statue of a beautiful woman who subsequently was brought to life. George Bernard Shaw used this theme in his play *Pygmalion* (later the basis for the musical hit *My Fair Lady*). The central idea of Shaw's work is that one person, by effort and skill, can transform another person into a more alive and useful being. Horizontal coaches have Pygmalion-like roles in supporting and stimulating functional behaviors.

A team leader or horizontal manager is not primarily present to give directions but to encourage the exploration and examination of behaviors and agendas. The horizontal coach does this with skill and artistry without being prominent and dominant. Being resourceful and communicative are the essential requirements for a horizontal coach.

Coaching is not done by exercising one's own leadership but by bringing out leadership in others. It is not done by having power over others but by releasing power in others. It is not measured solely by products and projects completed but by a measurement of growth in competence, accountability, and personal satisfaction in others. Indeed, in horizontal coaching situations, it is not always clear or important who is leading. What is important is that everyone has the opportunity to grab responsibility, learn respect, build confidence, be answerable, and become purposefully involved.

Leadership Artistry

The artistry of leadership coaching is found in a good sense of timing. Such artistry is usually treated as a "gift" or "intuition," rather than something that can be learned, as spontaneous rather than planned. The opposite is nearer the truth. Artistry in coaching is learned by bringing all of one's experiences into play at any given moment. Artistry of this kind is the ability to capture what is happening at the moment and to be in touch with the learning applications that can be made.

Too often, linear cause-and-effect learning makes people unable to see the multiple opportunities of a given movement. Individuals' skills are preprogrammed to the point that they become mechanical (this may happen particularly to speakers and teachers). A leader cannot afford to enter a situation with his or her skill tucked away and hope that spontaneous action will move everything forward. Nor is it enough to just have a plan and a strategy. A leader needs to have as many plans and options as possible. It is not enough to have a framework for diagnosing a situation and prescribing action. A leader has to have many frameworks and many prescriptions. It is not enough to get one's head into work. The heart must also be involved.

The artistry of a leader and a coach should be in line with that person's readiness and ability to engage in coaching. There needs to be a ready acceptance that the idea of working on behavior, including one's own behavior, is okay. There needs to be eagerness to work with other coaches. There should not be glaring deficiencies in the coach's own behavior. A person with artistry in coaching is not the subject of negative discussions by others. When artistry is present it shows in the values a person has toward others and toward the horizontal process. These values need to include an attachment to vitality, imagination, work, and learning. Coaches need to be glad to see their artistry applied to behavioral change. They also need to be able to connect the process of personal change with the process of organizational change.

The final test of coaching artistry is performance. There is nothing like real action to put artistry through the mill. Each situation presents a new opportunity for creativity. Little can be schemed or scheduled ahead of time. Skill will carry only so far. The artistry of face-to-face enhancing of leadership, problem solving, diagnosing, and bringing about of horizontal functioning by an accomplished coach must be seen to be appreciated. Yet neither skill nor artistry in coaching stands alone. Each relies upon the other. To be artistic requires techniques and skill. To be skillful requires intuition about people and situations. The utilization of inborn talent will increase artistry and skill. The practicing of techniques and maneuvers will increase artistry and skill. The coach builds on the natural and learned characteristics that are available to him or her.

To determine your own current level of artistry, take a good look at your natural capabilities and characteristics. Some questions to ask are: How well do you sense what is going on around you? Do you always see a process as well as a task in what others are doing? Do you see power in people? Do you have the ability to quickly clarify the cause of problems? Do you see the concept behind the issue? Do you work through ambiguity? Do you see beyond any particular situation? Do you always have an agenda? Do you always see possible consequences for a particular behavior? Do you always project a better situation? Do you invent new ways to communicate? Do you inspire others with your insight? The degree to which a person can answer these questions positively is the degree to which he or she has artistic coaching capabilities.

To become more artistic as a coach, you must learn how to learn. This means pushing aside traditional learning and learning anew about the world around you. Albert Einstein said it is impossible to get out of a problem by using the same kind of thinking that it took to get into the problem. So it is with the learning of the artistry of coaching. It must start from a different place than you started from in school. Experience is the key, not memorizing information for a test. Coaching learning is built on self-direction and insight. Experience underlies the coach's ability to be flexible toward what is happening and to track how the coaching is functioning. Learning must come out of every experience. The coach needs to be self-conscious about his or her own experience and value it. Learning is by doing.

Leadership Power

T. S. Eliot (1954, p. 169), commenting on the idea that in hell nothing connects with anything else, writes, "Hell is oneself, Hell is alone, the other figures in it merely projections. There is nothing to escape from and nothing to escape to. One is always alone." If people find work a living hell, maybe it is because they find no connection to anything that is important to them. A coach connects experiences and learning for people at work. There have to be connections to the world of others. There have to be connections between the perceptions people have and the development of new perspectives. There have to be connections between goals and values. There have to be purpose and pursuit. Joining principles and behavior, connections are what horizontal functioning is all about.

Making connections takes an effort from both the coach and the team. The coach's skill and artistry cannot overcome a team's lack of commitment. A team's commitment is of little use if the coach is unable to exercise proper skill and artistry. Success at work will not come without individuals' going through the agony of judging for themselves.

Bringing About Change

The inescapable conclusion we reach from both experience and observation is that those who would lead horizontal teams must begin by encouraging faith in organizational renewal and faith that people can become self-directed and make change. Team leaders must have patience as they help people move from past purposes, procedures, and skills to new ones through a variety of experiences in which they make mistakes, learn, and make corrections. Teams will need this learning later to work through additional challenges.

Leadership must be astute by not missing opportunities to work through restraints. Teams must plan for and be willing to work through the inevitable resistance and inefficiency that accompany the creation of a horizontal employee system. Those who lead the change should not overlook opportunities to show how old skills can be applied to new directions, and teams should identify the purposes and values from the past that should continue. Most importantly, teams should help individuals who have spent careers trying to embody certain values, or to acquire certain positions or specializations, through transitions in a fair and sensitive manner. If employees lose their confidence in the team's commitment to fairness and their own sacrifices to develop new self-directed approaches, then they are unlikely to make the changes necessary to succeed. However, people and organizations can survive relative incompetence for some time if they believe that eventually they will develop a successful team culture, become highly competitive, and see the rewards of their efforts. Similarly, people can accept a feeling of ambiguity about the purpose of teams if they believe that their efforts to develop a new order will eventually be rewarded.

We coach team leaders to keep journals of their experiences. One leader produced the following statement of learnings as a journal entry after eight months of team leadership:

> I have learned that communication is the most sought-after requirement for getting things done with teams. Because of improved communication, the team approach has been the key issue for change. I have found that accepting responsibility and desire for follow-through are the preferred behaviors for team members. Although change is afoot, sometimes nothing means anything to some people. Yet, I maintain a drive to eliminate bad behaviors. There continue to be moves for and against bringing this organization together. We sure need more supportive leadership. Our roles and relationships remain unclear and we are bumping into each other. There is a struggle with the mix and mixture of some of our work groups and teams. Some are wanting a more specific phase plan for this betterment. Some are learning that being self-righteous and being bothered by everything doesn't work. It is interesting how we are creating a greater awareness of the need to change behavior, not personality. Making a difference and greater contribution is the best leverage for our growth. The trouble begins when people think they know more than they really know.

The situation this leader describes illustrates why the crucial attitudes needed from leaders of team initiatives are faith, fairness, courage, and emotional maturity. Regretfully, these are the very traits many executives demolish first when they try to motivate employees into teams by attacking the "old ways." Effective team leaders develop faith and confidence in teams even as employees are complaining and holding fast to the former way of doing things. They will especially give help to newly created teams with negative self-images, teams made up of misfits and has-beens. Equally, they will protect fledgling teams from the incursions of the rest of the system. And they will help struggling teams develop distinctiveness through new skills and contributions.

Organizational Support

Team leaders cannot fulfill their roles as we have described them here without organizational support. An organization's support of each team leader can be assessed by asking such questions as these:

- Will he or she be empowered to set direction, or just to translate and communicate it?
- How much authority needs to be designed into the role to legitimize and support teaming?
- Can the leader's role be designed so as to foster rather than usurp the horizontal function of the teams?
- What kind of support system will the leader require to create ideal conditions and to harness needed resources?
- How can the role be designed to strengthen the leader's influence upward and outward?
- What kind and how much information will the leader need, and with whom will he or she need to collaborate and coordinate on a regular basis?
- Can access to relevant data and contact with key colleagues be designed into the role?
- Will the organization tolerate leaders who challenge established norms or routines to create conditions required for effectiveness?

Questions as these should be reviewed before designing leadership roles and casting people into them. The challenge for each organization is to have a design that matches the answers that are right for the organization's particular set of circumstances.

Tools and Actions for Team Leadership

Clearly, leadership of the horizontal revolution is a more important and a more demanding undertaking than that of managing traditional organizations. The primary leadership function is to help create or model those conditions that contribute to the establishment and maintenance of high-performance activity. If a leader manages, by whatever resource, to ensure that all functions critical to both task accomplishment and team maintenance are adequately taken care of, then the leader has done his or her job well. Two types of basic behaviors are key tools for the leadership of teaming: monitoring and initiating.

* *Monitoring* is obtaining and interpreting data about performance conditions and events that might affect them. When monitoring teams, the leader asks himself or herself such assessment questions as these: How is the team doing? Is the team appropriately skilled? Does it have process assistance and support from the organization? Are necessary resources available? Are there indicators that problems exist in the task work, in the team's ability to work together interdependently, or in the quality of individuals' experiences in the team? Is ample coaching provided? How can the team's planning and future implementation process be assisted? Monitoring should begin with knowledge of the outcomes or results the team is to achieve and then work backwards to identify process and performance conditions. When problems, unrealized opportunities, or negative trends are noted, the leader needs to be aware of what is going on and what the team plans to do about it.

* *Initiating* is creating or maintaining favorable performance conditions for the teams. Initiative action complements monitoring, creating positive outcomes from performance conditions. Action agendas can be focused within a team to improve its ability for high-performance activity and externally to sustain excellent performance—for example, to coordinate cross-training opportunities, to mediate a relationship between an outside consultant, or

to broker rewards and compensations for outstanding efforts and results.

Experience tells us there are four key leadership actions that appear to foster and sustain effective self-direction in a team:

- Provide clear and workable directions for the team to develop performance strategies around.
- Nurture competent performance through contingent information sharing, training, and rewarding.
- Coach, at appropriate times, performance strategies, knowledge, skills, and efforts.
- Make available adequate resources to improve conditions and accomplish tasks/services toward the realization of appropriate objectives.

The first key action provides the overall frame within which the team operates; when present, it intensifies the dynamic impact of the remaining actions. The final action provides the means for getting tasks accomplished. The middle two actions—nurturing and coaching—together increase the probability that a team will achieve effectiveness in knowledge, skills, and performance.

Facilitative Skills

To develop an understanding of the differences between a directive and a facilitative leader, it is helpful to observe successful leaders of teams—those who get the best results over the long run. A facilitative approach yields positive results, including generating new ideas, identifying hidden problems, capitalizing on the synergy of the team, and building on the ideas of others. Good facilitators reduce negative feelings between people and enhance cooperation. They increase trust within the team and create an open atmosphere in which members are willing to share and exchange ideas. They promote professional development and growth because they encourage team members to improve. Basically, facilitative leaders will focus most of their time and attention on how to provide the appropriate resources, experiences, and information needed if team members are to do jobs successfully in the team.

One of our consulting approaches for facilitation training is to ask teams to respond to a series of statements in order to get situations for team leaders to role-play or to practice their facilitation skills on. These statements all begin, "There are two kinds of . . ." The following example is taken from our work with a technical team.

- There are two kinds of people in this team:

    Those who bust their butts and try to do the impossible.

    Those who are just getting by.

- There are two kinds of approaches in this team:

    Fight, flight, and manipulate, which amounts to win-lose.

    Learn confrontation, problem-solving, and win-win skills.

- There are two kinds of people who say things in this team:

    Those who say one thing and do another.

    Those who say things you can believe.

- There are two kinds of problems in this team:

    Those imposed by the system.

    Those which individuals have because they are unable to handle themselves.

- There are two kinds of people affecting work conditions in this team:

    Those who crap on others.

    Those who get crapped on.

- There are two kinds of people with strategies in this team:

    Those who fight to change the system.

    Those who work on personal growth.

- There are two kinds of people dealing with responsibility in this team:

    Those who burn-out due to the frustration of inequalities.

    Those who are accountable and face the responsibility for their impact.

- There are two kinds of people with attitudes about conditions in this team:

    Those who are so cynical they can't see how to work out their problems.

    Those who have a personal touch and positive outlook for betterment.

- There are two kinds of people with attitudes about change in this team:

    Those who are impatient because things don't change.

    Those who are involved in the step-by-step process that makes change.

Team leaders participated in role-plays based on these character-izations in order to help them develop good facilitative skills for reducing frustrations in the team.

In addition to the skills discussed in the previous chapters for leaders and facilitators, facilitation focuses on initiating discussion and raising questions, mining hidden information from within the team, and sharing all information. It looks at all sides of issues and reduces the amount of tension among team members with different points of view. The facilitator pauses from time to time to make sure that all members know exactly what has gone on and what has been stated. Information is summarized and members are assessed on how they feel about their contributions and their readiness to continue toward their objectives. Good facilitative skills encourage contribution. When members are reluctant to reveal what they have on their minds, the facilitator draws them out. He or she also finds ways to pull together the best of different points of view to arrive at compromises and helps the team look at the viability of the net effect of their recommended solutions.

Resolving Intra-Team Conflicts

"I saw a bumper sticker on the way to work this morning," reported a team leader. "It had the inscription: 'Caution, I move from zero to bitch in seconds.' This is representative of the problems in giving feedback to the team."

When two teams members clash, inevitably they focus on who is right and who is wrong. If one member has a history of disagreements with the other member, this will cause even the slightest of disagreements to become representative of past encounters and conflicts. Skill in handling intra-team conflict is critical to the whole team. Three distinct questions need to be worked through (with the help of a leader or facilitator) by both or all parties involved to minimize the conflict.

How are things now and how would one person like to see it differently; or, What would make the other person's position right? Intra-team conflict is often the result of rational, well-intentioned people simply seeing the team operation differently and thus focusing on different perspectives. Facilitators should not allow members to dwell on who is right, but rather on trying to better understand why each one sees the situations as he or she does. A facilitator can ask, For the other person to be correct, what views or information would that person need to have about the situation in general? With an understanding of how each team member sees things, the team can objectively discuss the basis for different perceptions. It is easier to discuss different perceptions, how people arrive at those perceptions, and what could change those perceptions than it is to force someone to change a position he or she is locked into.

What do we have in common; or, What is there to unify us? Instead of criticizing each other when there is disagreement, two team members can find out what they have in common. Focusing on areas of agreement will minimize the conflict and make it more manageable. Facilitators can ask, Is there a unifying factor or force powerful enough to overcome the elements of conflict? The barriers of differences and attitudes of individuality should never be as important as the common thread that binds the team together.

If we were to agree in the future, what would that agreement look like? Asking this question allows individuals of different cultural orientations to focus together on a positive future vision in the team that can clarify and direct their interactions at present. From that perspective, areas of disagreement tend to be secondary.

Resolving intra-team conflict is no easy thing to do, yet through skillful facilitation, major strides can be taken toward increasing inclusion and achieving more harmonious relationships.

Expanded Roles of the Team Leader

Managers can help team leaders by paying special attention and providing needed support to the newly emerging roles required of the team leader if he or she is to maintain an appropriate authority balance that ensures accountability in others. This help usually begins with a basic team leader job description and expands to describe additional roles that must be understood by all in a high-performance setting.

As their roles expand, team leaders represent the team in coordinating activities. They become boundary managers who act as organizational designers, infrastructure builders, and cross-organizational collaborators. Part of the function of managing boundaries is to be a barrier buster—the individual who runs interference for the team, challenges the status quo, and removes artificial barriers to the team's performance. When the team leader takes on this expanded role, the team becomes focused on the big picture and high performance instead of becoming mired in the daily throughput tasks for which the team has primary responsibility. All together, as we have described earlier, the role of the team leader in an empowered organization is to act as a living model, coach, business analyzer, facilitator, barrier buster, and customer advocate.

Many times, we have discovered team leaders who lacked knowledge of the basic business workings of their own operation. Some could not identify the end use customers for their products or services. Others were unaware of the products or services and the strengths of their competitors. Yet others were unaware of basic personnel policies or government regulations that would affect them or of new technologies available to help them accomplish their work more effectively. We found that this information was, for the most part, obtainable for the asking within the leaders' own organizations. Here are some common business variables for which team leaders should have answers, to give them real-time fuel for effective operation.

- *Customers/markets.* Who are they? What do they need from us?
- *Technologies/technical changes.* What are the options? How do they affect us?
- *Competition.* Who are they? How do they affect us?
- *Environment.* How do we eliminate contaminants? Do activists affect us?
- *Political/governmental.* What laws affect us? Are there community concerns that could affect us?
- *Demographics.* What are the changing requirements of the work force?
- *Suppliers.* Who are they? How do they affect our work and customers?
- *Economics.* How is the current economy? How does it affect us?

Many managers express concern that their teams do not know enough about competitors. We often invite team leaders or different team members to go out and visit their competitors, take notes, and come back and report. The bottom line is this: business information needs to be disseminated to teams on a regular basis to create a forum for joint business analysis and for establishing realistic improvements.

Aligning Purpose and Goals to Outputs

Our onion model (Figure 5.1) illustrates the team leader's ongoing challenge of having to peel the structural/systemic onion back to its inner layers in order to answer the questions, What is our overall purpose? What is driving our performance goals in the team? The true construction of both an onion and a high-performance team is an inside-out process: from inputs to throughputs to outputs; from *common, meaningful purposes* to *specific performance goals* to *defined behaviors* to *specific outputs*. A team's outputs must relate directly to its overall performance goals and tough standards; otherwise, team members become confused, pull apart, and revert to mediocre performance. Focusing on outputs or outcomes, not good communications or good feelings, shapes teams more than anything else. Team leaders need to clarify and continuously translate common purposes into goals and behaviors that the team can measure through outputs.

Likewise, a team leader needs to focus on the environment surrounding the team, much as an onion farmer looks to irrigation, fertilizers, and conditions in the weather, which hold both potential risks and opportunities. The team leader focuses attention on outside conditions and issues such as monitoring customer and vendor interactions, assessing competitors and market opportunities, building communication links with other teams, and/or establishing important alliances, rather than spending his or her primary energy on the throughput process.

Defined behaviors produce the output. Putting the performance goals into operation, tracking milestones and deadlines, and executing contingencies are the doing. The team becomes stable and

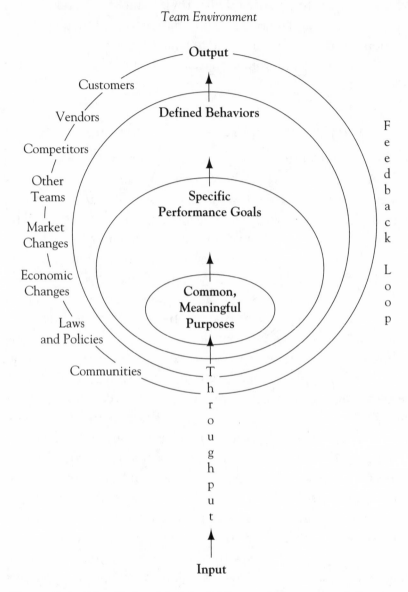

Figure 5.1. The Onion Model of Aligning Purposes and Outputs.

effective in implementing its plans through clear-cut policies and procedures. New team potentials are realized as a variety of team functions and individual roles are conceived. This process taps and develops diverse talents and resources of members.

The output—products, services, or information—is generated by the process and provided to others. The team "exports" its product to the internal or external community and decides what information, resources, roles, and values to develop and retain for future use and how to use them. Too frequently, teams put short-term expediencies and production quotas above the long-term steady growth that comes through a balance between dispositions and outputs.

Together, the four layers of the onion model illustrate a process that will guide, coordinate, and integrate needs, team member efforts, and resources. The idea is to have all the layers functioning in appropriate proportions, each coming forward with appropriate force at the appropriate time and each operating in unison with the other layers. Team leaders and members, in most cases, are working through more than one layer at a time. For most team leaders, the challenges are to maintain a balance in managing several projects (new onions) at the same time and to help the team adapt successfully to the environment.

Supporting Teams

Maturing teams that do not have what they need to perform effectively should actively and constructively seek through their team leader the needed guidance, support, or resources. One important type of support already mentioned is that the team leader should provide job reassurance, especially for supervisors if they are to support implementation.

Teams that know where they are heading will need continual support as they exercise these three process steps to get there: generating sufficient effort to get tasks accomplished at acceptable performance standards, bringing appropriate amounts of knowledge and skill to bear on the task work, and putting into operation strategies fitting the tasks and performance settings. When teams practice these processes, participants are more likely to engage in self-rewarding behaviors when they realize that they have done well and in self-corrective actions when they do poorly. Such self-influence supports effort in the absence of external controls and direct supervision.

As Challenging to Maintain As to Implement

Whenever organizations change the way they operate, employees may feel as if they are seesawing back and forth between the old and the new. Equally important as the challenge to implement teams will be the challenge to maintain them.

To meet the latter challenge, organizations should develop guidelines for leadership action that will be both powerful in affecting work performance and helpful in stimulating self-directedness. If a team leader manages, by whatever resources, to ensure that all functions critical to task accomplishment and to maintaining favorable performance conditions are adequately taken care of, then the team leader has done his or her job well. Team leaders should continually ask:

- What events might affect the creation and favorable maintenance of the team?
- Does the team have process assistance and support from the organization?
- Are necessary resources available from the organization?
- Are there indicators that problems exist in the task work, in the team's ability to work together interdependently, or in the quality of individuals' experiences in the team?
- Is ample coaching provided?

- How can the team's planning for a future implementation process be assisted?

Continuous, sustained improvement efforts will require the team leader to use processes that focus the team and at the same time clarify when certain management interventions are appropriate. Therefore, the leader's role often requires constraint, patience, and delegation along with time, attention, and constant leadership bolstering to maintain teams and help them see their accomplishments.

Managing Cultural Change

Managing horizontal functioning and cultural change is the team leader's greatest challenge, greater than all the other complexities and obstacles that come with uncomfortable, excruciatingly slow team implementation. As we have described, the process involves a major change in the roles and relationships between managers, supervisors, team leaders, and members of the teams and creates a major cultural shift in organizations. Traditional organizational forms and management practices have been so pervasive that, like the invisible air we breathe, they have become people's second nature. It is hard to alter something so normal that you no longer even see it. It is not until people are in a situation where they start choking because the old air is being withdrawn that they realize how much they depended on it. Nowhere are the changes demanded by the horizontal transformation more acute than in self-directed work teams. All the issues that we have been discussing in the pushing down of information and decision making; participative management; decentralization of resources; building of supportive, problem-solving coalitions; and helping each person to understand his or her organizational role, develop a higher level of organizational commitment and self-directedness, and take more responsibility have their biggest effects at the team level. Therefore, once change is happening, it is especially difficult when a team leader is unsupportive of change. In some cases, the only viable solution is to wait until a new leader emerges. But, in other circumstances, champions and advocates can be found higher up in the organization who can broker influences on behalf of the team as needed to sustain it through a rough period.

Measuring Leadership

Leadership is measurable through the degree to which it coaches successfully. Useful coaching allows people to realize that, more than technical know-how, mutually supportive relationships with each other are prime. Through coaching, leaders can comment on ineffective and inappropriate behaviors, knowing that these observations are critical if tasks are to be accomplished. Leaders who are coaches gain skills and experience on how to confront others effectively. They will use, and allow, fewer hidden agendas and subtle game playing. Feedback will be the food for conversations. As one leader asked us, "How do I address the gap between the theory of an issue and the application? We talk about people being important and we give them training, but we have not done a good job of everyday applications. There is a lack of basic preparation, coaching, and rewards. Historically, we have been protective of our people or we throw them to the wolves." Coaching is the way this kind of gap is addressed, and this leader accepted a coaching prescription to come across as being real, show change within himself, develop a system of measurement, accept and use feedback, develop a defining vision statement, constantly evaluate where he is and where he is going, and celebrate successes.

Another leader reported that, as the horizontal revolution developed, people who were accustomed to endlessly discussing the symptoms of their problems—only to leave the roots of their problems on their doorstep each day as they came to work—were now getting at the roots of their problems and solving them. Personal interactions, which had usually been win-lose, with whoever had the most clout or highest position winning and the other person losing (a who-is-right rather than what-is-right approach) were taking on a win-win approach through conflict resolution. Before, people had lived in two different worlds—the world of number crunching, budgetary pressures, and short-term objectives, and the world of people problems and long-term pursuits—and the priorities invariably went to the world of numbers and budgets, leaving people confused over commitments. Now, people were working on agendas, whatever they might be. Managing was once done by the "club." You had to be in the club to get ahead, be promoted, and find success at work. The club had given rise to cliques, and everyone gravitated toward a clique in order to talk about someone in another clique. Now, efforts to build teams have diminished the cliques.

Summary

One of the challenges of being a good football coach or a team leader is, first, to get commitment from your team, and second, to demonstrate, as team leader, the appropriate skills at the appropriate time, as the team requires. Expanding our football analogy, the team leader is an offensive or defensive coordinator, who reads the shifting plays and patterns of the opposition and then helps the team figure out how to respond. There is beauty in a well-coordinated team effort.

Team-based organizations need better, stronger, and more situationally correct leadership, not less leadership. Team leadership is not a universal concept that provides a unified set of principles applicable to all situations. The right leadership depends on what the team is trying to do. All teams are not the same, nor are the tasks and environments of teams in different settings the same. Team leaders are to be elastic, able to do coordinating, coaching, facilitating, and training; able to be leaders, models, boundary managers, business analyzers, barrier busters, and customer advocates;

and possessed with the ability to make others feel that they care. The work of getting to the point where team leader skills come naturally is not to be minimized. As one team leader said, "Preparing to be a team leader is like preparing to run a triathlon." Just as triathlon athletes must condition themselves for swimming, biking, and running, team leaders must learn to manage a change process with many different elements, and they must train not just themselves but the team too, which may include skeptics and resisters who choose to drag their feet. Though their responsibilities are difficult, most leaders are able to help teams continuously improve.

Chapter Six

Horizontal Coaching:
How to Keep Teams Fit and In Balance

I need to change. I have to be willing to listen and
change my approach. I have been brought up by this
organization and I only see things out of that
background. I don't have it all figured out. There is a
lot that is right about this organization, but there is a
lot that isn't. We need coaching for new leadership
and leadership behaviors.

—Executive becoming a coach in a large
organization in the process of a horizontal turnaround

One of the most useful ways to help employees through the revolution and realize new self-directed, leadership behaviors is through
coaching. Good coaching begins with a sincere interest in helping
and wanting others to personally develop and contribute to the
total effectiveness of the team. This chapter focuses on unique
coaching approaches and practical tools for optimizing performance
in horizontal teaming.

Why Horizontal Coaching?

The word *coach* first occurred in English in the 1500s, to refer to a
particular kind of carriage. Hence, the root meaning of the verb *to
coach* is to convey a valued person from where he or she is to where
he or she wants to be. Not until the 1880s was *coach* used in an
athletic sense (to describe a person who was tutoring rowers on a
river near Cambridge University), and then it retained its conno-
tation of moving a person (the athlete) from one place to another.

As horizontal functioning changes the us-them control paradigm to a commitment paradigm, leaders must switch from supervisory roles to coaching roles, taking people from where they are to where they want to be. A horizontal coach instructs, trains, and guides performers in some particular activity or endeavor. The coach's job is to identify the individuals' blind spots and provide whatever will enable performance beyond previous limits. The assumption is that this mutual commitment of performer and coach—this partnership—is what breaks down us-them barriers to horizontal activity.

The political, social, and organizational lessons of the day teach us that people at work are demanding less control from others and more power for themselves. They truly welcome coaching, not traditional management. In our experience, however, horizontal coaching does not come easily and, therefore, is in short supply. A frustrated team member accentuated this point in a recent conversation: "We feel isolated. We don't get informed. When we ask about something, they say it's in the mill. Nothing comes out of the mill, and the mill doesn't have enough input to produce anyhow." Coaches should be asking, What is in our organizational mills? What keeps these mills going? Where is the valid input that is needed to keep work teams operating?

Another work team observer said, "We have two types of people. Those who are so big on themselves that they act like they never make a mistake, and those who think so little of themselves that they are always correcting their mistakes." Coaches should be asking, What happens to those who do not accept that they can make a mistake? What happens to those who are always correcting mistakes? Why are people so polarized about mistakes? Why are mistakes not more of a vehicle for learning, for coaching!

A horizontal coach is needed in the workplace because bosses have lost their edge. A prevalent comment we hear is: "My boss says this is his shop, and he will do with it as he wants. All you have to do here to get ahead is suck up. I'm a nervous wreck because I've been told that if I speak of how it is, I'll get fired." Another angry person rings a familiar note with this description of her boss: "Instead of working on teamwork, you have to bury your head in the sand. It's depressing. When there is a problem, my boss brings me to his office and justifies his position. We are all victims of our boss's lack of management skills. He is difficult to approach because you are never sure of where he will be coming from and he talks down to us."

The boss mentality is turning the workplace into a battle zone. Follow the stages of the war as told to us by this worn-out warrior: "There are three ways we go about handling problems: first, *conflict* breaks out in the form of 'yes-buts' and denials. Then it goes to the battle stage, in which you argue over who is right, and finally, there is war, in which there are charges and countercharges, debates, and a win-lose situation. This pattern is well advanced, but is not serving us well." Perhaps the summary statement of what bosses have done, but can no longer do, comes from the workplace observer who said, "Just saying something will no longer make it fly—no matter who you are."

Coaching Capabilities

Coaches do things differently; that is why a coach is essential if the team is to perceive and interpret the present situation and outline a new perspective. A coach looks for breakthroughs in performance by finding new possibilities for action; expresses a dynamic vision of life in the workplace, based upon values, purposes, relationships, and results rather than hierarchical position, authority, credentials, and traditional ways of doing things; puts listening ahead of control; finds new ways to use the workplace, with all of its issues and purposes, as a "laboratory" for learning and practicing teaming; anticipates and uncovers possible barriers or breakdowns as progress is made toward the next level of performance; recognizes that breakdowns are the raw material for team problem solving; designs ways to close the behavior gap between intentions and impact; works for constant forward movement with a sense of reality about accomplishments to date; relates and communicates as a partner; and seeks the involvement of, and has respect for, people at work.

Some of the general assignments that a horizontal coach must accept are to develop a partnership and sense of mutuality among team members and management; provide new energy and drive for the employees through the enactment of a new vision and mission in the team; gain skills in speaking and listening so that innovation and new pursuits can come to the team; relate to the uniqueness of each person and situation; practice teaming with others as a concept and operating approach; establish skills in the team for coaching and being coached in horizontal functioning; and create vital team performance.

In this chapter, we present effective approaches to coaching team behaviors. These tools have taken years to collect, develop, and perfect. Much of what we do in working through a horizontal revolution with organizations involves the approaches presented here.

A Coaching Process for Horizontal Teams

Effective coaching is a key competency for the facilitator, team leader, team member/partner, and manager alike. The coaching process builds the confidence and capabilities of individuals in the team and allows mistakes to be a part of the continual learning experience, so that every mistake detected and corrected takes a person and the team toward more effective actions. A coach must be available to help people take effective action at work, just as a coach must be available to get the best from any sports team.

The actual coaching is performed as people apply behavioral principles to the purposes and pursuits of the team while they are doing their work. The process of coaching is essentially an information-giving, information-gathering, and feedback activity. In this process, a basic coaching message is given, critical issues are defined, new approaches are described, change options are prescribed, action is planned, follow-up is provided, and a support system is built.

If you are a coach, your basic functions are informative, diagnostic, and prescriptive.

Informative. Provide the person to be coached with background information about your purpose and approach as coach. Make this information interesting and relevant.

Diagnostic. Once information has been exchanged with the other person, it is your job to help this person see new issues or dilemmas surrounding his or her effectiveness, and to enlarge his or her experience about these issues. *You are responsible for seeing more than the other person sees.* From the other person's perception of things, you must develop new insights and understandings for that person. You do this by listening carefully and focusing your attention solely upon what is happening as you engage the other person.

Prescriptive. As you make a response to the other's information, you must help that person develop alternative approaches and a more effective plan of action. Your responsibility is to relate the other person's as-is data to principles and processes for better behavior. Always work on creating learning that has the capability of improving the person because it is based upon analyzed experience.

Coaching Agendas

Team members usually are so involved with task agendas and striving to survive that they are not accustomed to working on their next steps. Coaching agendas are lists, outlines, and plans for new behaviors to be accomplished, and because people are focused on the here-and-now rather than the future, a coaching agenda requires a coach (team leader or team facilitator) to assist in carrying out the agendas. Coaching only happens by doing; it never happens by talking about doing. A coaching agenda has the following five categories:

Direction: Determine where the team is headed.

Behaviors: List the types of behaviors that are necessary to move the team forward.

Norms: Prepare an assessment of team norms and how these norms are understood and accepted by team members.

Principles: Measure the level of service to others (respect) and accountability for self in the team, and also the way in which others accept responsibility for the ways things are and need to be.

Strategy: Prepare a report for your boss/coach on your design for the betterment of the team and pursue the options and alternatives that are made available after a discussion of your action plan.

Coaching happens through accountability within the team and through providing continuity of experience. This accountability and continuity can best be achieved through the use of two functional tools: keeping a journal and building coaching partnerships. Journal notes can produce continuity in the workplace function. Coaching partnerships can produce accountability for the workplace agendas.

Journals

Keeping a journal is an intensive process for restructuring behavior without being therapeutic. It uses specific procedures that give vitality to behaviors and movements for teaming. It causes new behaviors to be formed through channeling and assessing personal experience. The continuous learning from experience is the raw material for this kind of journal.

A journal can provide team members a fresh opportunity to renew behaviors. As experiences are organized and fortified in the journal, a new vision for the future is created. In addition, new perspectives are arranged and personal existence takes on new meaning and purpose. Keeping a journal can cause the writer to reappraise his or her behavioral history. It causes a prescribed pause in life's activities, during which a steadier and expanded perspective of one's place and purpose is secured. The far-reaching effects of a journal are not brought about by the mere act of writing. Results come from the special structure of the journal and the continuity of growing that it facilitates. The value of a journal lies in the cumulative effect of systematically probing personal experience and using a behavioral principle–based response to feedback. Thus, the most important steps in keeping a journal are identifying the relevant behavioral principles and then one's experiences according to these principles.

Behavioral Principles. The behavioral principles upon which a journal is based are the same as those all organizational members should be using: service to others and accountability for self. In the journal, the coach concentrates upon specific happenings and connects them to the behavioral principles. With this approach, there is continuity in learning. The process makes learning what it should be, a change in behavior based upon analyzed experience.

Steps in Keeping a Journal. A journal is not just a chronological record of events. It is not emotional elaboration in "Dear Diary" form. It is a self-analysis and self-record of experience, done in the language of the person doing the recording. There are three steps in keeping a self-directed journal:

1. The recording of team-related experiences, processes, events, and desires/wants as they occur to you.
2. The analyzing of your experiences and skills to determine their learning value for helping you achieve the results you want from your efforts at work.
3. The measuring of the progress you have made toward achieving production and performance goals because of taking a particular behavioral path.

In this way, a journal creates a record of a person's worklife. It structures a realistic look at personal capabilities, strengths, and weaknesses and becomes a vehicle for an analytical and diagnostic personal improvement study. Through careful, self-directed journal writing, events and connections in worklife take on new meaning and purpose. Critical incidents can be transformed into new perspectives for future behavior, and the past becomes a guide to the future. Journal writing is meant to be a personal not an intellectual experience, in which the writer focuses on answering these questions: Where was I in this situation? What is my perception of what I did? What is my perception of what others think of what I did? What is my perception of what others think I need to do now? How do I see this issue? Journal writing should always be a self-enlarging and self-sustaining behavior-adjusting experience, and a launching pad for continuous change and growth.

Agendas. The process of making a journal organizes a person for the next step in his or her empowerment. That is its essential function. It creates the structure for these key personal agendas:

- As-is agendas, which describe what is happening and how things are at this time.
- To-be agendas, which describe what needs to happen and how things need to be.
- To-me agendas, which describe what the person needs to do and is willing to accept a responsibility to do.

Journal Objectives. The journal objectives parallel the journal-keeping steps. These objectives are to secure a record of the essence of your work experiences in a timely fashion, to have a vehicle for enlarging your experience of your behavior at work, to build momentum for your self-direction at work, and to regularly retrace and recapitulate events at work in order to reshape your workplace existence. When you begin a journal, it may be appropriate to make a historical search of your workplace experiences. Large blocks of time can be covered in summary as a frame of reference for specific recent experiences.

Outline for Journal Action. Team members take these steps to start a journal.

1. *Getting ready.* Review the journal information provided here and identify areas of particular interest to you.
2. *Data gathering.* Reach out to at least ten people within your workplace and ask them for their perceptions of the climate in which they work. Sort this information into indicators of as-is and to-be.
3. *Recording.* Make a record of at least ten critical incidents (good and bad) you have experienced at work during the past year. Detail the type of involvement on your part, the strategy you used, the results you achieved, and your perceptions about the experience.
4. *Relating to work.* Intensify your work experience by involving yourself in more journal work. Over the next three months, spend two hours each week responding to the information you have accumulated. Keep some journal notes.
5. *Getting coaching.* Select someone in whom you have confidence to work with you as a coach at least one hour each month to pull more meaning from your journal-keeping experience.

Coaching Partnerships

A coaching partnership is basically a conversation between two people who work together and care about each other. It calls for a tone of friendliness and respect. A free exchange of perceptions is essential, and a warm expression of collegiality is needed for tensions to be removed. Common interests and helpfulness should be established, and both participants should work to create a relaxing environment.

The goal of the coaching partnership is to heighten each participant's job interest and desire for greater improvements. Before engaging in a coaching partnership session, the participants prepare an outline of points to be covered and make sure they have as-is, to-be, and to-me coaching forms.

During the coaching partnership session, each person asks specific questions and clarifies issues about behavior and agendas. Although each person probably has a general idea of the other's behavior and agendas, each must be prepared to give and take and, possibly, modify those perceptions. Each may bring up information that the other has not considered and that may make a difference in the to-be agenda. Unless each person incorporates, or at least ponders, some of the other's feedback, there will not be much to hold them together.

Objectives. Coaching partnerships are to be employed as companions to journal writing, and session information comes from each partner's journal. Objectives for each session include:

- Lessening the tension that surrounds talking with others about one's personal performance as it is and as it may become.
- Detailing a pattern for creating mutually acceptable expectations for future behavior.
- Recognizing how to use relevant concepts and techniques for self-direction and teaming.
- Learning to handle ongoing behavioral situations more effectively.
- Demonstrating active listening and effective handling of feedback.

- Understanding better ways of behaving and getting excited about behavior as an issue for the work climate.
- Establishing greater effectiveness as a personal and organizational trait.

By the end of the session, each partner should have a to-be agenda completed. This becomes a to-do list to carry into the coaching pattern. For each successive session, the previous to-be agenda bridges into the as-is agenda for the new session. The to-me agenda should provide an accurate idea of the improvement plan and action to be taken.

Before they schedule a time and place for the successive coaching partnership session, partners should always indicate their respect to each other for the guidance and support received.

Outline. The outline for each session has six parts.

1. *Warm-up.* Make quick comments, all with a positive and productive bent, about your expectations and purposes for this conversation.
2. *Target.* Focus on each of you as you really are and the need to improve your performance through mutual coaching.
3. *Grow.* Indicate some directives and concepts that have been learned through coaching and the need to deal with new areas for growth.
4. *Negotiate.* Discuss restructuring of each other's skills and capabilities in order to accomplish more from work.
5. *Commitment.* Work toward an action plan that includes a response to expectations, goals, support, and strategies for newness—personally and at work.
6. *Continuity.* Arrange for a time to continue and extend the process.

Ground Rules for Behavior. Coaching partnerships need to set ground rules for respectful behavior. A coaching partnership is a give-and-take situation using service to others and accountability for self as a framework. There must be an understanding that the discussion will be free of denial and of defensive, rationalizing, and blaming behaviors. The outcome should not be preplanned by either one of the participants. A coaching partnership session should not last more than one hour, and sessions should be scheduled to occur every three to four weeks. Partners should schedule enough uninterrupted time that neither feels rushed to finish quickly, but not so much time that they drift from their focus or tire of themselves and the process.

A good way to begin a session is for each person to briefly state what he or she expects to happen during the session. In other words, the partners agree on the specific purpose for the meeting. Then they work on putting each other at ease by making some constructive statements about each other and what can be accomplished during the time together. Each tries to find some outstanding accomplishment of the other as a beginning point for discussion.

Once the preliminaries are out of the way, they begin to work on their as-is and to-be items, always looking for ways in which they can improve and stretch. Each looks for items that may suggest the other person is glossing over factors that could impede personal growth. Each person's feedback should always be phrased as his or her own perceptions. They should not criticize or evaluate but provide a new way of looking at things and focus discussion on the change process that is to be undertaken. They should indicate some directions and concepts that are applicable to the behaviors that have been experienced and that are expected.

A coaching partnership session is no time for crude words and brave deeds. Each person is in the same boat. Each is doing well and wants to do better. Each is there to coach and be coached. If at any time the conversation begins to sour and words become brutal, partners should be prepared to turn the situation back toward the original purpose. Partners always encourage the searching for, and discovery of, new behaviors. They do not get into mind traps and become each other's therapists. This is not therapy. This is coaching. They must be specific and remain calm about the behaviors they discuss. They give examples, where appropriate, but partners must not chase examples, falling into the trap of defending themselves because an example is out of context.

At times, partners will need to be direct and, at other times, indirect in responding to each other. Be direct in guiding the conversation toward key issues and questions that need more clarification and exploration. Be indirect when encouraging the other person to expand more on points being made. Sometimes, perceptions will cross. One person will see something as the opposite of what the other person sees. Partners should not argue about different perceptions. The session is not designed to prove who is right but to find a better way for what is right. Different perceptions indicate that a new perspective is needed, and the new perspective will come through careful examination of where and why there is disagreement, what partners expect of each other, and how performance can become better. A disagreement is never catastrophic, but can be used to achieve clearer communication and pinpoint stumbling blocks. Find ways around the stumbling blocks. The goal should be to come to terms with information that reflects as-is behavior, at the same time expressing to-be behavior. Each partner may restate his or her to-me agenda in order to confirm what each is willing to do and allow each to know further coaching may be needed.

For a smooth session, partners should try to move naturally from one item to another. When either wants to start a new area of discussion, he or she can refer to a relevant statement or idea discussed previously, thus transitioning from one agenda to another. However, few sessions will follow a direct, logical line of conversation. There will always be some rambling. Partners should take responsibility to keep the rambling at a minimum, guard against irrelevancy coming into the conversation, and help each other get to the point. The main purpose of the coaching partnership is to provide guidance and support to a fellow team member, and that purpose will not be accomplished if either becomes inappropriately emotional. Partners can talk and listen as long as there is intensity between the two, but they should not say something just to break the quiet. They must take time to think and avoid interrupting the other and breaking his or her train of thought.

A Team of Managers Sets the Stage for Coaching Partnerships

The following conversation is made up of comments, taken in sequence, by managers during a team session that we coached. Weeks earlier these managers had been trained in coaching skills and had made out their coaching agendas. Observe how, in this session, they attempt to maintain and reinforce the coaching process with Paul, a new manager joining the team for the first time. Their comments reveal the change process for breaking bad habits that involve a know-it-all or there-isn't-anything-wrong-with-us position. John is the appointed team leader and he opens the meeting. All names are pseudonyms.

> *John:* Welcome to Paul. . . . We began these sessions six months ago. They have become an important thing to us. . . . We all bring in our own agendas. . . . We may talk about anything . . . . Great things have happened since we started. We can work on support of each other.
>
> *Terry:* We have worked on how we can improve during the last six months. We have to constantly improve.
>
> *Linda:* We have come together and developed comradery which has helped communications. Each has to see what the other side is.

John: We are not working that well together, as we assume. We are building walls with others. . . . We don't go directly to another person and deal with our feelings. That's what this is about—feelings, not technical stuff.

Our people judge us, and if we don't care, they don't care. We have to effectively communicate with each other. In the past, we haven't dealt with these things.

Linda: To deal with feelings is no longer a sign of weakness. This is the hardest thing to do.

Terry: We thought we were a team, but after a few sessions, we realized we weren't working as a team.

Linda: People do what is done to them, i.e., withhold information and [act out] group against group. When individuals become managers/supervisors, they vow to do all the bad things to others that have been done to them for many years.

Terry: Coming into management for the first time is a big change. Paul needs to realize that.

Linda: It is important to maintain yourself without a facade or without copying anyone else's style or bad habits.

Brian: You need to keep your eyes open and learn from others. Be receptive. Don't know it all. You have to learn beyond any class, seminar, or book. Draw from your own experience.

Linda: We change all the time in style of hair and clothes. We need to change our behavior as new situations and ways come along.

John: New things are happening around here. We are becoming more direct in dealing with issues with people. We have too much strife and coping.

Linda: We lack mutual respect and respect for the person regardless of rank, position, et cetera. Every job is important for our customers. We need to support each other. But, we have to worry about someone stabbing us in the back.

John: We have to adapt instantly once we learn new information, and all have to come together to coordinate and solve problems. It takes effort and communications to make things right.

Terry: We have to change from the old way of management in which you just tell people to get the job done and don't listen to them and coach. We have to be advisors, not dictators, to our people—and realize they may not do it my way. This is tough to do. It's easy to tell people what to do.

Linda: There are roadblocks out there. You aren't protected as a supervisor.

Paul: I'm willing to accept feedback without being defensive.

Our feedback to the managers about the content of this session and the process they used had seven major points.

- Openness and honesty are number one and have to be earned through involvement.
- Change and improvement are constant and relentless.
- Good is not good when better is expected.
- This is a movement toward creating a better place to work, and a better feeling about coming to work.
- This session is based on firsthand learning.
- We see the best way whatever it is. The responsibility of those who resist change is to identify a better way.
- As we coach each other, we learn coaching.

The action plan that came out of this meeting had three parts: to continue opening up, to bring examples of what is working and what is not working to the next session, and to set a priority to participate in the next session without being interrupted by outside calls.

Coaching the Whole Team in Teaming

What is a coach's responsibility when dealing with a whole team, as in the session just described? The following guidelines suggest a practical coaching approach that can be utilized by team facilitators, leaders, or coaches to identify and target behavioral performance issues.

Focus on team performance in need of change and communicate concerns out of a spirit of mutual respect and trust. It is critical to know how to focus on the appropriate things, in the appropriate order, at the appropriate time, with the appropriate skills. Describe clearly one specific performance area at a time to avoid overwhelming a team member. Explain why the skill is important, state clear expectations, and show how improvement will benefit the team and organization.

Seek team member perspectives. Pause and listen to the others' opinions to receive information and feelings about performance skills. Encourage their initiative and self-management in analyzing their own performance. Ask open-ended questions to stimulate thoughtful and objective analyses. Maintain a constructive relationship built on mutual respect. If the relationship is not well established, wait until trust is established before continuing. Clear expectations of performance need to be established up front, before providing the necessary resources and training.

Ask the team members to generate their best ideas to change performance. Allow team members to take responsibility in seeking out solutions before imposing your own perspectives. When given the chance, people want to express themselves, to learn quickly, and to resolve their difficulties. Through empathy and active listening, you can build cooperation, reduce tension, enhance self-image, and become influential. Take the time to see how team members feel and why they feel that way. From that base, you can guide them more effectively.

Respond to the team's insights and feelings through feedback and add your own perspectives. Encourage and reinforce others' workable insights and guide, teach, train, encourage, or refocus them if their insights are not sound. Open up other options or alternatives for them to follow in their plans for enhancing their performance.

Identify means and resources to enhance the targeted performance deficiency. It is important to establish agreement to take action and be accountable for results. This step of the coaching session requires building in a follow-up process and monitoring the situation for improvement.

Communicate confidence and support. Express belief in the team's commitment and ability to achieve performance goals. Articulate how reasonable support and resources can be provided to assist team members.

Effective coaches should always build and maintain trust before venturing on team improvement, especially in stressful situations. Take note from the managers' coaching session that the session coach listened and learned from the group before any prescriptions were formulated. Good coaches consider prescription without adequate diagnosis to be malpractice.

Behavioral Fitness

Coaching teaming, whether in sports or businesses, includes identifying threats in the behavioral arena that limit a player's ability to perform at his or her best. Indeed, the coach often looks out upon a host of inappropriate, unfit behaviors among team members, behaviors that drain energies, siphon innovation, inhibit learning, and undermine confidence and the ability to be highly productive. The U.S. workplace has evolved to contain a well-educated, well-trained, and assertive force of individuals culturally striving for personal success, too often at the expense of colleagues' or the team's success. Consequently, self-protection, arrogance, aloofness, insensitivity, or disrespectful behavior can set off counterproductive defensive routines throughout any workplace.

Behavioral fitness is an approach we developed to look at what team members do or do not do to improve service, accountability, and performance among themselves. It is to the organization what physical fitness is to the body—it gets it in shape to function better and do better. Behavioral fitness focuses on the two characteristics discussed before that are basic to all behavioral activities: service to others (which includes respect for other team members and self-confidence) and accountability.

Experience with employee work preferences shows that employees want to work with people who treat them with respect, and that their self-confidence is improved by doing interesting and challenging work. Creating a team culture that provides more self-confidence and respect is the starting place for commitment and motivation in teaming.

In many newly organized teams, some members, for one reason or another, will demonstrate inappropriate and counterproductive behaviors. Experience as coaches has taught us not to ignore but confront these behaviors. It is important to get team members to examine their own behavior by asking themselves such questions as: How tolerant am I of disagreement and conflict? How strongly do I value and support candor and openness? Do I strive for sound or acceptable decisions? By getting involved, do I sacrifice or diminish my responsibilities and timeliness? What can my team and I do to get in better shape? What can I do to achieve a proper balance of self-respect and respect for others?

Basically, everyone constantly chooses between respectful and arrogant behaviors. Respectful behavior leads to accountability. Arrogance behavior leads to disaster. Respectful behavior sets an example and arrogant behavior presents a warning. Arrogant behavior turns an individual away from behavioral balance, stops learning and growing, and discourages other team members and supporters. Arrogant behavior, if unabated, is costly in personal and team productivity. When coaching individuals struggling with their own and other behaviors in the team, we encourage team leaders to work through the variables of respectful and arrogant behavior and then invite team members to draft their own action agenda for changing behavior (Table 6.1 summarizes the contrast between respectful behavior and arrogant behavior).

Shaping Up the Team Culture

A work team may start out as a group of individuals coming together by the chance of being hired into the same unit. Their differences in personalities, talents, backgrounds, and work methods will naturally create behavioral imbalances. However, organizations that tolerate certain team members who remain behaviorally out of shape, no matter how competent they may be technologically, will produce shortfalls. Team leaders should periodically make behavioral fitness checks on their teams by asking themselves: What performance behaviors are fit in terms of high commitment and activity? How do team members' performance compare with the fit behaviors? What can be done to improve current behaviors?

When performance becomes fit, employees respond as a five-year employee of a large electronics firm did. Gary, as we'll call him, became interested in being coached, first as a member of a management-assigned task team, and later as a peer-chosen leader of his area team. Prior to this experience, he had been a quiet worker who did his job with little recognition and with skills lacking promotability. He says, "Coaching gave me the way to feel good about myself, and now I'm a positive influence on the others in my area. I've learned much more about myself and am more forgiving of my supervisors and managers now that they interface with me and my team. They taught me the techniques and helped me to find strengths I never thought I had." Similarly, after we held a

Table 6.1. Respectful and Arrogant Behavior.

Respectful Behavior	Arrogant Behavior
Exploration: To seek opportunities and ways for altering your behavior.	Denial: To refuse to accept a perception of you/your situation as true or valid.
Feedback: To receive course corrections regarding your behavior.	Defensiveness: To react negatively toward feedback regarding your behavior.
Acceptance: To receive feedback about you as valid and useful.	Rationalization: To give off plausible but unacceptable reasons for your behavior.
Ownership: To acknowledge responsibility for your own behavior.	Blaming: To escape responsibility for your behavior.
Continuity: To learn and build from each experience.	Avoidance: To withdraw and keep away from feedback regarding your behavior.
Growth: To constantly and continuously work at better behavior for yourself.	Déjà vu: Returning to the same pattern of problem behavior.
Accountability: To be fully responsible for your behavior.	Disaster: A great loss and disruption to your goals and direction.

two-hour coaching session with a manager and her supervisors, the manager said about one of those supervisors, "It was really hard to believe Mick would ever change. We let him dominate us. Mick didn't know what impact he had on others, and no one dared to tell him. Through this coaching we have developed a cleansing attitude. You have done in forty-five minutes what I and many others have not been able to do in twenty years. We are now involved in what's happening with each other, and Mick has stopped playing a role. This is amazing! We now know that there is no way we can have individual survival. We have to pull together and go forward."

In our coaching, we use these terms and definitions with teams.

Team Fitness Definitions

Team leader/coach: An individual who assists in the development process of (an)other team member(s).

Workout: A process for working regular behavior into teaming activity.

Position playing: A sense of ownership and responsibility that individuals take toward their personal role and function in the team.

Staying in shape: An ever-growing condition that individuals in the team develop as they balance their self-respect and respect for others.

Team-play: A togetherness that develops in the team through putting organizational winning ahead of personal and professional arrogance.

Winning work: The enjoyment that comes when work with the team is fun because behaviors are balanced.

Score: Results received through meeting and exceeding expectations. Teams score when they beat the competition to the punch without beating up others within the team.

The first step to team behavioral fitness comes when members realize that this fitness occurs when behavior is more of "what we do" than it is of "what we think" and that a host of similar redefinitions follow from that key redefinition (Table 6.2). The next step is to accept the importance of becoming behaviorally fit as a respectable goal. The step after that is to accept the importance of becoming behaviorally fit as a team. The final step, in line with the concept and practice of self-directedness, is to do something about becoming behaviorally fit.

Table 6.2. Behavioral Fitness.

Behavioral Fitness Is-

More of This		Than of This	
Behaviors:	What we do: results oriented	Behaviors:	What we think: activity oriented
Fitness:	To function effectively	Fitness:	To think well
Feedback:	Functional improvements	Feedback:	Talk about the need for change
Focus:	Real behavior	Focus:	Hype behavior
Learning:	Change in behavior based upon analyzed experience	Learning:	New information based upon available knowledge
Perspective:	Accountability	Perspective:	Informal organization
Purpose:	Continuous quality improvement	Purpose:	Creating excitement
Values:	Quality of behavior	Values:	Defense of behavior
Norms:	Appropriate actions, which produce acceptable behavior	Norms:	Selective action, which produces selective behavior
Expectations:	Making work fun and challenging	Expectations:	Making work work and routine

Team members are not likely to make drastic changes in their habits. They are likely to make some changes in their behavior first before making changes in their attitudes. The process is gradual, and with good coaching, it will profitably pay off. Team behavioral fitness comes complete with its own reinforcement. Team members will feel better. They will work better.

Unfits and Misfits

Coaches need to realize that some team members do not want to be team players. Some have already decided, consciously or unconsciously, that they want to avoid responsibility, be taken care of, be outsiders, or be victims. Consequently, teams experience disconnectedness and counterproductivity because of a few people. Coaches, especially, must realize that personality and behaviors are separate entities. An employee can have a healthy personality but behave like a jerk in a team workout. Lack of behavioral fitness relates strictly to a person's unwillingness and/or lack of skills to meet the standards and demands of his or her team environment.

If the team's work environment takes care of all their comforts, team members need to realize that their level of behavioral fitness will slump to what is appropriate—to the level they need to survive and no more. If things get upset suddenly, and if they are truly fit, they will adapt.

Some out-of-shape behaviors are easy to see in team members.

- Being either highly competitive or uninvolved
- Dominating conversations with personal references and accomplishments or having no accomplishments worth talking about
- Resisting or avoiding constructive feedback
- Quickly placing blame for wrongdoing
- Expressing a overly high or low opinion of themselves or others and having a way to make themselves and others look bad

- Seldom seeking ideas or help from others or giving ideas or help to others
- Demonstrating an exaggerated or diminished impression of their own importance

One of our test teams of about fifteen members was organized to solve a problem that had periodically plagued the organization for several years. The coach tried in vain, after many training sessions in interpersonal skills and problem solving, to get them to respond to management's requests for help. The behavior of the entire group was vindictive toward the company, management, and each other. After several months of unsuccessful meetings, two of the members become angry enough with the rest to challenge the mentality of the group's resistance. This challenge finally brought the behaviors out for analysis, and the group began to work through them together, a positive step that coaching alone could not bring about.

Behavioral balance is challenged the moment two or more members in a team make a contact that has a significant impact upon their work relationship. When this moment of truth does not better the relationship, the workplace environment is negatively affected, and the team loses time and energy and the capability to be more productive. Those moments of truth will achieve a balance point when members in the encounter show more self-respect and demonstrate more respect to the other person.

Communicating Respect

The communication of respect for ourselves and respect for others in the team is vital to high-performance activity. You show your respect for yourself and others through:

- Building relationships by exchanging feelings of high regard for the others

- Articulating expectations for yourself and others that show an element of respect and appreciation
- Listening to things you do not want to hear
- Expressing emotions without showing disregard for others
- Exchanging information with others without dehumanizing them and discounting yourself
- Using contact with others to build more confidence in yourself and respect for others

In communicating self-respect and respect for others, team members are strengthened to overcome defensive communication; view communication as a people process rather than a language process; improve communication by checking the balance between self-confidence and respect for others; recognize defensive behavior as the behavior that occurs when self-confidence is threatened or appears about to be threatened; overcome the temptation to diverge from respect for others through concern with winning, dominating, impressing, or escaping punishment; and replace tendencies toward defensiveness with concentration upon the message and the value of the other person.

To coach an individual in the team who wants to work on his or her own balancing, start by identifying a behavior that creates imbalance. Ask the person, Is it the way you respond [react] that is keeping you from accomplishing some goal in the team? It should be a behavior that the individual desires to change because it is causing problems for him or her and for others. We have found it effective to have individuals write the behavior down, underline it, look at it, and do the following three-step exercise.

1. List all the prices you pay for this behavior—that is, things that result from this behavior—until the total price gets too high. (When the price gets too high, obviously, the person will be motivated to discontinue the behavior.) List the ways

that you can minimize the prices and be free to discontinue your out-of-shape behavior.

2. List the techniques you use to activate your out-of-shape behavior. Your list might include discouragement, a comparison of yourself with others, impatience, or stress.

3. List the fears you may have when you think about eliminating your out-of-shape behavior.

Coach the team member privately to face his or her fears by testing them against reality—to let go of the out-of-shape behavior and see what happens.

Coaching to Achieve Team Balance

We were impressed when a manager in a client organization announced the following to his group of supervisors:

> *We are all going to become coaches.* This means that we have to be more honest and open to other values and it's not going to be easy. We have to . . . take leadership learning to our people; get more involved in getting others on board; be tactful and skillful; develop credibility and relationships; let others know how we see/feel about their behavior; find leverage for change; create a turnaround; instill confidence in our workers with no one being second-class; learn conflict resolution; move from our perception of how we see things to a new perspective of the world around us.
>
> Before you can coach, you have to have credibility as a coach. We have to become coaches because our workers are skeptical, and we must create a new vision.

Coaching is necessary because team members can range from those who really want to make a contribution and advance the cause of the company to those who are strictly maintaining the status quo and do not extend themselves beyond what they need to do to survive. Moreover, without proper coaching in the team, people will tend to magnify the mistakes and habits of the past and fail to create a vision of the future.

Two critical dispositions for high-performance work teams are *an energized quest for quality* (the team releases its own enthusiasm and energy through always improving products and services that will meet and even exceed customer expectations), and *a disciplined pursuit of performance* (the team exercises the courage and tough self-discipline to directly confront problems or barriers that must be overcome if team members are to achieve optimal outcomes for themselves to live by). Again, the coach needs to help the team understand the behavioral significance of these two high-performance workplace variables and then to develop a balance of the two. Too much disciplined pursuit of performance with too little energy toward purposeful quality causes team members to become *practicalizers*, getting lots of things done, but lacking meaningful direction and creativeness (see Figure 6.1). Too much energy spent on the quest for quality with too little disciplined behavior causes team members to be *idealizers*, achieving little significant result. Too little disciplined performance and too little quest for quality causes team members to be *verticalizers*, waiting to be directed what to do. The optimal course, obviously, is for team members to become *horizontalizers*—vigorous, purposeful, and self-directed.

Without both a quality orientation and disciplined behaviors, teams will lack clarity of purpose and action toward commitment and meaningful results. What is needed is to either hire "winners" or coach others to become horizontalizers. A coach needs to establish behavioral accountability and continuity of learning for every member of the team. This means that the coach does not use hype and quick-fix motivators for change. The techniques presented here are intended to work over an extended period of time to affect and maintain significant behavioral change.

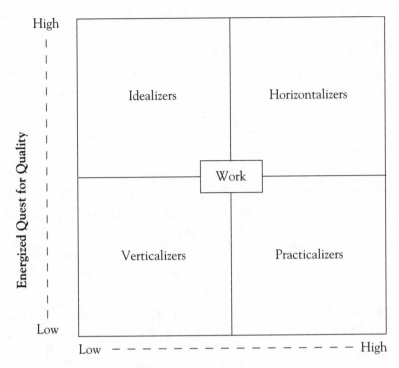

Verticalizers: Wait to be instructed what to do and sometimes do it.
Idealizers: All talk, no action.
Practicalizers: Get things done, but lack creativeness.
Horizontalizers: Vigorous, purposeful, and self-directed.

Figure 6.1. Team Balance Matrix.

Coaching Measurement

Good coaches are worth their weight in gold. They get more done with the same or fewer resources. Good coaching goes far beyond simply pointing out people's performance problems and urging them to shape up. A good coaching session is like a quality cheese; it takes more than a few minutes to develop into a quality product. Good coaching makes use of scheduled coaching sessions, scheduled performance reviews, and the numerous impromptu coachable moments in the course of any workday to collaborate with people in developing their potential.

From our observations and findings, a successful coaching session takes 30 to 40 minutes, which is often hard to eke out of a busy and demanding schedule. Common excuses to minimize, neglect, or avoid formal coaching sessions are: There isn't enough time; It feels awkward; or It will give people the feeling that something is seriously wrong. Unfortunately, some avoid coaching because they really don't care much whether people and teams develop. However, those who do prepare for high-quality coaching moments will focus on the right things, in the right order, at the right time, with the right skills. Effective coaches use current events, here-and-now concerns, and team problems that crop up on the job as opportunities to work with people.

Coaching effectiveness can be measured through the continual building of people's perspectives, skills, behaviors, and motivation base. Results are translated into more highly skilled and multiskilled people who can provide the flexibility and built-in extra resources that high-performance teams need. Ultimately, the consequences for not coaching are costly to the organization, because people and teams will not be as motivated, in shape, or skilled as they could be.

Summary

Horizontal functioning in teams requires a whole new set of attitudes and behaviors. Arrogance, passivity, and dependence on traditional paternalism and doing what you are told does not work anymore. Team members have to take responsibility, exercise initiative, be accountable for their own behaviors, and contribute toward productive outcomes. They have to communicate and coach more frequently and more effectively within and between teams and their customers. Experience shows repeatedly that whenever outcomes are important, preparing behaviors ahead of time contributes to a far better chance of success than does waiting for something to happen and then depending upon the available resources of the moment. The tools for coaching behavioral fitness are critical to developing a high-performance team culture and productive outcomes for the entire organization.

When the coach and/or team leader functions properly in coaching sessions, he or she allows team members to learn to be more self-directed through giving and receiving support from partners in the team. He or she uses such tools as journal writing and coaching partnerships to remedy the substandard job performances of team members who earnestly want to perform better but who need the kind of one-on-one personalized behavioral training that only coaching can provide. Coaches encourage teams members to examine their own performances and then plan ways to work better. Team leaders and coaches can make effective use of team training sessions, workouts, informal work progress discussions, and the numerous coachable moments in the course of any workday to help members develop their potential. They stress the importance of analyzing personal behavior and performance and then initiate steps to make it better. Likewise, they lead through their own examples of betterment.

Part Three

Keeping the Revolution Alive

Chapter Seven

Reward Success:
Tracking Performance and
Sharing the Gains

If our team or an individual makes a great
contribution, the result is usually a pat on the back
and a warm handshake. Don't [management] realize
that we can contribute too . . . but it has to be the
right incentive for me. . . . They have manipulated
me long enough so why don't they put their money
where their mouth is?

> —*New work team member in a*
> *large "Corporate America" organization*

This would not be a revolution if wealth were not involved. Wealth
is created at every level of a horizontal structure, and people should
be paid as much as possible rather than as little as possible. Why
not have one pay system for all levels of the organization with an
element of variable pay related to outcomes? What happens when
compensation practices are out of sync between management and
a team's pursuit of performance? Any mismatch between the heavy
demands on team members and their compensation and support
will show up clearly in employee dissatisfaction. A tension develops as teams mature and members gradually realize that they are
contributing more to the organization than they had before but that
they are not getting more back from the organization. A tension
also builds in cases where a team has surmounted a major work
challenge, yet rewards are provided only to certain individuals
within the team. As new members of teams find themselves responsibly doing more self-managing activity, they may also begin asking
themselves: Why am I doing all this? Why is the work going on

after hours and going home with me? Is it worth it? This state of affairs surely will undermine teaming over the long term.

Horizontal functioning needs a compensation system that values accountability for the success of the business, shares the wealth, and uses pay as a way of communicating and affirming mission. Design pay systems that pay for real outcomes of concrete value to the organization, that is, teamwork, creation of products, delivery of services, and so on. The emphasis on horizontal teams should not exclude recognizing outstanding individual contribution but should let teams determine individual efforts, while eliminating supervisory evaluations as the basis for determining pay.

A central task in implementing teams is to create a mission, values, and equitable circumstances around which high-performance activity and high employee satisfaction can coexist, and where appropriate, to sponsor financial initiatives at every level. We have found the following five key strategies helpful as an overall guide in team implementation:

- Establish a mission of circular linkages and value-added performance.
- Connect earnings to real outcomes of a team or a division of teams.
- Emphasize equity, flexibility, and autonomy.
- Provide financial rewards for exceptional individual performance.
- Pay as much as possible.

These strategies are discussed in this chapter in more detail under the themes of multiskill-based pay, pay for performance, gain sharing, and stock options and ownership.

A performance measurement system that works fulfills two vital criteria for horizontal teaming. First, team members must understand the behavior of key process parameters. Measurement systems make this possible by tracking and controlling scrap, rework, and other quality characteristics in a meaningful way. Second, reward and incentive systems must be based on measured contributions. The real strength of a performance measurement system is that the information is the tool of the team for measuring and directing itself. Teams do not need praise or reproach to tell them how they are doing. They know.

Management's Role as Sponsor

If teams are to spawn healthy attitudes about their work and aid their organizations in increasing productivity, innovation, and service, certain requirements must be fulfilled. First, a redistribution of power and privilege must go accountably hand-in-hand with team profitability. Redesigning the distribution of power and privilege means reassessing financial practices that are deeply ingrained in traditional thinking. Too many managers enthusiastically embrace the concept of teams but make minimal efforts to release to those teams greater control over money. Redistributing ownership and responsibility becomes credible when managers are willing to redesign their financial controls and practices to give more choice to teams close to customers. Teaming at the bottom of an organization does not work if highly centralized financial practices are maintained at the top. The financial commitment and support of the chief executive officer will in most cases make or break a horizontal initiative.

Second, teams accountable for outcomes must understand the economic realities of the organization, plus they must understand how they are to go about getting and spending money. True horizontal teaming means being fully informed about finances and understanding the economic consequences of the choices each team is to make. In the same vein, each team must be responsible for the budget that covers its operations and activities. Accountability for each team means choosing the restraints and ground rules by which it is to function. Management assist here through *building a financial infrastructure* that not only supports teams but also will build a total quality organization. Budget accountability, full disclosure and economic literacy, monitoring processes, spending authority, audit functions, and living within the law must become team-shared responsibilities. Skills training in financial management, process analyses, and team action must be thorough and ongoing. Positive reward structures for improvements and success must be in place. Unless top management are committed and actively involved in these efforts, teams are likely to perceive their own commitment and effort as futile.

Third, top management must allow teams to be responsible for creating their own standards of control against which they choose to be measured and to monitor their performances. Management's responsibility becomes one of providing resource people to consult and to teach the tools, skills, and strategies for creating effective controls and measures. We believe that with good information and good will, teams can make responsible decisions about what controls they require and whom they want to implement them.

Finally, if teams are statistically measuring and monitoring their own inputs and outputs, then managers should also receive training and be competent in understanding control systems, in knowing effective accounting practices, and in processing financial information and presenting it in helpful ways. Insights and resources from supervisors are needed to help teams identify and improve processes that have the greatest effect on customer satisfaction. Steering teams, too, should be well integrated into the organization's quality improvement initiative. These teams should be responsible for bringing employees together with the expertise and perspectives that are critical to the development of strong teams. The middle manager's role in this process is to serve as a resource finder or coordinator.

A Mission of Circular Linkages and
Value-Added Performance

Our visits to numerous facilities where well-designed and well-implemented teams were in place revealed strong circular linkages among teams who delivered added value, customers who responded with favorable returns, and managements that provided further opportunities for teams to exceed customer expectations. These linkages were translated into clear goals, commitments, values, responsibilities, standards, and guiding principles. Mission goals were generated at the top, and teams would own and support their portion of these goals. In these settings, management and teams were linked and aligned on purpose (Figure 7.1).

Antithetical, traditional structures will defeat this linkage process. Specialists from each unit will work toward their own goals. Accounting will align on score-keeping goals, supervisors on labor efficiency goals, quality on control chart goals, master scheduling on inventory accuracy goals, and sales on ship-and-bill goals. However, when all units align to a *company* strategy, their efforts become unifying. Quality, cost, and delivery, or a combination of these elements, become the standards against which all supporting acts are evaluated.

There are many approaches to developing mission statements in work teams. Most frequently, organizations sponsor off-site workshops for each team to define its mission and goal statements and its supporting or driving values. Alignment, for example, comes when conflicts between product quality and customer service are resolved with management and teams in partnership. Product quality might conflict with profit when research and development projects exceed budgets, causing one driving value to be compromised. In the off-site setting, team members can work out the kinks after coming up with four to six manageable driving values (having no more than six values will make alignment a realistic exercise).

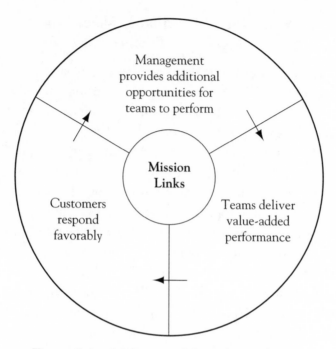

Figure 7.1. A Mission of Circular Linkages.

Mission statements on the team level need not be complex. However, the primary objective of this exercise must be met, which is to ensure that team members develop ownership and align around the mission. Another objective of these meetings is to ensure that all work team members understand the tasks that need to be accomplished. To this end, a team council monitors the team missions, goals, and task accomplishments.

Planning charts can be designed as visual devices to assist team members' understanding of the connection between mission, goals, and action agendas. Teams should use their own mission statements to establish meetings around the task of developing long-, medium-, and short-range goals. A team meeting is a good place to translate a mission statement into a concrete agenda. The following list summarizes the team development process going on at this early stage:

Team Development Process

- Mission and purpose of what?
- Desired future state of what?
- Present state of what?
- Transition plan
- How do we get there?
- What is getting in the way?
- How do we gain support?

Without an organizational network that shares a common mission and possesses a clear picture of the focus of teams, management and employees will continue to operate on their different social and political agendas and private time frames. The goal of linking mission statements is to align people, teams, and the organization in mind and heart—to expand vision, insight, and understanding in order to clarify purpose and to make the core values of the team culture congruent with the mission.

Policy Deployment

It is often difficult to define objectives in such a way that they are specific enough to be used as a measure of team performance and yet general enough that they remain current despite the fast-paced and ever-changing business environment. Internalizing new companywide policies on quality and team development can cause many shifts in the ways departments and individuals are to do their jobs. In many cases, these new ideas may be in direct conflict with decade-old policies and practices. Conflicts can arise from both written and unwritten policies. In either case, rules may need to be changed to allow the team transition to take place smoothly. Management teams and/or steering teams can make the necessary judgment calls in a timely manner and allow for changes to happen smoothly and quickly.

Then, as objectives pass from one level of the organization to another, they are increasingly refined and made more specific. Individuals and teams at each level of the organization have the opportunity to play "catch-ball," that is, negotiate with management to ensure that an achievable stretch goal is mutually agreed upon and documented.

There are a number of areas where changes are likely to occur and where specific problems must be watched for.

Labor grade structure. Many companies' labor grade structures are prohibitive to job structure changes and may also affect union practices. Proposed changes should be analyzed carefully before a decision is made that causes a ripple effect through the whole organization.

Cultural differences. Inequalities may include perks for salaried people, reserved parking areas, executive lunchrooms and/or washrooms, the use of time cards versus time clocks, hour lunches versus half-hour lunches, offices versus bays, and other possibly hidden differences that may seem minor to management but may be divisive in the horizontal revolution.

Misaligned departmental goals that impact on another area. For example, a shipping department's goal to reduce overtime may result in cutting the weekend coverage. Their goal is achieved at the expense of a timely shipment that a customer was counting on. The result is small savings on overtime, at the potential loss of a customer.

Process instructions, assembly instructions, job instructions, and so forth. It may be a requirement that these be accurate and current, but updating may not be the team's responsibility. When a team redesigns its work, it will require coordination with management to see that the required changes happen.

Areas of responsibility. Hidden boundaries and personal turf are lodged throughout an organization. When teams begin solving problems, some infringement on others' boundaries and turf is a reality. Clarification and cross-functional collaboration in these situations is essential.

Information sharing. Many companies, for whatever reasons, withheld information on costs, schedules, performance, and so forth. *Glasnost* must occur in an organization, through education and policy changes, in order to crack open hidden systems.

Latitude in lunch and work hours, personal breaks, and make-up time. As teams redesign their own work flow around tasks and people, a new, flexible approach to break taking and make-up time is needed.

Whatever the combination of issues, leadership must be sensitive to the needs of the team process and carefully listen to and act on issues that involve policies and procedures supportive of that process. Teams should address issues by using specific objectives that state the desired outcomes in numerical terms whenever possible. Objectives can be addressed and reviewed, then adjusted semiannually or quarterly to keep them current.

Self-Measuring Performance

Walk around horizontal companies, and you will see odd sights: widely available, easy-to-read charts tracking scrap, rework, on-time delivery, accident and error rates of all kinds, and customer service. The concept of measuring team activity should focus on a system of data-gathering feedback that the team itself uses to measure its own results and improve its own performance. That system's acceptance underlies all the rhetoric of pushing decisions down to the lowest possible level, of paying people for results, and of using teams to manage streamlined and reengineered processes.

How does a self-administered measurement system work? Look at your own work environment and ask yourself what your measured standard of performance is. On the one hand, if you are working in a support function, the chances that you have any formal performance-measuring criteria are almost nonexistent. You probably assess your performance based on the number of tasks you do in a given day.

A production or test job, on the other hand, is usually measured by a given amount of product achieved in a day. The standard is usually number driven, and a margin for defective products is built into the system. If you ask a production worker what he or she needs to achieve in a day, you usually get a reply along the lines of, "I need to build eighteen widgets, and sixteen have to be good." (Incidentally, the perception of that production worker is usually that "if I produce an additional 2 widgets, I can hold them over and count them in my numbers for tomorrow." This is not a case of a lazy worker; to the contrary, it is a case of management-conditioned expectations about performance.)

Management have historically given out the numbers to achieve, and production has met those expectations. The typical worker has had little or no ownership in an overall schedule other than knowing about the eighteen widgets he or she is expected to build. When companies get into trouble, the work force tends to blame management and vice versa. What is needed is a system that is aware that the production worker has ownership too, coupled with a performance standard that has a built-in feedback and scoring system that workers can relate to. Raising the level of awareness raises the level of performance. Increasing the ownership level increases the commitment. Teams must have ownership and a self-administered performance measurement that is based on improvement not punishment.

Starting a Measurement System

An organization's ability to establish good measurement systems within teams depends on those teams' established trust and maturity. Our experience affirms that some teams are ready to create their performance measurement system within six months of formation. Others will still struggle after a year or more, and even then their system may still reflect a level of mistrust because of their unwillingness to measure. A good approach is to begin training the team on aspects of performance measurement and the importance of measurable feedback. Past performance will reflect a comparative baseline for present performance and help establish realistic goals that teams can achieve.

Feedback has a positive effect on the rate of performance, and there are several methods to share it. The more immediate it is, such as daily or hourly, the better. Methods such as individual charts, team charts, area charts, or organizational charts are appropriate. (Training individuals in the charting process can take several sessions, in order to work out all the snags that teams encounter.) It is recommended that leaders consider setting up measurement systems in the following areas, and create a baseline of at least two years to determine past performance of the organization in quality and cost improvement.

Quality. Most companies have some sort of quality system in place and monitor the performance of their work force in defects per submittal or some other form of measurement. Establish the historical baseline for this measurement and then share it with the teams. Have each one set up and design some sort of tracking performance system and let them monitor it in their team meetings. Management must be committed and patient and work with the teams as they learn to monitor their own quality performance. Though most companies monitor performance, it is unusual to find individual areas that monitor and maintain their own performance charts. Teams may express some skepticism towards management, asking, "Are they going to use the information against us?" There must be clear communication about the goals of collecting the feedback if teams are to be self-correcting. Remember, if performance is charted it will improve; the better the feedback system, the better the performance.

Cost improvement. The ideal here is to establish an accurate baseline of past performance (some measurement of pure productivity that will work in the system) and then use the same formula to monitor the progress of the performance. Many companies base their measurement on labor hours, following the past costs, and comparing them to the latest figures. Let teams set the system up and be patient. This self-monitoring process may take up to a year before substantial savings are realized, although we have seen immediate improvement in a number of companies.

Scrap reduction. Teamwork makes a real impact on the area of scrap, especially when a team monitors how much it scraps and is then allowed to solve its own problems. Some companies may be reluctant to share the costs of the parts that make up their products, and in many cases, the work force is ignorant of the products' true cost. If managers are not presently sharing this information with their work force, they are doing a great disservice to cost savings. A cost-conscious work group is far more cautious and critical when it understands the impact that scrap has on profitability. Some kind of network system should be set up among teams in order to share scrap levels and parts costs on at least a quarterly basis. This way, individual teams know how much they contribute to the problem and see the need to make improvements.

Rework performance. This is an area often not measured in most work units. Teams create their own baselines and begin monitoring output quality. Rework performance will indicate to the teams how their product is doing at the next customer level. With an understanding of how rework hinders productivity, teams will find better ways to process and build. Again, it is recommended that rework information be shared with the teams on a quarterly basis. Many team networks monitor these criteria on a weekly basis and work on specific problems that are contributing to the causes. Elimination of these problems will reduce rework costs.

Human resources. Many tangibles can be monitored through the human resource department, and historical baselines can be established to determine the effect that team work has on the employee. Specific areas can be tracked for items like turnover, employee complaints, sick leave, grievances, and so forth.

Intangibles. The beneficial effects of teams go beyond tangible items and enter into the realm of things that cannot be measured, but are real improvements to the organization. They include:

- *Enhanced communication.* Both vertical and lateral communication improves with greater networking through team workouts and cross-functional activity.
- A *responsible work force.* Employees will accept more responsibility as they do more decision making and see a positive outcome of their efforts.
- *Professionalism.* Teams that have worked together for a long time and have shared in leadership roles and management presentations gain a higher level of self-esteem, direction, and maturity.
- *Integration of ideas.* Team networks integrate ideas and become more creative and innovative.
- *Trust.* A higher degree of trust is established throughout the entire work force. Teamwork emphasizes problem solving, not people blaming.

Encourage individuals to plot their own *tangible* and *intangible* results and then combine them to form a team rating. The idea is to set up a system of comparison among team members that advances their personal performance and that of the entire team. This system of measurement, if fair and consistent across jobs and people, will identify possible areas for improved performance.

There are four steps in establishing any team measurement system.

1.   Select the right things to measure and measure them in the right way. The team starts by discussing what the team outputs are and how they are currently measured. Typically, some people will focus on negatives; wanting to measure tardies instead of on-time products, mistakes instead of correct work, downtime instead of

uptime. Old habits and approaches are to be replaced by new ways of thinking about the work.

2.   Focus on several outputs of team performance. The facilitator helps the team establish an objective measurement system for these outputs, allowing team members time to work on their metrics and charts. Metrics are not valuable for continuous improvement purposes unless they are understood, owned, and actionable by those who can make a difference. One metric point starts a chart, two points a line, and three points a trend. Encourage team members' progress. It is imperative that they not be punished for poor performance but encouraged on the reasons for improving. Encouragement will solicit success and punishment will discourage any measurement.

3.   As team members begin to become familiar with techniques of measurement, introduce them to the aspects of goal setting and more sophisticated charting. At first, team charts can reflect overall team performance and not identify individuals. More mature teams will share individual performance numbers without apprehensiveness, but do not attempt this type of advanced charting in the beginning. It can cause serious setbacks. As teams become more proactive, they can begin to measure many more outputs of their business system and understand how individual performances affect overall productivity. It is best, however, to introduce performance charting gradually.

4.   Measurement is done and charted solely by the team members, who take turns with the preparation and presentation. Many teams can do all their charts and graphs on a computer with software programmed specifically to their measurement requirements. Their performance can be displayed in their areas, in a window or on a wall, for all to see. Teams may be at various levels of self-measurement, but all teams—including those in support areas—should have some sort of self-measurement system and a monthly forum for reporting, in order to aid their organizational learning, alignment, and development of people.

How do management manage the measurement system? They do not manage it. The system is monitored by the teams, and they submit a copy of their measurement system to management as a master report. These reports can contain numerous different styles and formats of measurement.

Teams should concentrate on the aspect of establishing a self-measurement system that allows them latitude to select what is best for them. Management can see the overall results in their accounting systems. Each team's primary concern should be continuous improvement based on its own measurement system. Encouragement and coaching by managers will elicit improvement.

Selection of the Indicators

It is not unusual to have a team that gathers data weekly on as many as forty different aspects of their product/service and that uses the data to monitor product quality and performance. Many areas also get weekly customer feedback that tells them how their product/service is performing. When areas of concern do not have direct measurements in place, the appropriate teams should begin by identifying the area not aware of performance, share information about the area, establish measurement and tracking, and mature the process from there.

The successful measurement of team performance comes from accurately measuring product quality, services, and/or customer satisfaction. Improvements may be measured in:

- Reduced operating costs through doing things right the first time
- Lowered inventory levels from improved predictability
- Improved staff motivation and commitment
- Increased sales from improved customer satisfaction
- Improved relationships with suppliers

- Increased market share
- Less shrinkage and theft

Productivity can be defined around a relationship between inputs and outputs. Customer satisfaction, for example, can be equal in importance to other productivity outputs such as revenue and inventory. Team productivity might be defined as the ability to achieve maximum financial return and customer loyalty from a team's efforts. Work teams can learn to weigh financial pressures against growing customer demands and expectations, short-term gains against long-term gains, and easy-to-control sales issues against hard-to-manage company issues. In other words, for each team to establish its own accountability system, it should identify its key quality relationships and determine its own inputs and outputs within the organization. From there, it can develop detailed, or strategic, quality improvement plans that identify means to further measure team performance. The objective of strategic quality planning is to establish a quality control system focused on continuous quality improvement. The plan may include specific activities to ensure implementation of cost-of-quality measurement and statistical process control.

Quality Cost Analysis. Quality cost analysis provides a practical management tool for the measurement and prioritization of functional quality program activities and results that affect organizational profits. The goal of a quality cost analysis system is to facilitate quality improvement efforts leading to operating cost reductions and to communicate the progress of a quality program in dollars, a language that management can understand and act on.

Statistical Process Control. Statistical process control (SPC) is a method of identifying and stabilizing uncontrolled variation in any production or service process. Once a process has been brought into a state of statistical control, SPC provides the tools necessary to measure the inherent systematic variation of the process. Knowledge of this inherent and predictable level of variation is vital to the production of quality goods and services.

Multiple-Rater Performance Appraisals

Horizontal structures—with fewer levels, fewer supervisors, and larger spans of control—make single supervisory ratings inadequate. Therefore, we recommend using multiple raters to appraise certain employees. Even though each multiple rater can deal with spans of sixty people or more, together such raters can give continuous and predictable information about wide range of performance criteria. Multiple-rater measures must be computerized to handle the data administration and scoring, and computer analysis also provides safeguards that ensure the best set of colleagues is providing evaluative information on the correct set of dimensions. When combined with artificial intelligence and expert systems software, multiple-rater performance measurements/ appraisals can greatly eliminate the bias, inaccuracy, and validity problems associated with rating employees belonging to several teams with no traditional supervisor. One popular multiple-rater system, Team Evaluation and Management System (TEAMS), includes thirty-two safeguards concerning rater behavior and data reliability, none of which would be available with a single-rater measurement system. These safeguards not only protect the integrity of the performance measures but enhance measurement credibility to users as well.

Team Member Performance Reviews

Although team member performance reviews are usually separated from the compensation process, they can be part of employee recognition. Typically, they are employed mainly as a developmental tool to help team members achieve expected performance standards, identify and overcome weaknesses, solve problems, and improve performance. At best, performance reviews qualify strengths, recognize outstanding performance, validate superior skills and contributions, and identify new directions for team members to pursue. At worst, employees who rate poorly in performance reviews can become bitter and alienated from the team.

Team member performance reviews are usually conducted once or twice a year by members of the team to evaluate individual members' performances over a designated period of time. Objectives established both by the individual and the team are the basis for evaluation. The review procedure focuses on the technical, administrative, and interpersonal skills that the team has agreed are essential for successful team membership. The more mature the team, the more responsibility it takes for determining its own objectives and standards.

We recommend that teams not review their own members until the team has reached the horizontalizing stage, when it also chooses its own leader. At that point, two members of the work team, one selected by the person to be reviewed and one selected by the rest of the team, conduct and deliver the team member performance review.

How to Measure Support Team Output

Support teams do not work directly on a product or service, but offer assistance to make the process work better. Support teams are found in accounting/finance, product engineering, maintenance, product flow, human resources, planning, scheduling, inspection, marketing, information services, production services, quality services, legal services, and so on. Usually these teams react negatively when approached with a proposal that they measure their performance. They are reluctant to establish any type of measurement system because they believe it is nearly impossible to measure what they do.

If any job in an organization cannot be measured, its value should be questioned. Every job has a customer, and that customer has expectations of what that job should do. Identifying and tracking conformance to these expectations is the basis of making support organizations accountable for their performance. It requires considerable effort, but support teams can succeed in creating some sort of measurement to monitor performance. If measurement remains a problem with a team, ask team members some clarifying questions to draw out measurement criteria.

- What is our accuracy?
- Who are our customers?
- What is our timeliness?
- What function do we serve?
- How do our customers feel about our product?
- Do we satisfy customers' needs, not just the specification needs?
- Who are our suppliers?
- Do our suppliers satisfy our needs?
- What are our methods for measurement?
- What are our throughput times?
- What are the best methods to satisfy our customer needs?

This type of questioning can bring about an internal customer focus that in many cases has not existed before in the support department. It will help in breaking down traditional department boundaries and also help teams focus on the internal customer for each job. Such questioning can bring about many positive changes in the way business is done. A clear understanding of customer requirements and a focus on improvement through measurement techniques can eliminate many work-flow problems and unnecessary procedures. Once a support team begins to gather data, the compiling and tracking of productivity/services will bring into focus various problems that each team faces. After extensive discussion of each issue, the support teams can begin to choose the real problems they have and focus on improving service to their customers. (There are several software programs currently on the market that help companies put support measurement systems in place.)

Coaches should help their work teams identify the support teams they need to work with. Those support teams' functions may be assimilated, according to work team responsibilities. For example, if a work team decides it is ready to do its own hiring, it might want to take over the interviewing and selection functions from human resources. It is recommended that teams and their respective support teams develop an analysis for all the tasks and processes they share together and decide how they want to handle them in the future. With the help of coaches and managers, implementation plans should be drafted identifying the hand-off timelines for the tasks and processes that are to be transferred. These are delicate sessions and sensitive care needs to be taken around the conditions of timing and hand-offs and people's feelings about new turf. A conscious effort may be needed to keep support staff people from feeling exploited, defensive, and resentful.

Recognizing and Rewarding Team Performance

Recognizing and rewarding team performance are critical for building employee commitment to the team. Guidelines and methods of recognition are set initially by the steering team and design team, and designing the most effective team-based reward and recognition begins with a clear understanding of team's type and the role the team is playing in the achievement of such business goals as customer service, venture or product development, problem solving, and continuous improvement efforts.

Recognition can range from special lunches to ceremonies that acknowledge extraordinary effort. Rewards can range from extra pay for learning new skills (in depth or breadth, or in leadership) to gain-sharing programs in which all employees receive bonuses when the organization reaches desired goals. Many organizations use various types of gain sharing or team bonus schemes, along with multiskill-based compensation plans. All these activities should recognize the team and reward the total team for its accomplishments. Positive and constructive recognition sustains effort, reassures teams that they are doing well, and promotes a sense of team identity by allowing teams to take pride in their progress and accomplishments. Whether recognition is given verbally or through modest team gifts, it can let evolving teams know they are on track and performing well.

Some inexpensive recognition techniques that give attention to team effort include providing a company wall to display such items as the team's picture, logo, banner, crest, certificates, schedules, and innovations; displaying a team plaque of distinction in the work area; holding celebrations or special dinners for team birthdays; arranging team competitions in company athletic events; and providing team mugs, pens, T-shirts, jackets, hats, or whatever the team finds distinctive to its identity and interests. Techniques that recognize team accomplishments should be especially sensitive to what the team would find appropriate. Some companies use "Team of the Month" or "Outstanding Team of the Year" awards, trips to Disneyland, pizza parties, and other public ceremonies. But remember, these are self-directed teams. In many cases, teams are delighted when management just give them the bonus money and the discretion to decide its use.

Before determining what rewards are best for your teams, three issues should first be addressed: how to pay employees for expanded skills and opportunities, how to reward teams for ever-higher levels of performance, and how to reinforce cooperation among teams. The pay issue will arise early in team initiatives because employees have changed from narrow, specific job descriptions to broader, more flexible job responsibilities geared to the self-management of the team. There are various pay systems to consider.

Multiskill-Based Pay

Multiskill-based plans hold a unique advantage because they focus on rewarding the number of skills a team member has mastered and applied, thus increasing production flexibility. Such compensation schemes encourage cross-training and reward team members on three levels: an entry level, where employees receive pay increases as they acquire skills that the team needs; a secondary team-rate level, where employees master all the skills assigned to their team; and a tertiary all-plant level, where employees master additional skills or horizontal skills in order to move around the facility. Here, for example, the team member learns such leadership skills as troubleshooting techniques, ways of training other employees, knowledge of safety procedures, and meeting management techniques that are used in all jobs and are required for successful team performance. Mature multiskill-based pay plans should add another tier that rewards workers for breadth of newly acquired skills and also for depth of knowledge acquired, to avoid post-tertiary-level topping out. Administered on an individual basis, the multiskill-based system often has each team establish its own criteria for evaluating mastery of technical skills.

Potential pitfalls of multiskill-based pay include not budgeting enough money for up-front additional costs, not making provision for a payback period that requires employees to perform newly mastered job skills for a specified period of time, and not planning ahead for times when newly trained employees might face long waiting periods before exercising their skills, due to a lack of job vacancies.

Pay for Performance

How to reward teams for ever-higher levels of performance is another challenge. Rewards are an essential component of teams driven by continuous improvement, but the rewards must be improvement oriented in order to achieve their desired outcomes. Initially, team participation is a reward in and of itself. Training can also be an important reward and can be vigorously employed by management to acknowledge outstanding performance and promote team member involvement in decision making. Along with knowledge and new skills come new challenging experiences—all rewarding to employees seeking development. For teams that have power to hire, evaluate, and discipline, authority can be a reward. It is a demonstration of management's trust in employees. In addition to increased responsibility, increased agency can be rewarding. Agency provides the right to choose one's own vision, the right to make mistakes, the right to invest today's assets in the future, and the right to benefit from one's self-directedness and diligence. Such rights are powerful rewards for many people. However, participation, training, authority, and agency alone will not be enough to motivate employees over the long run.

An effective pay-for-performance approach should create and reinforce team competencies among individual team members, address individual performance issues within the team environment, and allocate rewards based on external as well as internal measurement sources. Two essential issues need to be considered in order for pay-for-performance compensation to be successful. First, defining performance is a difficult task. Will you define performance by quality or quantity? In most cases performance consists of technical knowledge, application of knowledge, administrative effectiveness, work relationships and behaviors, response to coaching, leadership behaviors, and personal commitment. But performance can be anything an organization wants it to be, and often it is viewed as an entanglement of all these aspects. Each organization has to carefully write its policies, procedures, and job descriptions. And it will have to consider employees' definitions of performance in order to be realistic.

The second difficult issue is to link pay to the new team-based meaning of high performance. Giving out money may be a good thing; however, implementing this good thing is another matter. Pay for performance is not necessarily a way of saving money but a system to reallocate available salary dollars and to use these dollars to compete, challenge, and stay healthy in a rapidly changing business world. The crucial link is to build pay for performance on employees' turning their goals into objectives and action items for divisional, departmental, unit, and individual achievement. Making this link between the organization's success and the team's efforts and rewards is a turning point in raising the level of interest in and commitment to a pay-for-performance system.

A trap in recognizing people with monetary rewards is to put a team in competition with other departments or individuals. Money may give a team a special status that invites jealousy and may result in attempts by others to sabotage the efforts of the team. What is important to employees is equity of opportunity and fairness to all.

Finally, when designing pay-for-performance compensation programs, be sure to include objective criteria for advancement. Competency-based training should be developed for each group of skills. Satisfactory achievement on written or performance tests (the latter whenever feasible) should be required for promotion to the next higher grade.

Cooperation Among Teams

Rewarding teams for their own results raises a third pay issue. The organization must create cooperation among teams that have different objectives and reward systems. Organizations can minimize conflict between teams' goals by creating a series of team objectives that complement one another, from the executive boardroom to the shop floor. Teams at the top should have quality and earnings goals that translate into consistent performance goals for teams at each descending level. Set identical annual improvement goals for all levels. That is, every division and team should have the same percentage target for improvement, regardless of its current performance. If a division achieves its goal, then teams in that division are eligible for bonuses if they have met their team improvement goals.

Teams working in one department invariably will complain that another department has easier work, easier customers, and fewer problems. How can the challenges to the marketing department be equal to the challenges to the human resources department? How can the organization minimize competition between teams when they should be serving one another? To minimize conflicts from measuring and rewarding teams differently, compensation factors must be properly identified, defined, and weighted. A common method of evaluating the worth of jobs is to identify key or benchmark jobs (those commonly found in the job market), to survey pay practices relative to those jobs, and to determine market value for those jobs. Removing job evaluation from the confines of the personnel/compensation department and making it available to all employees (team-by-team) is a major step toward granting horizontal teams increased influence on issues of equity and other decisions that are crucial to their work.

Recognition and reward programs are not working for some companies because of limited coverage. At one organization we know, only about 10 percent of employees were recognized and rewarded. This organization is currently modifying its criteria to increase the opportunities for recognition to everyone. If teams are to be effective, most if not all employees must be recognized. The worksheet in Exhibit 7.1 is meant to be used by managers who want to review work systems, recognition needs, and opportunities for individual, team, management, and organizational efforts in their organizations.

Gain Sharing and Profit Sharing

Performance of teams also can be rewarded via gain sharing or team bonus programs. These programs reward teams for increases in productivity that exceed some measure of baseline performance.

Exhibit 7.1. Recognition and Reward Worksheet.

The work system encourages:

Yes	No		Yes	No	
		A cooperative/collaborative climate			Participation in decision making
		Dignity and respect from others			Opportunity for learning and growth
		Challenging work			Access to customer/job-related information
		Involvement in planning, doing, and controlling the work			Initiative/innovation
		Variety/multiskill development			Self-management

Individual reward system: What kind of pay for performance/knowledge should align to the work system we have designed?

Team reward system: What kind of team rewards should align to the work system we have designed?

Management reward system: What kind of management rewards should align to the work systems we have designed?

Organizational reward system: What kind of systemwide recognition should align to the work systems we have designed?

Gain-sharing or profit-sharing bonuses are usually distributed equally among team members (like the NFL Super Bowl bonus!), but occasionally, team members are asked to decide how to distribute the bonus among themselves. The performance threshold for gain sharing must be high enough to ensure the success of the business and to focus teams on excellence. Moreover, effective gain-sharing systems will contain a variety of yardsticks so that each team can see how it affects at least some part of the final outcome. When gain sharing pays off, everyone in a team should know that his or her collective performance was exceptional. By distributing equal shares, the company makes the teamwork message clear. It took the whole team to accomplish the performance and everyone receives an equal share of the achievement and the reward.

Gain sharing and profit sharing are most successful when implementation is a part of a total management approach or philosophy and not just a group incentive scheme. Gain sharing, in particular, provides a reason for employees to coordinate the work within and between different teams because it rewards organizational progress and, thus, encourages teamwork and cooperation. Both gain sharing and profit sharing can help communicate financial results and provide feedback about the fitness of the organization. Important favorable conditions for gain-sharing and profit-sharing incentives include small operations; employee-controlled production and costs; an open, trusting participative relationship between managers and teams; and a technically competent work force.

Effective team compensation schemes structure pay so that all team members receive adequate basic pay, additional rewards for increases in individual competence, and special bonuses or incentives paid according to team performance. No single reward system can support all the needs of corporate and individual goals. For example, gain sharing alone cannot meet the needs of management and professionals who are asked to work in teams or to join a cross-functional team and who are accustomed to being rewarded solely for their individual contributions. Thus, each system has its weakness as well as its strength. Experience offers several directives:

- Examine your individual reward systems (performance appraisal, merit pay, and so on) and determine whether they strengthen or undermine teamwork.
- Examine alignment of rewards. Do the rewards fit the purposes, goals, responsibilities, and roles of the teams?
- Examine dual- or multiple-track performance appraisal systems to ensure that career-path and pay issues are not diffused.
- Examine the degree of cooperation among teams to ensure that the reward system is equitable.

As organizational structures become more horizontal, the incentive system needs to continue to reward individual acquisition of skills as well as team skills, allowing people to develop more of their talents. It becomes not just a question of how people get paid but of how the organization learns and grows. The team itself functions as a steering/recommending committee for individual interests and selections. The philosophy is one of using team members' knowledge to make the team and organization more productive and innovative. Team members will select their own level of development or their ability will select it for them.

Stock Options and Ownership

The concept that employees should own part of the business in which they work has been around for some time. Stock options represent a relationship between individual wealth and that aspect of organizational performance that is measured by stock price. The benefits come from the employee's not having to buy the stock to guarantee the price offered in the stock option. The employee is given a period of time (years) to exercise the option. If the price of the stock goes up, the employee can sell his or her stock at that higher price and make money without ever risking any of his or her own money in investment. This is a fail-safe opportunity to benefit from improved performance and one that has been traditionally reserved for the management class. But restricting stock options to executive class compensation raises the question of who really delivers the profit.

To minimize the whole us-them condition in an organization, we truly believe that people at all levels should be given the privilege of no-risk earnings from the growth of stock price. Some companies are already offering such incentives at lower levels than before. Many companies are also referring to all their employees as partners, associates, colleagues, and so forth, to reduce class differences and are giving them a certain number of stock options as appreciation for the success of the business. Employee stock ownership plans (ESOPs) can underscore the organization's intent to treat employees as owners and partners.

Budgets

The implementation of a team process requires that the company establish a budget to support the efforts of the teams in their work session time, training time, additional time required for team-related projects, and miscellaneous time taken up in management presentations and other work sessions. Therefore, we recommend that companies establish a cost accounting and tracking system to measure baseline performance of teams; team hours used; overall plant effectiveness of the company since the implementation of the team process; and rework performance, scrap performance, and quality performance. This procedure should be set up as early as possible, for it will be an indicator to management of the performance of the team process and will serve teams as they mature in the performance improvement areas and pursue more prominent problems.

Celebration

Teams need to *celebrate* their successes, recognize one another's efforts, thank one another for help, and, in general recognize improvement. But in many team settings, celebrations are used sparingly, or not at all. All too often management send the message, "If you're having fun, you're not working."

When team projects are successful, it is important that everyone involved be acknowledged and that some kind of celebration be held in the work units. The celebration can be organized around something as simple as giving out plaques or mugs, offering donuts, or buying lunch for everyone, or on a more complex scale, conducting a special evening party or dinner or a weekend retreat. Recognizing the outstanding performance of a work unit as the result of the team members in that unit emphasizes teamwork. Sharing rewards communicates all-for-one and one-for-all commitments.

While celebrations, like high-potency vitamins, are an effective means of distributing something necessary for good functioning to all team members, they should be initiated by those respected and valued as team disciples and advocates. To ensure that the celebration given will be valued by team members, managers should, at the outset, assess what type of celebration is appropriate, meaningful, and timely for the team.

Summary

A work environment with interconnected task dependency is more likely to encourage success with team-based incentives than an environment in which sequential tasking predominates. Team behavior and results must be measurable and measurement accuracy must exceed that of eyeballing and taking hunches. A critical factor in the success of a team incentive program is the degree to which a sound and accurate mechanism exists or can be crafted to determine in a timely and accurate manner whether and how well each work team is meeting its own defined performance.

One of the most amazing things about the team structure is that improvement can be seen immediately. Solutions do not have to get worse before they get better. To see this improvement, the organization must give teams their own financial accountability and the freedom and support to make mistakes. People must be patient. Working in teams to achieve better and better results is an ongoing, never-ending process.

Management's new role is one of self-control and patience. Managers are responsible for the overall performance of the organization, and their own incentives must be linked to broad measures of strategic organizational performance. They should receive incentives only when total performance justifies them. In the horizontal organization, people do not really care what you say. They care what you do. This basically means adopting a new approach of sponsoring, monitoring, and recognizing real progress, and working with employees and associates in new ways.

The reward issue should not be introduced before teams have completed their horizontal movement. An untimely initiation of a team-based pay program to drive newly designed structures and/or lack of management commitment to making the rewards program work are principal contributing causes of failure. A rewards program that has the best chance of being successful is in large part conditional on where the organization begins and where it is headed in its redesign and integration of work processes, team systems, and profitability.

Chapter Eight

Revolutionary Prescriptions: Continuous Learning and Hard Work

When I first learned about the move to a horizontal
structure, I was never clear about my own agenda.
My purpose was faulty; my intent was vague. I had
hoped for certain rewards that never materialized
for I knew little then of the hardships of learning
that go with the struggle to reinvent our company
and ourselves.

—Executive caught up in the
learning of Carlos Castañeda's Don Juan
and his Yaqui way of knowledge

"Tradition," a beautiful song from the musical *Fiddler on the Roof*,
unfolds a story about change in a Russian village at the turn of the
century and how it affected the formerly stable and predictable
world of Tevya, the village milkman and the play's central figure—
a world in which everyone knew his or her place and the order of
things. Much of the trauma of tradition's giving way to revolutionary change comes from the villagers' dealing with the hardships of
learning how to change.

This chapter is about the applications that can be made
through a new type of behavior and learning. We also present further ideas for coaching and consulting for the continuous improvement that comes through learning how to learn. Those committed
to the horizontal revolution with its hardships of learning will combine their mastery of some specialized expertise with the multidisciplinary ability to work in teams. They will be driven by an
imperative that requires that they learn new ways to reduce their

skilled incompetence and learn how to continue learning. The coaching they must give and receive will consist of guiding and integrating the interconnected work of highly skilled people and flushing out all the causes of their less-than-desired effectiveness.

The revolutionary learning paradigm requires people in a horizontal system to coach one another in how to reason and act productively in multidisciplinary settings. That is a hard learning curve. Fear and defensive routines must be overcome, clarity obtained, and individuals shown how to become the ultimate learners. Confronting the reasonings people use to design and implement their actions is at the forefront of changing their behaviors.

Horizontal functioning thrives in a climate where individuals share information openly and broadly, increase others' capacity to confront their own ideas, remain open to inquiry from others, and are able to admit when they do not have all the answers. They make personal commitments to be flexible, knowledgeable, self-reliant, and self-confident in the face of change. Those commitments and concomitant skills enable them to master change rather than be enslaved by it. Those who accept the challenge and hard work of learning will enjoy the benefits derived from their efforts.

Individuals in the horizontal revolution must accept that change is a loaded word. Real change is accomplished by alterations in attitude and behavior; however, the prevalent response from people at work is to deny that their attitude or behavior is an issue. The greater the change is perceived to be, the more acute the reactions to it. The horizontal revolution requires dramatic change to achieve dramatic results. People will line up on the positive and negative sides of issues of change during this revolution, causing increased stress. People who are afflicted by change will have selective retention. They will selectively implement those parts of the change familiar to them. They will believe what they want to believe. They will retain feelings of dependency on the old organization as horizontal functioning begins to take shape. There will be many uncomfortable situations in which people will see change as a loss rather than a gain. The conflicts and the rewards of change will need management's utmost attention.

Learning the Learning Process

Going flat out for flat requires that the workplace become a learning organization where anything worth doing can be done better. Learning, as we have defined it in this book, is a change in behavior based upon analyzed experience. Taking on new roles, responsibilities, and relationships in an enterprise that focuses on continuous improvement opens new learning frontiers for all employees. It makes the ability to analytically reflect on one's own and others' motivations, behaviors, and work relationships a necessary part of one's work. The horizontal revolution is happening because there has been a functional lack of a valuable perspective on passing conditions. The onrush of new perspectives and resentment toward old perspectives has brought a bitter harvest of consequences in the workplace.

As the flood of change threatens those with outdated styles and trembling egos, leadership declines and policing increases; organizational sandbags are thrown into the breaches, but they cannot thwart the flow of change forever. Praise for what we are will not create what we need to become. Our coaching experiences show that we need less wringing of hands and more opening of minds and perspectives. The behaviors of yesterday can no longer hold hostage the requirements of tomorrow. Sometimes, the most conscientious need the message of the revolution the most. With the most honorable intentions, idealism has given way to cynicism. That is why there is a need for a new commanding perspective, and that is why there has to be a transformation of the grammar of work and the workplace.

The newer and younger-thinking members of organizations expect work to be different than in the past. They want freedom on the job but not an unrestricted experience. They want to be able to learn and to be allowed the opportunity to do their very best. The horizontal revolution is all about the new leadership that must emerge to satisfy this requirement. We have to slow down enough to retrain people in new skills for coaching and teaming. During the revolution, members of the organization must be put through a process that many will find awkward, in order to help them shove aside old baggage. The landscape of corporate America has taken on a new look. The human spirit and the fast, forward pace of technology have combined to overwhelm all semblance of the status quo. Old-style management is as dead as Elvis. New types of leadership are cropping up like spring grass. Those in charge of corporate America must set an organizational climate for learning and then get out of the way.

Building the Learning Workplace

The center of creating a horizontal learning culture is a strong shift in mind, a metanoia. In the metanoia that accompanies the horizontal revolution, each individual moves from blame to responsibility—from seeing problems as caused by someone out there to seeing how his or her actions create the problems, from being on his or her own and complaining to being connected to others and constructing. New learning causes a shift away from presenting a personal facade to discovering ways in which a new reality can be created.

This childlike learning is at the heart of what it means to be human. It shows individuals the many ways in which they can recreate themselves to gain new awareness of the world around them and their relationship to it. They become able to do something they were never able to do before because they could not see what was beyond their own blinders. Only through new learning can we extend our capacity to create. Coaching in the horizontal workplace causes the organization to continually expand its capacity to create its future. Yet the territory for building this learning in the workplace is still largely unexplored and will remain unexplored until many more people are coached to release their control.

Agendas for Learning

Coaching agendas for the new learning begin by helping individuals overcome patterns of defensiveness and blame that are deeply ingrained in the ways team members interact with each other. Organizations have to remake people's skills for interaction, but coaches make a mistake when they think people can learn to interact if they are just given new information. Horizontal functioning requires not just getting new information but using it. Learning to interact must come through the experience of interaction.

As teams mature, their learning does not revolve around the agenda of a charismatic leader. Instead, their learning agendas come from personal visions transmitted so that they become shared visions and collective action. The leader must have a vision, but this vision cannot be dictated, no matter how heartfelt it may be. Principles and guiding practices for behavior must be transmitted to individual team members as the process of coaching takes place.

To-Do's for Learning At Work

Coaches must accept that horizontal teams will retain some learning disabilities from the old structure. But these learning disabilities are tragic only if they go undetected and unresolved. Many managers and supervisors have stopped learning because they have taken an "I am my position" attitude. They have focused their lives upon their position at work and have difficulty relating to themselves as individuals apart from a job. For them, interaction occurs between position and position, and they take little responsibility for results because they find someone to blame.

Many workout sessions recycle us-them problems. Coaching must help people at work end the idea that the enemy is out there.

Coaching focuses directly on the here and now and the responsibility that needs to be taken by the people who are here and now. Part of the problem with accepting responsibility results from the illusions of greatness that individuals try to project when they are in a room with their peers. This drive for an illusionary image is what makes the hardships of learning difficult to face, since the focus of the learning is abolishing illusions. The coach's responsibility is to help each person see how he or she contributes to his or her own problems.

People at work are often so caught up in tasks and projects that they cannot appreciate process. Conversations in teams are dominated by fixations on specific events. Yet, effective horizontal functioning depends on understanding processes, not sudden events. Much of the remainder of this chapter is dedicated to the processes that must be learned if learning is to go forward in the horizontal workplace.

New Learning

Going through the hardships of learning is much like starting and driving an automobile. There must be something to spark interest and ignite the mind for action toward new functioning. There has to be a means, such as coaching, of accelerating the work of change. Brakes may be needed at times to prevent possible disasters. There must be shock absorbers to assist in overcoming rough situations. Lights have to be available to help learners see things that have been previously unseen. Mirrors, in the form of feedback, reflect the reality of situations and behaviors. Doors can open to new adventures in performing. But a poorly tuned automobile engine is a shell of its potential, and so is an organization that is not running well.

Coaching for new learning requires providing opportunities for each individual and every work group to move out of the political orientation that has built up over the years and to move through a personal growth pattern into a professional understanding of teaming and coaching. Personal growth goes beyond acquiring competence and skill to approaching one's life as a creative work. A coach operates on the learning principle that you do not pump meaning into people, you pull meaning from them. You also remove factors that limit learning.

Working the Revolution

Although there are many groups and teams involved in the new learning, much of it takes place within one-on-one coaching situations. The narrative that follows sums up typical coaching actions and learner behavior in the horizontal revolution as the horizontal movement reaches a pivotal point for the learner. We have chosen a narrative in order to suggest what really happens on the person-to-person level of the new learning. In this narrative, a coach and a manager work on many aspects of the manager's personal development and the manager's need to coach his or her own team.

Discussion of Purpose

> Coach: As a coach, I always begin my work from the premise of the other person's purpose. A typical purpose that operating managers have for using coaches is to be better informed on what is happening and to do a better job of continuous improvement. Often, the purpose will focus on individual behaviors and the need for particular change within the organization. Please tell me your purpose for my being here.

> Manager: My purpose is to learn what we need to do to reach a higher plateau with the performance of our people; to receive the experience of an expert in how to manage people; to learn to motivate my team and become an effective player throughout this organization in meeting our goals; to improve communications at all levels and to become a better listener myself; and to

create an environment in which others can best reach their potential.

Coach: We can begin the coaching with your purpose as our basis. Initially, I can give you these observations:

- Some of your people will be slow to change because they reject newness. If newness isn't ingrained into the behaviors and attitudes of your people, it won't happen.

- Being understood is hard work, but it is my job to be understood by you, and it is your job to be understood by your people. Those who may be objectionable to me and to you won't be doing it on purpose. They just haven't seen new learning and the overcoming of defensiveness.

- We can only create solutions to your complicated problems by breaking the problems down to their basic causes. Right now, it is safe to say, one basic cause will be your ability to remake yourself and your people's ability to remake themselves.

- How I come across to you, and you to others, should not be left to chance. We need considerable involvement, interaction, and working and learning together.

- Those who are creating the most problems in your organization are doing it through their attitudes. Those who are making it the most difficult for each individual to enjoy his or her work are those who have a bad attitude toward newness and new learning. Of course, they likely don't realize that they are doing this. You will find, to your concern, that too many workers are performing in concert with the attitude of management.

- It is a myth that if you have good in your heart and have good intentions you will do well. You need to stop measuring your people by their intentions and start assessing their impact.

- As we begin this coaching relationship, I would like you to do certain tasks:

Make a list of your people, in order of their effectiveness, with what you really want done.

Identify which of your people are "with it" and are making a positive contribution.

Identify which of your people needs to seriously change his or her attitude and behavior in order to grow personally and to do a better job as you expect it.

Manager: I would like to improve my ability to influence others and get the most from my people. I guess this is what you would call coaching. I need to learn the techniques to coach subordinates so they accept more ownership and responsibility for what goes on around here. I need ideas that can be put to use day to day to effect change. I need to know how to make coaching work more effectively. What else do I need to know? What are the skills?

Discussion of the Guidance Coaching Gives

Coach: I would like to reassure you that I will work with you in a partnership to meet your purpose and provide the skills you want. You have a new and vigorous organization emerging. We will work to change the culture, not the structure, to one that is based on collective action and self-directedness rather than control. We will actually be empowering employees to take ownership and responsibility. They will become more motivated to innovate, achieve, and challenge the competition. Much of your management processes will be done in lean, flexible, and responsive teams.

The expected outgrowth of the coaching effort is a flattening of the management structure and a streamlining of your work forces, and your becoming more quality and service directed. Eventually, you can expect increased productivity, lower costs, and a never-ending process of improvement.

One part of your problem at this point is getting everyone aboard. You have an organization that has talked team but has not been a team. Now, for the first time, you are learning how to use work teams and what must be done to make them succeed. You will tend to underestimate the total investment and the amount of training needed to help teams succeed. In too many instances, your supervisors and managers will be reluctant to give work teams the authority they really need to succeed.

As with any initiative to effect a change with people, there will be issues along the way, including personnel and personality conflicts, unwillingness on the part of your management to give up their power base, worker distrust of management, and a fear on the part of some that they may lose their jobs. You will need to work hard to learn the new skills that are required for our new thrust. You will need to do more to cross-train your people. We will be coaching for new job skills, as well as team building and problem-solving skills, and for skills in resolving conflicts and communicating. All employees will need to be more skilled in leadership in order to facilitate meetings, interact, and coach one another.

My job is to coach and to set expectations. I will do this through documented memos, reports, agendas, and journals. I will make the norms and ground rules clear, listen to your people and document their desires and anticipations, and build teams around those who develop the capability and motivation to perform.

During each work session, I will emphasize the sense of team purpose, mission, and role that is essential for each person and every work group. There will be some who will put themselves on trial with teaming concepts and processes. Those who have difficulty living up to these new ways of doing things will experience some personal distress. Some will hold to old allegiances and alliances and, thereby, create internal conflicts and peer pressures.

We will have constant conflicts between the old and new ways of doing things, and they will result in different standards of performance and different attitudes about diversity. The sources of resistance will be counterproductive and will distract people from the positive features coaching can bring to your organization. But significant efforts will be taken to counter the resistance within management and the front line. Where possible, I rely on strong professionals to overcome the lack of professionalism. I can massage the egos of those affected by newness. I can lay it on the line to those who choose to take contrary directions.

Management work groups will need to take time away from regular work to negotiate roles and responsibilities, to clarify relationships, and to establish the ground rules for their functioning. During this time away, each member of the work group will be given a model of desired behavior and incentives for appropriate performance management. Follow-up to everything we do is essential.

Manager: We recently had a brainstorming meeting and asked our people to identify, on a 3 x 5 card, a problem they were having. The results were extremely revealing. I am concerned that there are so many issues that my people don't seem to be able to do much about. Is this a starting place for coaching? These are some of the issues they wrote down:

- "We thought we were a team and now we realize that we don't behave like a team . . . but we don't know what to do to become a team."
- "[People make] up their own priorities, and if they don't like you or are mad because of something you've done, they won't help you."
- "Leaders are saying they believe in change, and that we have to give time to learning and doing it, yet the priority is still whatever the boss wants now."

- "We have been involved in a lot of team activity, but we are having a hard time keeping it up."
- "There is a person who works with me who I dislike and I don't know how to handle this situation."
- "Some individuals see themselves as being ideal employees, yet most others have serious problems with these individuals' behavior."
- "You are unsure as to why you should change when so many others aren't changing and seem to be getting by just fine."
- "One of our fellow workers continues to exhibit unacceptable and bad behavior, but no one will level with the person."
- "My boss is screened out and doesn't know what is really happening in our world, but he won't listen to anyone's point of view or insight."
- "My boss says all the right things about treating people with respect, but he doesn't do those things."
- "We are trying to get everyone to be proactive and yet we are mostly crisis directed."

Discussion of a Strategic Plan

Coach: Yes, coaching can do something about these issues. First, you must be prepared to plan. The starting point is with you and your staff. There are three critical questions you are required to ask all of your staff.

1. *Do I want to be a part of this?* This question lets your people know that horizontal teaming has purposes and a need for their contributions, and that everyone is on trial to prove himself or herself. Each person may select to become cooperative, as a part of what you are doing, or to withdraw and become apathetic. Egos are easily bruised. You need to know where each person stands before measuring his or her commitment to teaming. There will be a sharp separation between those who are

positive and those who are negative toward this question. This separation will give you a continuous flow of good news and bad news. You will need to continue to sell your staff on the merits of horizontal functioning and on being a part of teaming. You will want enrollments in this effort. You will need to massage the egos of those who need extra reassurance of their worth. You can do the ego massaging, but you can't make the commitment for anyone. Despite your efforts to enlist team players, there will still be some who (usually by subtle behaviors) show they don't buy-in to what you will be doing. Simply telling them to shape up or else is not likely to work.

2.   *What is expected of me here?* Three factors will interfere with individuals accepting new expectations from you. First, they will holding on to their old allegiances and ways of doing things. Second, they will start internal conflicts that wreck team development, such as back stabbing peers in an effort to gain power. Some will even orchestrate a mild revolt against you. Third, work groups that have their own informal rules and norms will demand that you support them. There will be some who consider themselves unique and think that no one can work with them unless he or she is part of the "in" group. As you deal with these three factors, positions and players may be set, but new job duties and responsibilities will require clarification and elaboration. As coach, I will be doing a lot of one-on-one and work group discussion. There is a new organizational chart in the making, which will explain who reports to whom and with what authority and responsibilities. You will be establishing new procedures for budgetary authority, communication formats, training, and teaming relationships. These procedures will be designed for all to work together to find common ground.

3.   *In whom do I have trust and confidence?* As the leader, you will be a role model for how you want others to behave. You have to give trust and expect trust. You have to break up the old-boys'-club mentality. You have to link rewards to indicators

of trust and confidence, and desired behavior. You have to lead with vision and values. You have to infuse your teams with a sense of your purpose and shared values. This will include a refining of team character, a sorting out of roles and relationships, and signing your staff up for the journey. Your work is to get all employees to trust you, and to trust each other, and to find goals and values that all can believe in and put into practice. You will have to help your people face the first hardship of learning: fear. Some of the fears they will have to face are going from the known to the unknown, losing control over the situation, losing visibility and credit for work accomplished, acquiring new responsibilities, losing old bosses and friends, learning new skills, healing wounds left by change, building trust and teamwork, integrating different cultures and functions, targeting new goals, improving processes, and finding new opportunities for advancement.

Manager: Okay, what do my leaders need to do? What learning experiences do we need to put them through? How do we involve the frontline people in joint learning situations? What new skills and capabilities are needed by management? Who needs to meet with whom, for what purpose, to learn what needs to be learned to make this a better place to work? What is your blueprint for the coaching and training that are needed for us to deal with all the issues that have been identified and that will be identified? What do we do about our work groups and teams? What are the objectives and tangible results that are a part of this undertaking? From what you are saying, we have to put together some agendas. Some of my concerns right now are these:

- How do we deal with those who withhold information and are not honest about themselves?
- How do we communicate the notion of newness and personal growth?

- How do we work on changing our attitudes and behaviors?
- How do we use feedback?
- How do we consolidate our objectives and determine our pursuit?
- How do we understand coaching, beyond your words, and really use coaching methods?
- How do we deal with our impact on our business and its future?
- How do we utilize coaching partnerships?
- How do we investigate and apply new reading and reference material?
- How do we handle fear as you describe it?

Coach: As your coach, I will have to be able to sit with your people and present and discuss the following two items. First, they are creating a lot of newness in this organization. They cannot handle all of this newness without some coaching. Everyone needs to work with a coach and get assistance in handling new situations better and in getting better results.

Second, coaching needs to become the organization's business strategy. Coaching is needed to get from where the organization is to where management wants it to be. Coaching is over and beyond administration. Coaching gives new insights and awareness that wouldn't otherwise happen, and it is the guide for taking the next step.

Manager: What do you see as being the next step? I believe in mission statements. What is our mission here? What does all this say about what our objectives need to be? How can all this be summarized into a one-statement vision message for us? How can we communicate this newness and coaching throughout the organization? What do we do to provide a focus for people, and get them all pulling in the same direction in the pursuit of this new look? How do we use this statement to identify the critical skills and capabilities that we need to build a foundation for greater success? I have a lot of questions and I am asking myself some of them more than I am asking you. But they all need to be dealt with in moving from here to where we are talking about. I believe leadership is critically needed for us to have any success whatsoever in developing a coaching and teaming approach. I believe strongly in beginning with vision. We also have to condition our people to become more honest with themselves and each other. This will not be an easy task. Our people can never rest in their comfort zone if your coaching is to be successful with us. You are talking here about a new kind of association and networking. There will be some who will resist. Others will welcome the opportunity, primarily because they see opportunity in everything that happens.

Discussion of the Approach

Coach: People change their thinking and behavior through observation and interaction, not argument. Management and coaches have to exhibit proper behavior and attitudes and encourage all to move in that direction. We are all in the behavior business.

My coaching needs to make this a learning place to work. A workplace in which everyone learns from his or her experience and goes on to do things better as a result. Action is secondary to vision. People have to see before they say. The basic approach is to lessen the effects of hierarchy and authority and increase the effects of responsibility and accountability. Heavy emphasis on hierarchy and authority has brought out the dependence of people who work here. Responsibility and accountability will bring out the integrity and respect in people.

We have to appreciate that those who are most harmful to this organization are those who think they are doing what is right when they aren't. Some of your managers tend to give more attention to the tricks of the trade than they do to the trade itself. We have to be much more concerned about what is right than who's right.

There are several new agendas that need to be placed in the worklife of your people. Some of these new agendas are to accept ownership for themselves and the process of newness, to deal with whatever is blocking them and others from being more effective, to get involved in making a greater contribution and in being more accepted as they accept new tasks and ways of doing things, and to constantly explore new agendas and develop realistic action plans for improvement of themselves and this workplace.

Managers and coaches have to equip all employees with new learning and new tools, knowledge, insights, skills, and artistry to work with individuals and work groups.

Manager: It sounds like I have a job to do, to lead the way. You seem to be indicating that much of the commitment for coaching and teaming lies with me, and that you provide the skills and artistry. I suspect that if my commitment is down, your skills and artistry are not going to do much good regardless of how good you are at what you do. Okay, so I have to create a vision and direction for this stuff. I have to get my people enthusiastic about the purposes and meaning of what we are doing. You will provide appropriate coaching and connections to prepare our people for greater teamwork, togetherness, and less us and them.

Discussion of the Concept

Coach: This organization resembles a huge ocean liner making a U-turn in the middle of the ocean. It takes time and energy to get it turned around. It is now turning, but it will take a boost in engine power to get it up to speed and some critical navigation to keep it on its new course.

Relationships within this organization are like two icebergs. As long as they are apart (that is, when no one is talking about performance and behavior), they are okay. But, when they start moving closer together (that is, when we start talking about issues of behavior), something underneath the surface will start to grind. Those who cannot build trust, caring, and credibility in this organization will become more and more awkward in their relationships in the organization. But, over time, coaching processes will build supportive and collaborative relationships.

Those touched by the horizontal movement will expect the work climate to be different than in days past. They appreciate more freedom on the job. They want to be able to learn. They want the opportunity to do their best without controls from on high. New leadership must emerge to satisfy this requirement, or these people will select other options that will give them meaning. Also, the organization has to slow down enough to train some people in the skills for one-on-one coaching, teamwork, performance assessment, leadership, facilitation, and action planning. Some must be put through an awareness process to help others shove aside old baggage.

Manager: So it is an extended journey. It will take time and effort. We have a lot of control in us. It will take a lot of coaching to get some of us out of control. We plant fear in people because it is the only way we know to get them to do things. You are saying that we need to create more understanding and awareness of values and common goals. We have to examine how new leadership and coaching capabilities can affect decisions concerning our personal and organizational goals and aspirations. Let's go to work.

Discussion of Vision

Coach: Behaviorally, we have a long way to go but, fortunately, we can be productive at the same time as we learn and change. The biggest problem to face lies in each person's accepting responsibility to personally grow and change as a result of feedback and interaction. Growing can be painful. It can also be exciting. There are some who tend to avoid uncomfortable situations and resist the risk of needed self-exploration. Some must give up their tendencies of fight, flight, and manipulation.

Manager: We have to change. We no longer are unique in our business. I cannot carry the burden for all that has to be done. It all comes down to behaviors. We do have to change; we just aren't sure how to change. Our main objective is to get better results by creating new energy. There has to be a better way. We have to get out of command and control behaviors. We will achieve more if we work as a team. This does need to be a long-term approach. We have to leverage our abilities and develop our talent. Fear strikes people dead. We are dealing with people who have mixed priorities and a lot of individual discretion. Some have tunnel vision, which precludes them from seeing all that has to be done. People here believe that if you leave something alone long enough, others will forget about it. People withhold information and the whole story to keep power. We have individuals who are unqualified to do the job they are assigned to do, but they cover up rather than face the fact that they are misfits. We also have a problem here with people often being judged by a single mistake. This keeps the fear in place. Some people keep their thoughts very close to the vest and present a facade. We have to know more about where all of our behavior is coming from. Certainly, before some of our people can coach, they will have to build some credibility. I clearly see that this is a process and not another training program.

Coach: Let me review. My role as coach is to provide you and your organization with firsthand learning, to coach as things are happening, to handle frontline change, to establish the skills and tools to make this a learning organization. This work is through coaching accountability and takes continuity to be effective. The coaching function in an organization needs to be considered a cost of doing business as the organization moves, through the social interaction, to some behavioral conversions. You have to appreciate that it isn't what your people know that is so important. It's what they know that ain't so.

You have outlined two to three years of coaching work. During this time, one of my goals as coach will be to work with you to deal with these issues without becoming an issue myself. I have to be sure that I am not a problem for anyone except those who are a problem. As your coach, I accept the responsibility to provide artistry and skills for a relentless drive toward learning.

Discussion of Building a Network

Coach: Now that I have detailed some of the coaching responsibilities that I have and that you have with your people, let me identify some information you need to share with your boss. You do not direct your boss, but you do have a responsibility to communicate. You have a responsibility to find a time and place to meet with your boss and review some of the processes with which you are becoming involved, and some of the probable ramifications of these processes on the bigger system. This process may go in these stages:

Thank your boss for anything he or she has done to provide a vision and make you feel more a part of a team.

Point out that you believe there is a need to promote an "air of positive discontent" in this organization. A place where trust is felt, risks are taken, and failures are discussed openly. Indicate that continuous improvement demands that people talk about how they do things, not to criticize but to encourage everyone to see alternatives.

Mention some of the problems you see and some suggestions you have for improvements.

Emphasize that your boss's vision is needed to help people pull together as a team.

Point out that most of the management skills people learn come from observing someone they admire and, therefore, coaching is new learning that requires a new type of training.

Suggest that every employee become involved in some discussion of quality and vision. Elaborate the need to always maintain a high standard of quality through a measure of performance. Question the direction in which this organization wants to go.

Reiterate that continuous improvement requires continuous learning. Stress the need to learn more about this thing called management. Provide some of the awareness you have on coaching and new learning. You may also suggest that your boss take some responsibility to set up and support a steering group, made up of top leaders who aren't afraid to say what needs to be said.

Outline some viewpoints that could bless your work for change if they were to come from higher up in the organization. Some of these viewpoints are: continual learning is essential, the way we are doing things has to change, individual and collective accountability has to be looked at, we have to know how to set expectations within our work environment that go beyond anything we have had previously, we have to use our collective mentality, and we have to stop getting caught up in hierarchy; instead, we have to get caught up in teamwork, empowerment, and our creative component for doing business. It can be painful, and it will take courage.

Manager: My boss says change is needed. We have discussed how we are looking toward a whole new organization. I think we are ready for the labor of learning. My boss has a military style so we will have to test the difference between saying and doing. It will be hard to get rid of some autocratic ways. We will have to work according to my boss's desires, but not require his involvement in all things. Eventually, everyone will get in sync. We have to spread the message to everyone that everything here is changing. I'm changing. This organization is changing. Each person is expected to change. We have to get coaching and learn how to coach. Ego has to go. Change has to start with "my" attitude. This is a continual learning process. A new identity. We expect all to jump on the bandwagon. Each has a personal responsibility to take ownership. We have to take the initiative to give feedback and resolve old issues with people. This is a new experience for us. A new kind of involvement. We have to accomplish tasks at the same time each of us becomes a people person. Everyone has to recognize that this is for real and that I am committed to being a new person. Others will have to look at what I have done to change and what I am doing now that is different from what I did in the past. We have to develop a new perspective toward leadership.

Revolutionary Prescriptions

We stress once again that prescription without adequate diagnosis is malpractice. Prescribing, like making plays in sports coaching, comes only after the coach has seen the team practice and play. Here are some specific prescriptions for sustaining horizontal viewpoints when certain symptoms of particular issues appear in yourself or others.

Issue 1. "I cannot tell you what I really think. I'm not going to suffer from political backlash."

Prescription 1. Take the chance to speak openly about the issues that bother you in this workplace. Just do it in a positive manner and within a group context. Be seen as a major part of a team instead of a small function of the complaint system.

Issue 2. "We need to change behaviors and attitudes. People hold grudges and make you pay when you give them feedback."

Prescription 2. Improve your skills for giving and getting feedback. Begin a community spirit of self-improvement and help others to identify and deal with change from their particular perspectives.

Issue 3. "People make you feel stupid by the way they put you down when you talk to them about changing things. They are demanding."

Prescription 3. Become less dependent on others for approval. Assess your values and passion. Lead with your reasoning of what makes sense given all that is happening.

Issue 4. "We aren't working together. For me to put this team-ing program together, I need input from all areas and many people. I get discouraged and refuse to call a person from whom I need information. I just go ahead and do what I can regardless of the extra expense."

Prescription 4. You have to get rid of those people who behave toward each other as Felix and Oscar did in "The Odd Couple." Those who think differently and do differ-ently are not to be considered odd. Become more aware of the problems outside of your particular section and cause people to come together to talk about their problems.

Issue 5. "Frontline people won't tell managers how they see them. Managers are shaken when they learn they are seen as difficult to deal with."

Prescription 5. Most managers would get hate mail from Quakers, sometimes just for being there and other times for things they have done from their hierarchical position. This is a revolution that is creating a greater reality and your responsibility is to clarify that reality for others.

Issue 6. "So many people protect their egos and make others look bad."

Prescription 6. As the revolution reaches the advanced stages, it will become obvious that key people are all wrapped up in themselves and have become self-absorbed. Self-protection is a sign of some sense of inadequacy. Do not make it any harder for people to grow. Create greater confidence in how people work and relate to you.

Issue 7. "We don't communicate with others. There are mixed feelings about our managers. We had a bitch session without management. We talked about problems and attempts to get our message to management. There is fear of retribution."

Prescription 7. So management have a 911 personality. It is not uncommon that the horizontal revolution will give the impression that management lack only a few obnoxious traits to be perfect. Stop and think how your actions affect others and put yourself in their shoes. Learn more about how to approach management in different situations.

Issue 8. "Petty things go on and on. People get in groups and talk about others. They give them labels. Are we having fun? No! We need to get closer."

Prescription 8. You need to consider more carefully what is important and what is not important. Then ask yourself fundamental questions about yourself and the way in which you operate. Someone has to set the example around here.

Issue 9. "We need new leadership skills to continually identify things to do: the next game plan beyond this crisis. We need perpetual agendas."

Prescription 9. The prime strategy needs to have positive consequences that encourage good performance. This can start with you. All you have to do is convince everyone in this organization that however bad the news is, the end result is going to be better for him or her.

Issue 10. "It is not uncommon for a boss to take credit for things someone else does and to take advantage of that person's work. This leaves you in bad shape when it comes to merit increases rated on performance. Many of my achievements have been advertised as someone else's accomplishments."

Prescription 10. You cannot direct the wind, but you can adjust your sails. Enthusiasm is the propelling force necessary for climbing the ladder of success. Show positive enthusiasm, and you will get ahead. Remember, getting ahead is going to take a different path in the future than it has in the past. Enhance everyone's ability to grow and do a better job as you now see things.

Issue 11. "I am discontented. How do I stand up for myself? How do I get through to my boss? What am I good for? How do I deal with being seen as negative, emotional, and too honest?"

Prescription 11. It is better to be right half the time than half right all the time. Sometimes you feel when you ought to think, and you think when you ought to feel. Think about extending your capabilities and expanding your learning to become one of the organization's major leaders. Feel the excitement of opening up and learning new abilities and possibilities and of seeing new ways of doing things and developing a brighter future.

Some of our standard prescriptions for working in the horizontal organization are these:

- Stop referring to all you know. Start articulating your action plans.
- Stop waiting for someone else's agenda. Start having an agenda always ready.
- Stop saying, "It will work out." Start relating to what is happening and get involved.
- Stop having answers. Start working on alternatives.
- Stop being obsessed with tasks and events. Start giving more attention to new learning and long-range planning.
- Stop focusing on others' needs for transformation. Start creating and defining your own transformation.
- Stop being so available to everyone. Start spending more time with key people.
- Stop dealing with problems in general terms. Start defining action plans and needed pursuits.
- Stop reacting to decisions that are counter to your beliefs. Start being proactive in creating leadership for the new way.
- Stop relying on buzzwords, slogans, and jargon. Start processes for the application of useful ideas.
- Stop being an advocate for the latest fad. Start being an advocate for ways to continually improve.
- Stop nagging and bugging the higher ups. Start marketing who you are and what you are doing.
- Stop being on the sidelines and join the action. Start taking charge.
- Stop continuing to push movements that have had their time. Start getting ahead of what is happening today.

Maintaining the Revolution

Once the horizontal movement has passed through the four teaming stages, and prescriptions for new behaviors are being taken on a regular basis, people are going to look at what is going on and say, "What a great experience!" But they also will start to falter because the next steps will not be so obvious. It is easier to go from the bad to the good than it is from the good to the better.

Maintaining the revolution requires a new map and a new process for mapping the way. Some mapping questions that can sustain the movement of the revolution are these:

- What gaps exist between the way things are working out at present and how you would like to see them work out?
- How do you see those areas where you have new scope for discretion and new freedom of action?
- How do you see those areas where your behavior is no longer prescribed and you are no longer constrained by procedures, routine, or traditional patterns?
- How do you think others would answer the previous questions?

This mapping exercise should constructively move teams beyond everything else that has happened. The major issue is to sustain employees who understand the revolution and are committed to the process as they continue working to accomplish results. Appropriate mapping will reveal that the present culture is still inadequate and that inadequate interpersonal communication is the greatest barrier to productivity. Maintaining the revolution often means fighting the chain of command; fighting the "it's my job" attitude; fighting mood swings and the burying of problems; and fighting continued manifestations of resistance to a learning commitment.

During the stabilizing of the revolution, land mines will still be planted. Management are required to become even more intensive and committed than they had originally planned. This is the beginning of a long-term effort to build a learning environment. This environment is the answer to surviving the horizontal revolution. Making it happen will depend upon everyone's becoming a visionary, and bringing his or her vision to those involved in areas of change.

Learning environments are designed, developed, and maintained through such action items as stopping the rumor mill; beginning a strong, targeted communication campaign; making your commitment clear; achieving buy-in at all levels; accepting responsibility and making accountability the preferred behavior; removing the risk of fear; stopping back stabbing and politics; educating oneself; talking in terms of team strategies; and practicing self-evaluation. As the revolution reaches its high learning point, and managers stop being referees and start being coaches, teams are able to design the continuation of the learning and teaming process. The following outline was developed by just such collections of workers, as part of their revolution maintenance process.

Teaming Accomplishments

Motto: Working Together for a Change

Purpose:	We are committed to using our collective resources and teamwork to evaluate, facilitate, and support continuous improvement in our working relationships within the company.
Philosophy:	Bringing people together will make the difference.

Goal:	To work together as a team to unite the organization through behavioral skill development.
Objectives:	To maintain an environment where learning, feedback, team building, and coaching are a way of life.
	To stimulate continued awareness and innovation to balance quality service with fiscal responsibility.
Action Items for us as a team:	We will acknowledge the needs of the organization in the change.
	We will come up with strategies and designs.
	We will implement and facilitate new learning experiences.
	We will continuously examine the processes and requirements of the team.
Action Items for us as individuals:	We will establish and maintain team credibility.
	We will set an example of leadership for the times.
	We will extend ourselves to others.

The Managers' Last Roundup

No one at work wants to have his or her survival at the cost of someone else's freedom. The horizontal revolution should have removed micro-managers from the scene. New meaning, cohesion, and connections for doing work should have been established, but without trivialization. People lose their freedom at work when managers manage through the tyranny of trivia. Horizontal structures are not built on hype or charisma, or on detail-directed managers.

The continued "doing" is done when everyone has agendas for improvement and is constantly tuned to the next game to win. Factors that limit such action have to be identified and resolved.

Management styles during the revolution must be a combination of direction and involvement. Managers need to give up tight control in order to gain new control over what counts: results. Managers, as they have never been before, now need to be honest and clear in describing what responsibilities they are taking and what roles they are asking their people to assume. Management may be showing signs of being more competent, responsible, and performing, but they will still face a crisis of legitimacy. They will need to give even greater attention to the ways in which they motivate, measure, and develop their people. Unless managers make the transition to coaches, employees will still go out of their way to not communicate with them and not develop a sense of harmony. In particular, managers must:

- Recognize that they have moved up the line without being trained for what they are now doing
- Appreciate that they have a lot to learn about how to deal with people
- Do a better job of letting others know where they are coming from
- Do more to let their people get somewhere with them
- Not defend their behavior by saying, "That's the way it's always been!"
- Do more to allow people to use their own common sense
- Give more recognition, praise, and respect for good work

Managerial Ground Rules

We also have some ground rules for managers who have made the transition to coaches.

Have confidence. Stay in touch with your purpose. Use your skills, your experiences, and your work to bear upon the situation at hand. Stay away from getting trapped in other people's behavioral problems. Constantly remind yourself that you are not responsible for other people's learning. You are responsible for being prepared and for creating for others an opportunity for learning (for a change in behavior).

Show respect. Turn yourself on rather than being dependent upon the situation for your enthusiasm. Generate your own enthusiasm through your respect for others with whom you are working. Focus on the challenge of working with each work group and situation and get excited about what you can do for your work and not what your work might do for you. Respect the value of the moment.

Work expectations. Live in several worlds without being swallowed up by any of them. Recognize that the worlds in which you work are full of irrational behaviors and that you are adrift in a sea of ambiguity. You do not have to make sense out of everything or be responsible for straightening out everything. You do need to listen to and learn the expectations of those with whom you work and work those expectations into a viable format for action.

Be answerable. View the consequences of your work as well as your impulses for doing it. Your impulses need to be constantly checked against the consequences of what you are doing. Ask for feedback. Search for indications of your impact. Be accountable for what you do, not just your intention for doing.

Revolutionary Guidelines

The following guidelines are useful in keeping the movement in place. These guidelines can best create learning if they are accompanied with as-is, to-be, and to-me agendas. They represent items that are already well established but are continuing to be improved.

Identify: Name specific improvements
               State clear expectations
               Define achievable pursuits
               Determine meaningful measurements
Involve: Obtain cooperative commitment
               Develop participatory problem solving
               Program well-being improvement
               Gain decision-making input
Capture: Record projected steps
               Monitor success track
               Prescribe measurement indicators
               Prepare key agendas
Coach: Strategize improving performance
               Process work and progress
               Establish listening and encouraging
               Mandate self-directed assistance

Memo to the Coach

Your challenge is to get people to present issues they have uncovered and to keep them working on the issues as their issues. Ownership builds commitment. Use agenda making as a means to keep them focused on themselves and not on you. As they identify issues, clarify the issues with them and help them see that the issues are as-is agenda items. Then ask them to identify what conditions they would like to-be instead. Once the agendas are clear, ask them what they would like to do and help them create their to-me agenda. This is the process of taking ownership without blame.

Work to stretch each individual's knowledge of the real behaviors in his or her work environment. Help people see that behaviors are what people do. Indicate that all team members can get into the behavioral change business by using coaching skills and behavioral principles to guide their insights and communication skills. As each situation arises, use some aspect of coaching to help team members get more meaning and an expanded view of the situation. This expanded view comes as they search to see more than anyone else sees about the behavioral happenings of the moment. You will need to come up with strategies and alternatives in the form of agendas to fit the constantly changing situations.

The learning process is working when people make the leap from knowing about their behavior to doing something about their behavior. They see behavioral improvement is fun and greatly rewarding but recognize that it requires effort. Certainly, they recognize that learning is not listening to lectures or motivational speeches or reading self-help literature. It is built on self-reliant behavior and helping one another with increasing the level of competencies, improving behaviors, and being successful as an organization.

Changing attitudes and behaviors to reach this stage of learning is the design and purpose of coaching. Unfortunately, when people think in negatives, they tend to act in ways that prevent them from trying new ways or taking risks. We use a worksheet to list the ways in which change is being communicated at this stage of learning. The worksheet has spaces to describe change in yourself, change in the teams, change in management, change in the organization, and action items.

The coaching role expands across the organization as change broadens and deepens. Figure 8.1 suggests the skills in which different organizational areas typically require coaching. These skills fall in the three categories of coaching, team-building, and leadership skills.

The coach's role is never done. There is always the next step. As the process magnifies, your coaching skills and artistry must extend and expand. Here are some summary tips for coaching during the organization's learning experiences:

- Provide new learning experiences designed to cause individuals and teams to continually expand their capacity to create another future.

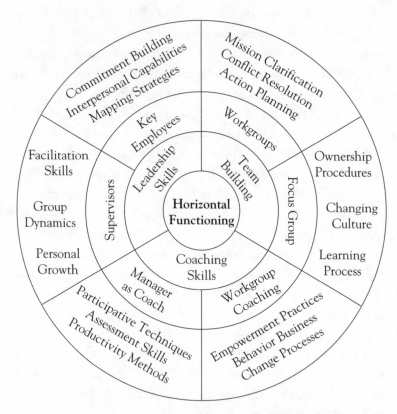

**Figure 8.1. The Learning Organization's
Coaching-for-Change Work Plan.**

- Coach team members to be more effective by changing from seeing problems as caused by someone out there to seeing how their own actions create the problems they experience.

- Work toward a greater emphasis on team learning, with interaction that leads to behavioral conversion and is free of defensiveness and blame.

- Move learning beyond taking in information and into individual firsthand experience and shared visions.

- Guide the change process through using the principles and guiding practices of the horizontal revolution. Avoid the cookbook approach.

Summary

Those involved in the horizontal revolution are to be seen as refugees. They are constantly going through a worklife passage. There will never be a time when they will not have the potential for discontinuity in their worklives. The revolutionary life at work involves adapting and readapting. It is a burden and it often has the hardships of learning. There many things about the horizontal revolution that throw icy water on the human spirit.

Maintaining the movement is difficult to plan and dangerous to coach. The battle between those who initiate change and those who are merely lukewarm continues. The frozen mind-set of significant people is always a challenge to confront. The creation of new anticipations, flexibilities, and acceptances of continual improvement and learning is even more demanding. We firmly believe that people are insightful enough to see themselves; strong enough to treasure values; attentive enough to listen; brave enough to welcome feedback; and wise enough to recognize and correct their mistakes.

The phoenix is a legendary bird represented by the ancient Egyptians as living for five or six centuries in the Arabian desert, being consumed in fire by its own act, and rising in youthful freshness from its own ashes. Similarly, the organization that undertakes the horizontal revolution must boldly destroy its old life before it can start anew.

Epilogue: Guiding the
Transformation to Teams

A new and fundamentally different organizational approach is replacing the outmoded, adversarial approach that has grown up between management and labor and that now threatens the competitiveness of our corporations. The experiences, insights, and practices that we have cited throughout this book are a witness to the fact that almost every aspect of corporate life will be profoundly challenged and subsequently altered when companies organize around core processes and develop multifunctional teams from different departments to manage everything.

The artistry and skills of teaming become all-important as both the people inside and outside companies become complexly networked. Increasingly, teams are linking up with customers to understand the customer's business, the customer's real needs, and the ways the customer is going to use the team's products or services. The design and redesign of basic business processes are realized in this team-customer consultative partnership.

Occasionally, through hit-and-miss practice, a team eventually evolves to the productive and collaborative operations described in our stage four, transforming. Our experience affirms that most team-oriented work design ventures will never achieve this level of optimal performance with their customers without skillful guidance and coaching. In reality, many groups stall and lose their potency. Others regress to earlier stages of team development. Still others call themselves teams when in fact they are little more than a segregated collection of individuals with nothing more in common than working for the same company or having their names on a team roster. And for those whose management team won't give up control, team work is analogous to having to back over the metal one-way prongs when pulling out of a parking lot. Of the few teams that reach the transforming stage, many do so only after painful months and years of unnecessary struggling.

In days past, when business was less turbulent and more predictable, the wisdom and advantages of self-directed work groups or self-managing teams became obvious. Indicators of their efforts reported higher productivity and quality and cost effectiveness. Teams also reported improved job satisfaction, motivation, and employee morale. All seemed well and fine.

However, heightened global competition and the ever-increasing speed of technological change have raised the ante on the game of work. We are now being forced to reinvent or reengineer ourselves to manage work processes that are more complex. Prepared or not, teaming is now thrust into a new generation and asked to actively participate in an information systems revolution. That revolution is demanding that teams take on a more challenging and expanded role in bureaucratic dismantling, that is, bringing on another revolution by tilting the pyramid and building the new horizontal order. Although we have identified the stages of team development for horizontal structures, the barriers along the way, and the guidance and coaching skills needed, we have covered only part of the movement, as readers who attempt horizontalizing in their own company will discover. We have fundamentally focused on the horizontal development of teams and not on reengineering the organization at large.

Horizontal teaming does not run a predictable course. Likewise, there are no premixed solutions to every organizational problem. We have seen companies rushing to galvanize employees around processes without linking those processes to the organizations' key goals. It is profoundly important to first conduct an analysis of what it will take to understand and win markets and customers. Only then should the organization begin to identify the most critical core processes to achieve its objectives and determine how a teaming redesign would fit into the management of those processes.

We are often asked if our four-stage teaming model is a direct pathway to the horizontal organization. Our model represents a natural evolutionary path for most task-oriented work groups that pursue horizontal activity and are capable of resolving developmental and systemic issues and barriers along the way. But there is a critical difference between free-form team development (typically described as form, storm, norm, and whatever) and a guided and coached approach with a purpose. In our guided approach, teams are helped to get things done while they are facilitated toward developing strong roles and relationships, which are needed for preventing several undesirable things from happening. Departments that house teams must be laterally organized and managed in ways that guide teaming efforts without pushing them from the top. Without this horizontal guiding and coaching approach, juxtaposed with reengineering efforts, teams will weaken and easily lose their way.

We also wish to reemphasize the critical role of the team leader. It is the team leader's task to bring the team to maturity; help the team work through interpersonal, task, and authority issues; and be skilled in nurturing a cohesive, effective team. The skills a team leader requires are the hands-on skills of direct involvement and full membership in the team. Flexibility, shared collaboration, and coordination are characteristics of healthy teams and team leaders.

Finally, team development must be an ongoing process of diagnosis and feedback—supplemented by sufficient training and direction—to improve on strengths and shore up weak spots. Only then will teaming approximate and sustain the behaviors needed in performing work around processes that are multifunctional, voluminous, and complicated.

It is a shame that much of our work force has already lost its freshness, its resolve, and its ability to face up to hard work. Change is never easy, but with appropriate spirit and effort, we do promise you a rose garden. You just have to roll up your sleeves and keep working at it and working at it until you smell the roses.

References and
Recommended Readings

Argyris, C. *Knowledge for Action: A Guide to Overcoming Barriers to Organizational Change*. San Francisco: Jossey-Bass, 1993.

Argyris, C., Putnam, R., and Smith, D. M. *Action Science: Concepts, Methods, and Skills for Research and Intervention*. San Francisco: Jossey-Bass, 1985.

Argyris, C., and Schön, D. A. *Theory in Practice: Increasing Professional Effectiveness*. San Francisco: Jossey-Bass, 1974.

Beer, M., Eisenstat, R. A., and Spector, B. "Why Change Programs Don't Produce Change." *Harvard Business Review*, 1990, 68(6), 158–166.

Blines, D. "Semi-Autonomous Team in the Zoo." *The Journal for Quality and Participation*, July/Aug. 1990, pp. 93–95.

Bolman, L. G., and Deal, T. E. *Reframing Organizations: Artistry, Choice, and Leadership*. San Francisco: Jossey-Bass, 1991

Byham, W. C. *Zapp! The Lighting of Empowerment*. New York: Harmony Books, 1990.

Carnevale, A. P., Gainer, L. J., and Meltzer, A. S. *Workplace Basics: The Skills Employers Want*. American Society for Training and Development and U.S. Department of Labor Report 0–225-795-QL.2. Washington, D.C.: U.S. Government Printing Office, 1988.

Cherns, A. "The Principles of Socio-Technical Design." *Human Relations*, 1976, 29, 783–792.

Cherry, R. "The Development of General Motors' Team-Based Plants in the Innovative Organization." In R. Zager and M. P. Rosow (eds.), *The Innovative Organization: Productivity Programs in Action*. Elsmford, N.Y.: Pergamon Press, 1982.

Drucker, P. *The Practice of Management*. New York: HarperCollins, 1954.

Dubnicki, C. "Building High-Performance Management Teams." *Healthcare Forum Journal*, May/June 1991, pp. 19–24.

Dumaine, B. "Who Needs a Boss?" *Fortune*, May 7, 1990, pp. 52–55, 58, 60.

Echols, D., and Mitchell, R. "Champion or Victim? The Supervisor? New Role in a Team-Based Work System." Paper presented at the Seventh Annual Fall Forum of the Association for Quality and Participation, Denver, Colo., Oct. 1990.

Eliot, T. S. *The Cocktail Party*, in *The Complete Plays of T. S. Eliot*. Orlando, Fla.: Harcourt Brace Jovanovich, 1954.

Emery, F. *Limits to Choice*. Canberra: Australian National University Center for Continuing Education, 1978.

Emery, F. E. "Designing Socio-Technical Systems for Greenfield Sites." *Journal of Occupational Behavior*, 1980, 1, 19–27.

Gladstein, D. L. "Groups in Context: A Model of Task Group Effectiveness." *Administrative Science Quarterly*, 1984, 28, 499–517.

Goodman, P. S., and Associates. *Designing Effective Work Groups*. San Francisco: Jossey-Bass, 1986.

Gwynne, S. C. "The Right Stuff." *Time*, Oct. 29, 1990, pp. 74–84.

Hackman, J. R. "Group Influences on Individuals in Organizations." In M. D. Dunnette (ed.), *Handbook of Industrial and Organizational Psychology*. Skokie, Ill.: Rand-McNally, 1976.

Hackman, J. R. "The Commitment Model: From 'Whether' to 'How.'" In R. Hayes and K. Clark (eds.), *The Uneasy Alliance: Managing the Productivity-Technology Dilemma*. Boston: Harvard Business School Press, 1985.

Hackman, J. R. "The Design of Effective Work Teams." In T. W. Lorsch (ed.), *Handbook of Organizational Behavior*. Englewood Cliffs, N.J.: Prentice-Hall, 1987.

Hackman, J. R. (ed.). *Groups That Work (And Those That Don't): Creating Conditions for Effective Teamwork*. San Francisco: Jossey-Bass, 1989.

Hackman, J. R., and Walton, R. E. "Groups Under Contrasting Management Strategies." In P. S. Goodman and Associates, *Designing Effective Work Groups*. San Francisco: Jossey-Bass, 1986.

Hall, J. "Americans Know How to Be Productive If Managers Will Let Them." *Organizational Dynamics*, Winter 1994, pp. 33–46.

Hammer, M., and Champy, J. *Reengineering the Corporation: A Manifesto for Business Revolution*. New York: HarperBusiness, 1993.

Hauenstein, P., and Byham, W. C. *Understanding Job Analysis*. Monograph 11. Pittsburgh, Pa.: Development Dimensions International, 1989.

Herzberg, F. *Work and the Nature of Man*. Cleveland, Ohio: World, 1966.

Hirschhorn, L. *Managing in the New Team Environment*. Reading, Mass.: Addison-Wesley, 1991.

Hoerr, J. "Getting Man and Machine to Live Happily Ever After." *Business Week*, Apr. 20, 1987, pp. 61–65.

Hoerr, J. "Work Teams Can Rev Up Paper Pushers, Too." *Business Week*, Nov. 28, 1988, pp. 68–69.

Hoerr, J. "The Cultural Revolution at A. O. Smith." *Business Week*, May 29, 1989a, pp. 66–68.

Hoerr, J. "The Payoff from Teamwork." *Business Week*, July 10, 1989b, pp. 56–62.

Hoerr, J. "Sharpening Minds for A Competitive Edge." *Business Week*, Dec. 17, 1990, pp. 72–78.

Hoerr, J., and Pollock, M. A. "Management Discovers the Human Side of Automation." *Business Week*, Sept. 29, 1986, pp. 74–77.

Homans, G. C. *The Human Group*. San Diego, Calif.: Harcourt Brace Jovanovich, 1950.

House, C. H. "The Return Map: Tracking Product Teams." *Harvard Business Review*, Jan./Feb. 1991, pp. 92–100.

Howard, R. "Values Make the Company." *Harvard Business Review*, Sept.–Oct. 1990, pp. 132–145.

Jacobsen, G.. "A Teamwork Ultimatum Puts Kimberly-Clark's Mill Back on the Map." *Management Review*, July 1989, pp. 28–31.

Jessup, H. R. "New roles in Team Leadership." *Training and Development Journal*, Nov. 1990, pp. 79–83.

Johnson, R. "Volvo's New Assembly Plant Has No Assembly Line." *Automotive News*, July 10, 1989, pp. 22, 24.

Katz, D., and Kahn, R. L. *The Social Psychology of Organizations* (2nd ed.). New York: Wiley, 1978.

Katzenback, J., and Smith, D. *The Wisdom of Teams: Creating the High-Performance Organization*. Boston: Harvard Business School Press, 1993.

Ketchum, L. D. "How Redesigned Plants Really Work." *National Productivity Review*, 1984, 3, 246–254.

Kotter, J., and Heskett, J. *Corporate Culture and Performance*. New York: Free Press, 1992.

Lawler, E. E., III. *High-Involvement Management: Participative Strategies for Improving Organizational Performance*. San Francisco: Jossey-Bass, 1986.

Lawler, E. E., III. *Ultimate Advantage: Creating the High-Involvement Organization*. San Francisco: Jossey-Bass, 1992.

Ledford, G. E. *The Design of Skill-Based Pay Plans*. COE Publication 689–15. Los Angeles: University of Southern California, Center for Effective Organization, 1989.

Lee, C. "Beyond Teamwork." *Training*, June 1990, pp. 25–32.

McClelland, D. C. "Achievement Motivation Can be Developed." *Harvard Business Review*, 1965, 43, 6–24.

McClelland, D. C., and Burnham, D. H. "Power Is the Great Motivator." *Harvard Business Review*, 1976, 54, 100–111.

McGrath, J. E. *Groups: Interaction and Performance*. Englewood Cliffs, N.J.: Prentice-Hall, 1984.

Manz, C. C., and Sims, H. P., Jr. *Superleadership: Leading Others to Lead Themselves*. Englewood Cliffs, N.J.: Prentice-Hall, 1989.

Mohrman, A. M., Jr., Resnick-West, S. M., and Lawler, E. E., III. *Designing Performance Appraisal Systems: Aligning Appraisals and Organizational Realities*. San Francisco: Jossey-Bass, 1989.

Moskal, B. S. "Is Industry Ready for Adult Relationships?" *Industry Week*, Jan. 21, 1991, pp. 18–27.

National Center of Education and the Economy. *America's Choice: High Skills or Low Wages*. Rochester, N.Y.: National Center of Education and the Economy, 1990.

Near, R., and Weckler, D. "Organizational and Job Characteristics Related to Self-Managing Teams." Paper presented at the International Conference on Self-Managed Work Teams, Denton, Tex., Sept. 1990.

O'Dell, C. "Team Play, Team Pay—New Ways of Keeping Score." *Across the Board*, Nov. 1989, pp. 38–45.

Orburn, J. D., Morgan, L., Musselwhite, E., and Zenger, J. *Self-Directed Work Teams: The Next American Challenge*. Homewood, Ill.: Dow Jones-Irwin, 1990.

Ostroff, F., and Smith, D. "The Horizontal Organization." *The McKinsey Quarterly*, 1992, (1), 148–168.

Parker, M., and Slaugher, J. *Choosing Sides: Unions and the Team Concept*. Boston: South End Press, 1988.

Pasmore, W. A., and Sherwood, J. J. *Sociotechnical Systems*. San Diego, Calif.: University Associates, 1978.

Robenstein, S. "Don't Fear the Team, Join It." *New York Times*, June 11, 1989, sec. 3, p. 2.

Rosen, N. *Teamwork and the Bottom Line*. Hillsdale, N.J.: Erlbaum, 1989.

Rummler, G. A., and Brache, A. P. *Improving Performance: How to Manage the White Space on the Organization Chart*. San Francisco: Jossey-Bass, 1990.

Semler, R. "Managing Without Managers." *Harvard Business Review*, Sept./Oct. 1989, pp. 76–84.

Senge, P. M. *The Fifth Discipline*. New York: Doubleday/Currency, 1990.

Sheridan, J. H. "America's Best Plants." *Industry Week*, Oct. 1990, pp. 27–64.

Stayer, R. "How I Learned to Let My Workers Lead." *Harvard Business Review*, Nov./Dec. 1990, pp. 66–83.

Sundstrom, E., Demeuse, K., and Futrell, D. "Work Teams: Applications and Effectiveness." *American Psychologist*, Feb. 1990, pp. 120–133.

Taylor, F. *Principles of Scientific Management*. New York: HarperCollins, 1947.

Tichy, N., and Sherman, S. *Control Your Destiny or Someone Else Will*. New York: Currency/Doubleday, 1993.

Toffler, A. *Powershift: Knowledge, Wealth, and Violence at the Edge of the Twenty-First Century*. New York: Bantam Books, 1990.

Trist, E. L. *The Evolution of Socio-Technical Systems*. Occasional Paper no. 2. Toronto: Quality of Working Life Centre, 1981.

Trist, E. L., and Bamforth, K. W. "Some Social and Psychological Consequences of the Longwall Method of Goal-Getting." *Human Relations*, 1951, 4, 1–38.

Verespej, M. A. "Are Your Teams, Teams? Not Always." *Industry Week*, June 18, 1990, pp. 103–105.

Walton, R. E. "Quality of Working Life: What Is It?" *Sloan Management Review*, 1973, 15, 11–21.

Walton, R. E. "Work Innovations at Topeka: After Six Years." *Journal of Applied Behavioral Science*, 1977, 13, 422–433.

Walton, R. E. "Establishing and Maintaining High Commitment Work Systems." In J. R. Kimberly, R. H. Miles, and Associates (eds.), *The Organizational Life Cycle: Issues in the Creation, Transformation and Decline of Organizations*. San Francisco: Jossey-Bass, 1980.

Walton, R. E. "From Control to Commitment: Transformation of Work Force Management Strategies in the United States." In R. Hayes and K. Clark (eds.), *The Uneasy Alliance: Managing the Productivity-Technology Dilemma*. Boston: Harvard Business School Press, 1985.

Weisbord, M. R. *Productive Workplaces: Organizing and Managing for Dignity, Meaning, and Community*. San Francisco: Jossey-Bass, 1987.

Wellins, R. S., Wilson, J., Katz, A. J., Laughlin, P., and Day, C. R., Jr. *Self-Directed Teams: A Study of Current Practice*. Survey report. Pittsburgh, Pa.: Development Dimensions International, Association for Quality and Participation, and Industry Week, 1990.

Wesner, M., and Egan, C. "Self-Managed Teams in Operator Services." Paper presented at the International Conference on Self-Managed Work Teams, Denton, Tex., Sept. 1990.

"What Workers Want: The Gap in Management's Perception." *Behavioral Sciences Newsletter*, June 27, 1988, p. 1.

Williams, T. A. *Learning to Manage Our Futures*. N.Y.: Wiley, 1982.

Zemke, R. "Sociotechnical Systems." *Training*, Feb. 1987, pp. 47–57.

Zenger, J., Musselwhite, E., Hurson, K., and Perrin, C. "Leadership in a Team Environment." *Training & Development*, 1991, 45(10), pp. 47–52.

Index